The Use of Voice in Music Therapy

Kelly Meashey

The Use of Voice in Music Therapy

Copyright © 2020 by Barcelona Publishers

All rights reserved. No part of this book may be reproduced, stored, or distributed under any circumstances, without prior written permission from Barcelona Publishers.

Print ISBN: 9781945411533
E-ISBN: 9781945411540

Barcelona Publishers
10231 Plano Rd.
Dallas TX 75238
Website: www.barcelonapublishers.com
SAN 298-6299

Copy-editor: Jack Burnett
Cover Design: Matthew King
Production Manager: Dr. Demi Stevens

ACKNOWLEDGMENTS

In the spring of 1979, I was trying to sleep in the back of my dad's Bobcat station wagon while being driven from Lebanon, Pennsylvania, to Philadelphia for an interview with Dr. Kenneth Bruscia. In my then laid-back style, I began filling out the interview questions in a moving car with a runny ink pen, and by the time I got to Temple University, the paper was a mess.

Nonetheless, the interview began. Pleasantries were exchanged, with a few easy questions as a warm-up. Then Dr. Bruscia turned to ask what characteristics someone might need to be a music therapist, and the exchange grew in intensity. I said, "Patience." He said urgently, "What is patience?" As I stumbled around for an answer, he kept pressing me to come up with an acceptable reply.

"Tolerance," I said. He asked emphatically, "Tolerance?!" I stared at him blankly.

In a final dramatic gesture, his very expressive concert pianist forefinger hit the desk as he asked, "Are YOU tolerating ME!?" I was far too sleepy and spacey to get ruffled. Like a cow chewing its cud, I calmly replied, "I think you're tolerating me."

With his signature charismatic smile and twinkling eyes (I think he was quite amused with me), Ken Bruscia extended his hand and said, "Welcome to Temple University's music therapy program."

I knew from that moment on that he was an amazing teacher, but I didn't know that through undergrad, grad, GIM training, qualitative research, and book-writing, I would still be learning from this man 40 years later.

Thank you so much, Ken, for guiding me on this beautiful music therapy road.

My guru-ess, Diane Austin, taught me, through endless hours of supervision, how to flow from verbal to music and back, as well as how to stay with clients who are struggling and in pain. From this training of being present, I have learned compassion for others and for myself like I never dreamed possible. You are an amazing woman, Diane!

I must acknowledge Demi Stevens, who has become a friend and who has held my hand and guided me forward with great clarity as I journeyed into the writing world. Without you, Demi, there would be no book.

When I told my husband, Steve Heitzer, that I was overwhelmed about writing acknowledgments, he said, "Kelly, you don't have to mention me. I don't care about that." It has been so liberating to be encouraged to pursue my own dreams independently as an individual yet still share these life dreams with someone. And also, thank you for your Sibelius wizardry.

My son, Sam, taught me how to be a good enough parent. From this, I learned how to better parent myself and how to support clients as they learn the same. Thanks, Sam!

Along the way, there have been so many people who have supported, pushed, confronted, cheered, listened, hand-held and patiently allowed me—sometimes awkwardly, and excruciatingly slowly—to grow as a music therapist. There are far too many to list here. I hope that I have already thanked you, that you know who you are, and that you know how much you mean to me.

And … oh! … my clients. I don't think there are words in the English language to describe the experience of witnessing you in utmost authenticity moving through profound disabilities, intense struggles, and deep pain in order to heal and grow. It has been an honor to accompany you.

Thank you so much for singing with me.

Acknowledgments

SPECIAL THANKS TO ...

Molly Hicks, MMT, MT-BC
Music therapist and bereavement coordinator

Anya Ismail, MA, MT-BC, LCAT
Hospice and palliative care music therapist

Bryan Muller, PhD, MT-BC
Organizational assistance

Kathleen Summers, MA, MT-BC
Music therapist, Children's Hospital of Philadelphia

Lisa Sokolov
Embodied VoiceWork

Jim Wade, BME
Former music therapist, Cascade Center for Aphasic Adults

Lydia Westle, MMT, MT-BC
Music therapist, Children's Hospital of Philadelphia

ABOUT THE AUTHOR

Kelly Meashey has spent her career in music weaving together various professional pursuits, including clinical music therapy, professional singing, and teaching vocal performance and music therapy voice in higher education.

As a self-employed music therapist, Kelly has worked with clients with severe/profound intellectual, learning, and physical disabilities; cerebral palsy; muscular dystrophy; brain injury from trauma and stroke; dementia; impaired vision/hearing; autism; eating disorders; depression; anxiety; trauma; and psychosis. She has her bachelor's and master's degrees in music therapy from Temple University and has completed training in GIM and Austin Vocal Psychotherapy.

She also won the music therapy research award for finishing Bruscia's qualitative study titled *Re-Imaging Client Images: A Technique for Uncovering Projective Identification* (Bruscia, 1998, p. 549). Kelly currently practices privately as a music psychotherapist in Philadelphia.

In the heyday of Kelly's singing career, she worked over 200 gigs a year performing at Atlantic City casinos, the Philadelphia Four Seasons Hotel, and the Philadelphia Art Museum and as a featured artist for jazz festivals in Pennsylvania and New Jersey. She has co-led on two albums: *Inner Urge* on Dreambox Media, and *Songs of Living* on CIMP (Creative Improvised Music Projects) Recordings. In a review of *Songs of Living*, *Cadence Magazine* wrote "[Meashey's] style reflects the study of horns (as seen through her phrasing) as well as the passion of Soul and jazz performers."

Her voice was featured on the soundtracks of two films: *Takao Dancer*, which was presented at the Tokyo Film Festival, and *Duck Painter*, written and produced by Wen-Shing Ho.

As a voice educator, Kelly has taught classical and contemporary voice at The University of the Arts and Community College of

Philadelphia, jazz voice at Temple University, and music therapy functional voice at Immaculata University and Temple University.

She also teaches a performance anxiety class at Temple University that helps musicians and others to gain tools for accepting psychological performance issues and reconnect to the joy of performance.

TABLE OF CONTENTS

Acknowledgments iii

About the Author vii

Chapter 1: Introduction/Experiential Introduction 3
  The Voice in Human Development 4
  The Voice in Adulthood 5
  The Voice in Music Therapy 6
  Therapeutic Benefits of Singing 8

PART ONE
Therapist Training

Chapter 2: Using the Musical Elements 15
Chapter 3: Exploring Your Own Vocal Range/Limits 29
  Basic Vocal Technique Exercises 32
Chapter 4: Improvisation 43
Chapter 5: Simplifying the Voice When Working with Clients . . 51
Chapter 6: Vocal Identity and Self-Expression 55

PART TWO
Working with Clients

Chapter 7: Ethics of Self-Awareness for Vocalists 65
Chapter 8: Methods for Awareness of Therapist/
  Client Dynamics 71
Chapter 9: Goal Areas and Methods 81
  Establishing Safety 81
  Levels of Utilizing Methods 86
Chapter 10: Maintaining Goals as the Focus 89
  Grounding/Empowerment 90
  Toning 92
  Call-and-Response 98
  Songs of Empowerment 100
  Singing and Rhythm 101
  The Blues 103

	Final Thoughts 104
Chapter 11:	Sense of Unity (Group Cohesion/
	Individual Connection) 107
	Singing Songs in Unison 108
	Singing Harmony 109
	Singing Fun, Silly Songs 109
	Vowels 110
Chapter 12:	Stress Reduction/Relaxation 111
	Vocal Exercises 112
	Chant 113
	Singing and Imagery 114
	Singing and Mandala 115
Chapter 13:	Cognitive Behavior, Rational Thinking,
	and Emotional Regulation 117
	Singing Songs for Core Beliefs 118
	Simple Lyric Writing 119
	Songwriting 121
	Mindful Singing 123
	Singing with Bilateral Stimulation
	and Grounding Techniques 124
Chapter 14:	Self-Expression and Communication 127
	Listening 128
	Dialogue 129
	Dialogue with Nonverbal Clients 129
	Dialogue with Verbal Clients 130
	Fill-Ins and One-Word Phrases 135
	Dynamics and Tempo 137
	Singing Songs 138
	Short Songs 138
	Singing Songs and Planned Dynamics 138
	Singing Songs at Different Tempos 139
	Sharing Songs, Receptive to Singing 140
	Sharing Songs in Individual Sessions 140
	Sharing Songs in a Group 141
	Receptive Listening and Mandala 142
	Singing for Clients 142
Chapter 15:	Support for Emotional Pain 145
	Toning 146

	Singing Songs	147
	Vocal Improvisation	149
	Songwriting with a Goal of Singing	150
	Vocal Psychotherapy	151
Chapter 16:	Support for Physical Pain	153
	Toning	155
	Singing for Entrainment	155
	Songwriting and Singing	158
	Singing Songs	159
Chapter 17:	Social Interaction and Relationship-Building	161
	Sing-Alongs	163
	Client's Choice	165
	Fill-Ins	166
	Call-and-Response	167
	Tempo and Dynamic Changes	168
	Silly Songs	168
	Songs to Promote Functional Skills	169
	Singing to Promote Social Skills	171
Chapter 18:	Cognitive Development	175
	Singing for Reminiscing	176
	Singing for Label and Object Recognition	177
	Melodic Intonation Therapy	178
Chapter 19:	Physical Development	181
	Vocal Exercises for Speech Articulation	181
	Monotone and Arrhythmic Speaking	182
	Singing for Diaphragmatic Strength, Lung Capacity, and Fluid Speech	183
Chapter 20:	Psychotherapy	185
	Training Requirements	185
	Grieving	187
	Healing Deep Wounds	188
	Transpersonal Experiences	189
Chapter 21:	Toolbox	191
	Call-and-Response	191
	Chant	192
	Dialogue	193
	Dynamics and Tempo	194
	Fill-Ins and One-Word Phrases	194

	Listening 195
	Lyric Writing 196
	Receptive Methods 197
	Sing-Alongs 198
	Singing and Imagery 199
	Singing and Mandala 200
	Singing for Entrainment 201
	Singing in Harmony 201
	Singing Lighthearted Fun, Joyful, and Silly Songs . 203
	Singing Songs in Unison 204
	Songwriting 205
	Toning 207
	Vocal Exercises 208
	Vocal Improvisation 208
Chapter 22:	Conclusion 211

Appendix: Lisa Sokolov Duet Games 215

Song Resources 219

References 225

Index 245

The Use of Voice in Music Therapy

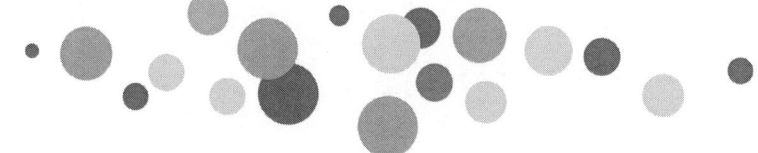

Chapter 1

INTRODUCTION

EXPERIENTIAL INTRODUCTION

Before reading this book, take a deep breath. Feel your feet on the floor and your back supported by the chair. Now place your hands on your chest and your stomach. Feel the hand on your stomach rise and fall. Take another deep breath and this time imagine that you are breathing all the way down to your feet.

    Now begin to hum on your favorite note. Don't worry, you'll find it. Continue humming. Change notes if you like. Hum only for 30 to 60 seconds. Stop. Now notice how you feel. Do you feel the shift? If not, hum longer. Now pretend you have been sitting in a wheelchair sleeping all day and the music therapist has come right up to your confused face so that you could see and hear him and asked you to hum or sing "Hi" a few times. With guitar in hand, the music therapist exclaims, "Great job, Harry!" and then asks you to sing a few more notes before moving on. You are now breathing a little more deeply, your body is slightly more relaxed, and, when your vocal cords vibrated inside your body, you realized that you had a body and that someone had seen and heard you. You realized that you existed, and, for that moment, you were aware of self and other in a pleasant way. You were connected with another human being.

    Now try singing some syllables. Sing *ma ma ma* in different rhythms … or *ba ba ba* or *doo doo doo*. Notice how your mouth opens and closes, and each time that it does so, you feel tickly vibrations in your face that open into a louder sound and vibrate in the roof of your mouth and nose. Or, you can explore the D consonant and feel your tongue move. Imagine that you are a nonverbal individual with profound developmental delays as well as autism. You usually use these sounds to shut out the world, but now a music therapist is playing sounds on the piano and singing back and forth with you, sometimes on the same notes, sometimes echoing you. It actually feels nice to have another vibration with yours. You begin to sing even more, and sometimes you even look at the music therapist. For the time being, someone has found a bridge to your isolated world, and, in that moment, you feel less confused and less alone.

Finally, play a recording of your favorite song and sing along. Be aware of which part of the song you connect to most. Turn off the recording and sing that part for 60 seconds like you are chanting. Notice that your inhales become deeper, your mind becomes clearer, and you feel less tired. You are even aware of negative thoughts shifting to positive, rational thoughts. Once more, imagine that you have just been placed in a psychiatric facility for severe depression. The depression is so painful it feels like knives are cutting you inside. The music therapist in group puts on Bob Marley's "No Woman, No Cry." When the song is over, she asks everyone to play drums and sing the vamp, which states, "Everything's Gonna Be Alright." You sing a little but mostly feel as though the song actually understands you. You notice that you have been able to breathe a little better and that the vibrations of the drums and voices bring a sense of comfort to your body. For this moment, the jagged edges of the depression have softened a bit.

These three opening singing/imagery exercises exemplify the simple power of using one's voice and encouraging clients to use their voices to connect to self and others.

THE VOICE IN HUMAN DEVELOPMENT

Our first connection to the world at birth happens through our voices. Our first experience of ourselves outside of the womb takes place when we inhale and release the journey of birth by vibrating our vocal cords with intensity. It is a powerful, beautiful, anguished, and awe-inspiring expression of life and the fact that "I am here!"

When an infant cries, the diaphragm engages and the vocal cords vibrate freely with no tension or holding back. An emotion happens and the body knows exactly what to do to sound that emotion. The body and the voice are completely connected.

Over time, as we grow, we begin to use our voices to say "Dada" and "Hi," to learn our ABCs, to recite book reports, to call football plays, to order food, to complain to the gas company, to quarrel with our partners, to teach a class, and so on. Our voices become less connected to our internal experience and more connected to engaging with the outside world. Rather than using our voices from our bodies, we use our voices to please others, to communicate important concepts, to negotiate, and to work.

As infants, we self-soothe with pleasureful babbles and delightful body sounds of endless creative combinations. Very soon we learn not to make these sounds and self-soothe in this way for we are too old and must now use words. At around age one to two, we learn that when we speak words, this fills the adults around us with delight. We have made them happy. From age five on up, we begin to learn not to cry ("Don't cry"), not to express anger, and not to speak or laugh too loudly ("Use your inside voice"). In teenage years, we absolutely must use our voices in the same way as our peers or we will be ostracized. Consider the relatively new phenomenon of young women speaking from their vocal fry (Wolk et al., 2012).

THE VOICE IN ADULTHOOD

By adulthood, unless we are very unusual, we are mostly using our voices with an outward focus and to be a part of society. This encourages more focus on "other," and there is a gradual, persistent move away from using the voice to connect to and express from the body. Even professional and amateur singers most often use their voices to please others first and themselves second.

In 2009, I started a Singing for Stress Reduction class in a local adult community night school. The class attracted individuals who did not want to sing in a choir or in church. They did not want to rehearse or be required to make a commitment. They simply wanted to reconnect to their voices and sing for fun, pleasure, and relaxation. None of the members of the group were musicians or experienced singers. The group members were not asked to share their stories, but as the group bonded, the stories emerged. Often, the men stopped singing when their voices changed. The women also felt "not good enough" to sing. One woman, while singing with her class in school at age nine, had been told by her teacher to "mouth the words" or stop singing. This woman had just lost her father and was trying to hold back tears while singing, so her voice had sounded strained. The teacher's direction was quite effective because she stopped singing for a long time.

In working with individuals with autism and developmental disabilities, I have received quite an education in the astounding range of sounds that human beings are capable of generating from two little folds of mucous membranes located in the larynx. It was freeing and delightful to find my own voice could make these sounds, too. Yet, it became clear to me that most of us are very limited in our range of expression and that as we become socialized, we inhibit our expression to adhere to what society deems appropriate.

For this and many other reasons, encouraging our clients to use their singing voices as authentically as possible is an important therapeutic tool. While it would be unrealistic to believe that every client's therapeutic process is in their voice, in working with many different populations, I have found that most clients can benefit from some singing. Of course, some clients' journey of growth lies solely in their voices.

THE VOICE IN MUSIC THERAPY

Although it may be difficult and there may be resistance from certain clients or specific client populations, this does not necessarily void the therapeutic benefits of singing.

Consider, for example, one of the toughest populations to motivate for singing: 11- to 14-year-old boys (Ashley, 2015). Dr. Martin Ashley interviewed 400 boys ages 11 to 14 in order to understand why they had stopped singing in choirs. The main reason they listed was fear of being seen as "effeminate." Second, boys claimed they had stopped singing because they did not sound like the performers on *American Idol*. Third, voice changes greatly hindered their singing comfort level. Consequently, a program called "Boys Keep Singing" was initiated in England.

It is important to keep boys singing through their voice changes not just for physiological reasons, but for psychological ones as well. A 13-year-old client, upon hearing a recording of his pure boy soprano voice singing a song from a musical performance, burst into tears and cried, "I'll never have that voice again." This client, after expressing his grief, continued singing in musicals through cracks, breaks, and yodels. Due to the possibility that there may be boys and girls and clients of any population who truly wish to sing but cannot admit this, it is valid to introduce singing methods on some level. Even when the client(s) seem(s) disinterested, continuing to gently provide opportunities is therapeutically indicated.

While working with adolescents ages 10 to 16 with learning disabilities, I found there were two songs that they would sing while drumming loudly: "We Will Rock You" (May, 1977) and the interlude/vamp to "No Woman, No Cry (Everything's Gonna Be Alright)" (Ford, 1974). In a 40-minute session, singing lasted for 1 to 3 minutes on a good day. Still, a brief opportunity was provided for any clients who truly wanted to sing.

It is our job as therapists to move through our desire to be liked, to allow momentary discomfort, and to hold the tension by introducing significant therapeutic interventions so that we are not enabling our client's resistance to growth. I am not saying that we should force clients to sing, but I *am* saying that if we have an intuition that singing would help a group or individual process and don't initiate a vocal technique, this is as though we are saying, "You're right. Singing is too scary. Let's not do it."

Admittedly, it can be.

Many times in my work, I have felt strongly that the client needed to sing, but at the same time I have felt shy or frightened because I knew this would move us to a new intimacy. In these moments, I try to remember how important voice work has been for me, take a deep breath, and, as Ben Folds Five says (Folds, 2012), "Do It ... Anyway!"

To this day, I still feel anxious when introducing singing in new situations (new clients, new feelings, new experiences). While mistakes in initiating music therapy vocal methods do happen, most of the time singing has deepened the therapeutic relationship and provided an avenue for working on trust.

On a similar note, a vocal method that exists in the receptive domain of music therapy includes listening to recorded voices as they express for the client. While this method can promote deeply effective therapy, this book is mainly focused on encouraging therapists to sing in vivo.

THERAPEUTIC BENEFITS OF SINGING

The health and therapeutic benefits of singing have been well documented in research.

Only a small amount of the research is given here. It is my hope that this book will be used (torn, tattered, and coffee-stained) on site as a clinical hands-on, user-friendly manual. I imagine the reader having a need for ideas to facilitate cognitive development, for example, and turning to that section. Once there, the reader will find not only methods but also motivational research and mini case examples embedded into each goal area. The research is significant, and the case examples are authentic, meaning that the therapeutic outcomes described in each case example can actually happen. By weaving this information into the methods descriptions, I am saying, "Here's a recipe, and here's how delicious it can taste if you take your time and trust the process."

To get you started, here is a brief summary of the research.

One study that stands out was completed at Frankfurt University; it found that singing in a choir increases immuno-efficiency and improves emotional state (Kreutz et al., 2004).

Other studies have found a connection between singing and lowered blood pressure (Niu et al., 2011), increased lung capacity (Bonilha et al., 2009), development of stomach muscles, improved posture (Stacy et al., 2002), and release of endorphins (Dunbar et al., 2012). Singing has been increasingly used by people with Parkinson's disease to maintain vocal and respiratory control (Stegemoller et al., 2018), as well as speech production (Elefant et al., 2012; Yinger & Lapointe, 2012).

Further research has connected singing to feelings of well-being (Grape et al., 2002), group trust and cooperation (Anshel & Kipper, 1988), pain management (Bradt et al., 2016), decrease in depression and anxiety (Trimmer et al., 2016), improvement in cognitive processing for dementia patients (Satoh et al., 2015), recovery from nonfluent aphasia (Schlaug et al., 2010), and impaired speech due to brain injury (Tamplin, 2008).

This is indeed exciting information for music therapists employing vocal techniques, and yet there is a deeper part of human life that can be reached by singing in a therapeutic relationship.

Introduction

As stated earlier, voice is our first expression of self, and with this, there exists another level of benefit beyond the quantitative researcher's eye. Even the simplest of therapeutic vocal interventions can reach to the unconscious part of the mind and effect psychodynamic change. When people sing together, their heartbeats and breathing synchronize (Vickhoff et al., 2013). Furthermore, the vibrations of vocal cords, whether one set or many, produce a very pleasant vibro-acoustic sensation. This can connect individuals in an intimate way quickly or slowly, depending upon each unique client. This connection of breath, heartbeat, and vocal vibrations replicates being held in infancy and early childhood and can create a relationship of trust and safety that goes way beyond words.

At the time of therapy, Gloria was an 83-year-old woman with advanced Alzheimer's disease. She had essentially regressed back to infancy and was completely nonverbal except when she was singing Baptist hymns. When singing hymns, she could remember first, second, and third verses and descant parts. She also enjoyed scatting with wild abandon. Gloria was seen once weekly for one and a half years until she suffered a stroke and died a few months later. During this time, the only interaction she had with another person was while singing. At all other times, Gloria's eyes were closed and she was being fed or bathed or sitting in a Geri chair.

Gloria's chart revealed that her mother had died in childbirth. While singing, we would sit facing each other. As we sang together, she would lean toward me, often so close that our foreheads would touch. Once we were this close, she would just listen deeply to my voice. This would produce an intensely deep and powerful feeling of connection. It was as though some deep sorrow was being held.

We can never know, but the possibility exists that as Gloria regressed to a state similar to infancy, she was getting a second chance to be held before the end of her life. Thus, simply through singing together and sitting together with another, she may have been enabling her subconscious wounds to be companioned. She may have experienced less loneliness as the singing bridged her diseased, nonverbal mind to a caring "other."

Of course, not every client needs to or wants to work psychodynamically; however, as with a good recipe, there is always at least a little psychodynamic "salt and pepper" in the singing soup.

Like an elevator, music therapy vocal methods can carry you down to the depths of the building or can stay on the ground floor. Vocal methods can be highly effective in physical, mental, emotional, and psychodynamic areas of therapy. The methods discussed in this book will provide ideas and techniques pertaining to all four of these therapeutic areas.

However, the methods are organized not within these areas, but instead within the focus of goals. This distinction is being made in order to encourage the idea of flowing from one area to another and the thought that one technique can cover more than one area at the same time. The importance of goals as the focus will be considered later.

The necessity for the therapist to maintain an honest and grounded connection to their own vocal expression will be discussed as well. I hope that the book will encourage those therapists frightened of singing to do so as well as encourage veterans of singing to remember the powerful effectiveness of their work.

As a new clinician and for the first 10 years (and beyond) of my work in facilities, I was constantly searching for materials, ideas, and new ways to use the same songs with very limited populations, but, most of all, I needed to know that I wasn't just "singing a song" with someone ... that I was, in fact, making therapeutic change.

Even today, 30-plus years later, I have moments when I am thinking, "I have no idea what to do." I have learned this is a beautiful part of the therapeutic process in creative arts therapies. After all, we are creating in the moment, and sometimes we need to just be with our clients—whether through music, words, or silence—until the right method presents itself.

So, I also hope that this book will inspire readers to take risks and create their own vocal methods or take my ideas and change them.

Finally, voice is the only mode of musical expression that does not require an object outside of the body. A music therapy session can be run entirely with only singing. If you would like to gain a new insight into voice or are feeling stuck with your sessions, try this experiment: With no instruments in hand, introduce a simple chant. You can encourage hand-clapping, knee-patting, or foot-tapping while you simply keep singing. If you need to move in closer to your clients, do so. Move around the group (possibly in a chair with wheels) to sit or stand right in front of each individual or simply sing from the top of the semicircle. Try to stay with this for 30 to 60 seconds, even if no one else sings. Just say, "I really like this chant, and I want to share it with you." If you choose to do this little research project of self-inquiry, you will have explored something about the intimacy of voice. You will have raised the bar in terms of allowing your own vocal vulnerability and will also receive information about your clients.

This self-inquiry exercise, though not a requirement, is an interesting way to begin the Therapist Training section, which includes basic vocal exercises as well as use of the voice for self-exploration.

PART ONE:

THERAPIST TRAINING

Chapter 2

USING THE MUSICAL ELEMENTS

There are many music therapy publications, both articles and books, with extensive information on using musical elements in therapy. Specifically related to musical elements and voice, *Functional Voice Skills for Music Therapists* (Schwartz et al., 2018) holds excellent information and techniques. On this basis, therapeutic uses of musical elements in voice will be briefly covered here.

Rhythm

Just like drum, piano, and guitar, the rhythm of a voice can be used to connect with a client over time. Imagine playing with a baby by putting silly sounds to her movements. When the baby begins to realize that she is in control of the sounds she hears, she laughs with delight and her movements increase. Watch this baby explore, expand, and challenge her environment by creating new and bigger movements.

Making vocal sounds and singing in the rhythm of the client, or the rhythm in which you want the client to be, can promote confidence in one's environment and other, a sense of safety and trust (you see me), and a bridge for communication (you hear me).

This may be an elusive concept because we most often think of nonvoice instruments as the rhythm section.

> *MAGGIE was diagnosed with mild autism and began music therapy at the age of 2 to work on social interaction. She had no interest in sitting with the therapist, but, rather, preferred to spend the half-hour running around the room. The therapist spent the half-hour making up words and singing in rhythm to Maggie's movements. As Maggie was*

> running, this was mostly singing on eighth notes and sounded like, "Maggie's going to run and run and run and run and stop!"
>
> This extreme attention to Maggie's movements with sound and words was highly pleasing to her and promoted social interaction, as she would stop on cue, turn, and then look at the therapist. The therapist sang the rhythm of the notes exactly when Maggie's feet would hit the floor. This kind of social interaction allowed her to be in control of the connection and gave her complete freedom to move.

Pulse

In ensembles, it is the percussionist's job to keep good time. Yet, think for a moment about an individual who accelerates as they speak. What kind of listening experience does this create for you? Does your head spin? Now, think about someone who pauses frequently with "um's" and "uh's." This time, what is your experience of this person's communication? Do you perhaps hold your breath and forget to inhale during each pause? Do you want to complete their sentences for them? Once more, imagine someone speaking at a consistent and steady pace. Assuming this person is talking about something pleasant, does your body begin to relax? Do you inhale and feel a sense of safety? Do you find that you can listen with ease?

Whether singing with a faster pulse to motivate a client to reach a goal or singing in a soothing pulse to calm and empathize, it is important to maintain consistent pulse. This doesn't mean that you can't syncopate, observe ties, or breathe. It does mean that you need to know at all times where the downbeat falls and be able to communicate this through your voice.

I have heard singers pause often to correct a note or move the screen on their phone to see the chord chart. This creates anxiety for the listener. If your hand misses a chord, keep singing anyway. Make a ring binder full of your chord charts so you don't have to pause and scroll, or you can memorize the music. Practice with a metronome or while drumming or marching.

If you sing with a steady, consistent pulse, you communicate to the client, "I am steady and consistent. You can rely on me."

When using a steady pulse to sing with or for clients in deep distress, I often feel like a "good enough" parent soothing and rocking a child. I will admit this is difficult. It takes, patience, willingness to renew focus on each note, and rock-solid diaphragmatic support (with open throat and raised soft palate). However, the client's powerful response provides motivation.

If pulse is used with this knowledge over time, here is a place where safety and trust can be established with clients of all levels of disabilities, abilities, and diagnoses. No verbal processing need be done. The pulse of the voice can go way back to the mother's heartbeat in the womb and infancy. As well, the vibro-acoustic nature of the voice provides an experience of holding without any physical touch.

> *SARA is a 50-year-old woman being treated in a psychiatric facility for severe anxiety and depression. She arrived for her individual music therapy session having witnessed an upsetting event and was triggered into trauma. She was trembling; her heart was racing. The therapist picked up a singing bowl, encouraged Sara to feel her feet on the floor, and began to sing a steady pulse of "Mi–Do" on "ah."*
>
> *When Sara indicated that the sounds were okay, the therapist began singing in synchrony with Sara's breathing. As Sara's breathing slowed, the singing slowed as well. Sara was able to take a deep breath and describe what happened.*

Tempo

Tempo can be used to elevate heart rate or to slow down and calm an individual. Party band leaders play cover tunes much faster than the original version because they want people to dance rather than sit and listen. Relaxation recordings use slow to very slow tempos to encourage deep breathing and tension release. The resting heart rate is 50–75 bpm (Davidovic et al., 2016), depending on age. So, playing music faster or slower can affect an individual's physiology.

Because tempo is a powerful intervention, it is important to be able to sing at many different speeds. Issues that can occur when singing at faster tempos include articulating coherent lyrics and learning to inhale quickly by using the diaphragm. A brief inhale is called a catch breath and is a rather muscular practice. Singing at slow tempos also requires sustained breath support.

There is another consideration in singing various tempos, which is knowing your own natural rhythm. After I had been working clinically a little over one year, my supervisor, who was not a music therapist, wanted to video some of my groups. When I watched the recording, I was appalled to see that my tempos were consistently too slow and lacking energy, especially for the adolescent population with which I worked. When I thought about it more objectively, I realized my natural rhythm was mellow.

I had grown up in a Pennsylvania Dutch farm area in which people would drive 25 miles per hour down the main street, and Sundays were spent driving on country roads behind horses and buggies. While I realized that my natural rhythm was perfectly fine, I needed to step it up many notches to be an effective therapist.

Being aware of your innate tempo and honoring it is just as important as embracing various tempos.

> *The Recovery Choir was getting ready to begin rehearsal. The music therapist noticed that the overall energy of the group was hyper and anxious. She knew the choir needed to focus in order to be productive, so she introduced a fast vocal exercise on "ha" requiring consistent diaphragmatic support and release. This fast, athletic singing produced results much like an aerobic exercise and helped the choir members to release the excess energy.*
>
> *With each consecutive exercise, the tempo slowed until reaching 80 bpm. At this point, the mood of the choir was calm and attentive.*

Meter

Meter is all about the downbeat.

Just as with any instrument, when we sing, we need to emphasize the strong beat of the measure as well. For clients who are confused, withdrawn, or struggling emotionally, physically, mentally, or socially, observing the strong beat can help with mental clarity, with motivation to play or sing, and with locating the self in the present.

Sing the song "Daisy Bell" (Dacre, 1892) with a good emphasis on the downbeat of each 3/4 measure. Do you notice the energy you feel? Now sing "When the Saints Go Marching In" (Armstrong, 1938). Sometimes you will only be accenting the first beat, but in other sections you will be accenting all four beats of the measure. Singing in this way compels others to sing along, drum along, tap a toe, or listen.

A wonderful old hymn that emphasizes every beat in the measure with accent and text is the "Battle Hymn of the Republic" (Steffe & Howe, 1861). This song is a great example of a march in 4/4 meter. As singers, we can use not only the breath to emphasize a note but also the lyrics. Specifically, consonants help to provide accents. Practice feeling and singing meter in this way, with and without words, using scat syllables.

Practice singing in varied meters. Which meter do you like best? Which meter do you use most with your clients? Why? I can honestly say that I sang mostly in 4/4 when working with individuals with developmental disabilities. This meter choice was made for no other reason than it worked extremely well.

Clinically, it's okay to experiment with meter as long as there is a therapeutic reason. In the same way, it's okay to play mostly 4/4 if this meter accomplishes goals and objectives.

> *While running a coping skills group in a drug and alcohol rehabilitation center, the music therapist was aware of the group members having shared intense emotions with regard to their struggles and fears. She introduced "Amazing Grace" in a slow, 3/4 meter for two verses while observing the effect of the singing on the clients' breathing.*
>
> *Once the singing had effectively created deeper, slower breathing, the therapist smoothly shifted to a 9/8 time signature, being careful not to shift tempo. This inspired the clients to sing with gospel phrasing and to experience internally a brief shift from despair to hope and faith.*

Melody

Melody is the heart of a singer's expression. When we sing openly with authentic expression, our heart and soul connect to our voice and the melody flows. In these moments, the structure of the melody, the notes used to express the experience for the client—re-created or improvised—doesn't need any planning, analysis, or theoretical background: The therapist simply will pick and sing the right notes. Through melody, the therapist helps, encourages, leads, doubles, and sometimes solely expresses the thoughts/ feelings/ insights/ pain/ hopes of (and for) the client.

If pulse is the bridge for creating a safe connection to the client, melody is where the client and therapist meet in the middle of that bridge. Sometimes the therapist sings solo while the client listens. At other times, the client sings and the therapist listens. Once this happens, a conversation—a true duet—exists.

We sing established melodies, paraphrase, or create the music in the moment. We sing step-wise, arpeggios, octave leaps, one single note, and two- or three-note melodies. It does not matter, because when we sing from this experience of understanding, we will intuitively feel the client resonate when we hit a note and know how to compose or choose the next melody.

A melody can cause someone to cry, feel young again, remember how to speak, express a difficult emotion, feel less alone, be reminded of beautiful memories, or have an aching heart soothed. No melody is too simple.

What are your beloved melodies? Go explore and find some.

Then, use your vocal tools of resonance, breath, diction, and so forth (see basic vocal exercises), look at your client(s), intuit what they need, and sing.

> *ERIN was a high school senior who lost her mother to cancer and had sought vocal music therapy for grief support. She had been singing in musicals since the age of nine and possessed a powerful voice. Erin came into her tenth session excited to share that she had won the lead in her high school's current musical.*

> *As she shared, her triumph suddenly turned to active grief when she remembered her mother would not be there to hear her sing. While describing her anger and pain, Erin began to imagine Idina Menzel's expressive voice singing "Defying Gravity"(Schwartz, 2003). Erin knew the words were not about grief, but the therapist found the music and she began to sing.*
>
> *The challenging melody which moved up and down the scale continuously, dared the singer to persevere through intervallic ascending and descending leaps. In some measures, the melody would leap up a 6th and back down a 7th. In another, the singer was asked to leap up an interval of an 11th and land on high Eb.*
>
> *Erin was able to use the energy of the melody to wail on the high notes and express her pain in a raw, natural way without feeling inhibited. Once finished, the therapist and Erin talked about how the melody was bullying Erin just like her grief. It was forcing her to experience the highs and lows from elation to despair. In fact, the melody was making Erin angry and helping her to express just that. Erin left feeling sad and calm.*

Harmony

Harmony is an amazing intervention. In an improvisation class, Colin Lee asked students to experience each interval of the major scale and, in a spontaneous way, throw out words to describe these intervals.

We used words like "tense," "scary," "stable," "open," "sad," and "happy" to describe minor seconds, open fifths and fourths, minor thirds and major thirds. We had been studying music so long that we were no longer aware of the world of emotions living in between two notes.

Now, I welcome you to explore this world. In your favorite vocal key, play *Do* on any instrument. While sustaining Do, move up the scale while singing in half-steps. Notice the unique vibrations and how each interval feels to you. This is truly all the information you need to use vocal harmonies with clients.

In my first years of practice in serving individuals with developmental disabilities, I could not use harmonies, as my clients were not capable of this skill. Now, working with trained musicians, I still use harmonies mindfully. If an individual is working deeply, they may need to sing in unison for years. When moving to harmony, use those intervals within the chords that provide the most resonance for your voices. Ask "How was that for you?" Also, when moving to harmony, there must be a therapeutic purpose, such as modeling "It's okay to explore" or "It's okay to separate from the melody." A person can feel separation anxiety if the therapist moves to harmonies too soon. More often when using harmonies, holding the ground with a low Do or So can provide consistency and security so the client can explore freely while you stay present.

Harmony can be used toward many other goals, such as sense of independence, social interaction, building confidence, awareness of self and other, stress reduction, encouraging creativity, and so on. In summary, use harmony consciously. Do not use harmonies because you are bored. Move to harmony only when doing so will help to accomplish a clear intention.

> MARVIN was an 18-year-old young man diagnosed to be functioning at a 5-month-old mental age. After a year or so of tactile exploration and vibro-acoustic therapy with autoharp, drum, and cymbal, this young man began to play instruments. One instrument he loved was piano. He would take his two pointer fingers and play while exploring the keys with his tongue.
>
> With just two notes, Marvin would explore tension and release and make beautiful music happen. For years, he expressed on piano using two notes. It was in these moments I learned to see him not as a disabled individual, but as a man who knew something I didn't. He knew how to live for 18 years with profound physical and mental limits. I can hear Marvin saying, "See, Kelly, you have this whole, big piano, but I only have these two notes. So, I'm going to make them beautiful!"

Dynamics

Dynamics are synonymous with energy. Dynamics, or the force of a sound wave, are measured in decibels. For example, a whisper is 15 decibels, a normal conversation is 60 decibels, and a rock concert's decibel rate is 120 (Garden, 2020).

Dynamics can express a soothing energy—*pianissimo*; a surprising energy—*sforzando*; a fading energy—*diminuendo*; a powerful energy—*fortissimo*.

Just like tempo, dynamics can be used to quickly effect changes in a client's state. Often, working with seniors in drum/percussion circles requires medium to medium-loud voice volume, while working in hospice and in the NICU can require sustained, soft tones.

But let's assume for a moment that you are running a group or an individual session in which you can use dynamics at your discretion. How will you choose to use this element of music? How do soft and loud feel to you? Do you like all of the dynamic levels in between?

Find a short song you enjoy and sing it through, using many different dynamic levels. There is a tendency to change speed with dynamics. Refrain from getting slower when singing softly or speeding up when singing loudly. Just use a different dynamic for each verse. It's amazing how this single element completely changes the feeling of the song and the meaning of the words.

This is a wonderful tool that can be used to create various musical experiences with one song. It is also helpful for providing variety on familiar tunes when the population requires short (30-second) songs. It can be quite effective after singing many verses of a song like "This Little Light of Mine" (Loes, 1920) or Leonard Cohen's "Hallelujah" (1984) to suddenly sing *pianissimo*. With this technique, the words suddenly seem more emotional, and a prayer-like quality can appear in the singing.

Another technique that creates emotion is directing the client(s) to sing little swells of *crescendo/decrescendo* within one or two measures of a song.

These are just a few examples, as there are many variations for using dynamics. Create your own and watch the spontaneous emotions happen.

HILLARY is in recovery for an eating disorder. She loves to sing in her music therapy sessions. She consistently requests the vocal warm-up with the pretty chords. The warm-up is simply an ascending and descending pattern on thirds with major and minor seven chords. The chords have a soothing quality, and, as Hillary and the music therapist sing in unison, they crescendo and decrescendo through the two-measure motive.

The therapist can sense a swell of emotion when the dynamics swell. When they finish, Hillary says that when singing like this, it is one of the few times she feels a sense of well-being.

Timbre

Vocal timbre is subjective for the listener. Janis Joplin's voice was scratchy and raspy yet reached many people's souls. The high soprano sounds of opera may be blissful to some and shrill to others. The scream technique used in heavy metal music provides release to some and pain to others. Rapping is monotonous to some and poetry to others.

It is actually not beneficial to wonder whether our clients like our voices. It is way more important to pay attention to the client.

Most of the time, we are encouraging clients to sing along or play along, so our voices just become part of the musical landscape when we are not leading. Yet sometimes, such as in hospice care, we are doing the singing for the client. In these times, producing a timbre that is therapeutic is an intuitive process of watching the client, sensing tension and relaxation, and observing breath and skin tone.

When client and therapist are entrained, the client's responses to the tones and vibrations of the therapist's voice become much clearer. It is highly possible when in a deeply resonating musical relationship to understand that the client needs the therapist to sing low, earthy tones or that the client feels permission to cry when the therapist sings high, soft sounds.

Of course, over time, as we get to know our clients, the best timbre to help them express or feel understood becomes familiar.

When singing with clients, whether in groups or individually, unless there is a need for modeling a vocal goal, it is best to duplicate the timbre closest to the client's voice. In this way, the client is being doubled and reflected throughout the music-making.

> ELIZABETH had received a diagnosis of terminal cancer and requested a session with the music therapist. As they spoke, Elizabeth began to sob. The therapist began singing softly in the mid to mid-high part of her range with open oohs, ahs, and ohs. As she sang, she felt Elizabeth's sorrow and allowed this sound to come through her voice.
> When Elizabeth could speak again, she said that was exactly how she had felt. She had wanted to express this but couldn't make a sound.

Texture

The human voice is the only living instrument. While it is true that we are all born with a specific vocal quality, sound is also shaped using the lips, cheeks, soft palate, nasal passage, tongue position, and jaw.

If you scan your playlist, you will probably find a variety of vocal textures. My playlist contains the various vocal textures of Chaka Khan, Sarah Vaughn, Steven Tyler, Michael Bublé, Bill Withers, and Amy Winehouse. Chaka Khan can belt to a high G. Sarah has the flow and vibrato of a classical singer. Steven's voice is a hard-edged shriek. Michael sounds akin to the smooth baritone-tenor voice of Frank Sinatra. Bill has a warm, natural, easy voice that sounds almost like speaking. Amy's soulful, crusty contralto is incomparable.

Also take into account the many instrumental textures of Bobby McFerrin and Al Jarreau, as well as those of beat boxers. The human voice is capable of tremendous flexibility and sound variety.

Self-calming behavior for infants includes vocal play such as lip buzzing, tongue exploration, shrieks, and slides.

While working with individuals with profound disabilities, I realized there were many more textures in my voice than I used on a daily basis. The freedom of expression without words was exhilarating. Explore the textures of your voice by singing, "Old MacDonald Had a Farm" (Crosby, 1959) and imitate various animal noises; try making percussive sounds with your mouth, tongue, and voice; visit a baby and communicate with them. You will find or remember the flexibility of the human voice.

While this wide range of textures may not be appropriate for working with all clients, it is still beneficial to expand and stretch the voice so that we have them in our "utility kit" when needed.

> GERALD *is a six-year-old boy on the autism spectrum who attends individual music therapy sessions. His interaction with the therapist is minimal except for the times when the therapist imitates his vocal sounds and inserts them into a song. The therapist imitates lip buzzes, laser gun sounds, low growls, nonsense syllables, high-pitched shrieks, and slides as he becomes adept at fitting these sounds into a song pattern.*
>
> *When Gerald is echoed in this way, social interaction increases as he ceases rocking, looks at the therapist, and continues to make sounds. On one or two occasions, Gerald has dialogued briefly with the therapist.*

Form

Whether improvising or re-creating, when musical form gets complicated, clients are most often no longer working on therapeutic goals and are moving toward music skills goals. Therefore, simple forms such as *A* ("You Are My Sunshine," Davis & Mitchell, 1939; "Amazing Grace," Newton, 1779), *AB* ("Stand by Me," King, 1961; "Greensleeves," Hollens & Faust, 2018), *AAB* (traditional 12-bar blues; "Let It Be," Lennon & McCartney, 1970), and *AABA* ("Hey Jude," Lennon & McCartney, 1968; "To Make You Feel My Love," Dylan, 1997; "Girl From Ipanema," Jobim, 1964) are highly effective in creating a container for therapy.

With a beginning, middle, and end, a predictable road map provides the client with a holding structure and room to explore.

In jazz, the road map or form is used for solo journeys. Musicians can signal in the moment where to go in the form (e.g., hand on top of the head for da capo, finger to the nose for the bridge).

Musical form is an excellent way to improvise. If a client shows a particular connection to lyrics, chord texture, or melody in any part of a song, the form can be changed immediately in the moment and intervention can be based upon that section of the song. The therapist can go back to that section frequently, repeat it as a chant, dialogue musically upon it, write new lyrics, and so forth. It is amazing how many times the entire session can boil down to one simple sentence or phrase, the simplicity of which is a powerful bookmark for remembering a resource from that session.

When the therapist listens to detail, senses the client's connection, and varies the form in response, the therapist is saying, "This is important. Let's sit in this together and just allow. Let's take our time."

> *As the music therapy bereavement group session was coming to an end, MATT was still actively crying. He needed help to ground his emotions and feel safe to close. The therapist introduced "Sunshine on My Shoulder" (John Denver), a song he knew had brought Matt comfort. After singing verse/chorus, the group was guided to repeat the chorus and then to simply repeat the opening line of the chorus, "Sunshine on my shoulder makes me happy."*
>
> *This section of the song moves back and forth from major to minor chords. This, along with the words and the vibrations of the voices, helped Matt to shift from deep distress to calm sadness.*

Text

As a performer, I won't sing a song if I don't believe the lyrics in the moment. This includes singing cover tunes, music theater tunes, classical, and jazz. The only song I ever refused to sing for a bandleader was Madonna's "Hanky Panky" (1990), which was about physical abuse. Otherwise, it was my job to connect with the lyrics.

As music therapists, it is also our job to connect with the lyrics. Sometimes singing a song week after week can get old; at other times, the connection doesn't come right away. Still, striving to feel the meaning of the lyrics with a client is part of what sets us apart from non–music therapist performers. Especially if there is no verbal processing happening in the session, helping the client to express the words while singing may be the only verbal therapeutic intervention.

80-year-old ETHEL is singing with the music therapist at the senior center. Her vocal cords are bowed and stiff, so she cannot possibly come close to singing the melody of "Misty." Yet, she knows every word and sings on one or two pitches. As she sings, in her mind she is 20 years old and dancing for the first time as a wife with her handsome groom now long deceased.

Chapter 3

EXPLORING YOUR OWN VOCAL RANGE/LIMITS

When I started teaching in a private studio, occasionally a young student would confess that upon being asked for voice lessons, a parent would incredulously proclaim, "What do you need lessons for?! Just open your mouth and sing!"

Au contraire. Would that it was so simple.

Students

Music therapy functional voice class is usually geared toward basic technique. However, a student's psychological and biographical connection to the voice is markedly present. Some students are comfortable singing slow, soft to medium-soft soothing sounds but fearful of using the voice to lead and direct in a medium dynamic with punctuated, march-like textures. Others love using the lower part of their vocal range (G below middle C to G above middle C) but exhibit reluctance to choose keys that center the vocal melody higher than that. A few students love improvisation yet struggle to accurately re-create composed melodies. Most students, however, are frightened of vocal improvisation.

Vocal majors, or those who have experienced success and self-esteem in the vocal performance world, feel sad or angry upon being asked to sing more simply. Some singers struggle with letting go of R&B or jazz melodic stylings, while others use rock-and-roll inflections or country twang in their diction. This portion of the book brings students and therapists face-to-face with their connection to their own voices as well as their strengths and weaknesses.

Just as in any voice class where students need to become aware of their limits and strengthen their vocal technique by expanding range, learning to sing correct melodies in tune, executing open vowel diction, and singing at different tempos and dynamic levels, the same holds true for music therapists. However, the focus of this book is not about performing but instead about meeting the vocal needs of clients.

Professionals

As vocal professionals, music therapists need to find ways to maintain these vocal skills over time. Maybe your client, Harry, used to be a high tenor and loves to sing high Cs. Maybe Sara really doesn't like R&B. Perhaps Ethel's wedding song was "Fly Me to the Moon" (Howard, 1964), and when the therapist changes the original melody, she feels alone. Perhaps Joey will not drum or sing unless the tempo is fast and percussive.

Therapists in the field are called upon to continue to expand and connect to their voices. It takes diligence and perseverance to use the voice day-to-day with energy and a focus on helping clients to achieve self-expression.

In working with seniors with developmental disabilities, I was called upon to reinvent my interest in singing the same songs over and over again. While it was not practical for these individuals to learn new songs at this point in their lives, they knew many from their past.

> *BRAXTON's whole face shone with love for "By the Light of the Silvery Moon."*
> *SYDNEY became a cabaret singer/dancer during the group's rendition of "When the Saints Go Marching In."*

My former client Jeanette became radiant with beauty when singing, "Take Me Out to the Ball Game" (Norworth & Von Tilzer, 1908). About two years into running this group twice a week, I began to feel dread about singing "Take Me Out to the Ball Game." It was compelling to imagine the scenario of not singing it anymore. Then, one morning as I watched Jeanette's face, I was struck with a realization. Jeanette told me that she had been a patient at a mental hospital. She probably would have been placed there as a child, which was not an uncommon practice. When state facilities began downsizing in the 1960s, Jeanette would have been in her 30s. History is rampant with stories of abuse of and inhumane conditions for institutionalized patients. In this moment, I got the strong sense that "Take Me Out to the Ball Game" had been there for Jeanette through difficult times. Even if she had not experienced or witnessed abuse, being separated from her loved ones may have been traumatic enough.

Regardless of whether this was true, the thought provided me with a way to reconnect to the song and, in turn, to Jeanette. In my mind, I was no longer humoring her with a cute song; instead, she was sharing with me an experience of a song that had brought her joy. Like a little gift box, the song became a container that held her resilience and wisdom about surviving life. No longer was "Take Me Out to the Ball Game" boring.

In another setting, while running groups of nonverbal adults with severe mental disabilities, I had one client named Susie who communicated vocally solely by crying and wailing. In order to interact with her, I had to play guitar in a minor key and wail along. I knew the care workers were rolling their eyes. In all honesty, it must have been difficult to listen to. But the members of this group were so withdrawn that I felt it was important to initiate interaction with each one. Susie was absolutely giving me clear vocal expression, so, each week, I wailed with her. It felt agonizing, but I couldn't ignore Susie's plea.

These are the challenges we face every single day when choosing to sing (or not sing) with our clients. A music therapist might choose to sing only with verbal clients because nonverbal may require improvisation. A music therapist could choose to sing only in lower keys because higher ones are more revealing. A music therapist can choose to sing with jazz inflections because their self-esteem is connected to sounding that way. A music therapist might avoid singing certain song material or with certain clients altogether. A music therapist might choose to make up a melody because it's too much effort to look up the original version. A music therapist can avoid a song because it makes them cry.

Burnout and Vocal Self-Care

In my journey with voice, I have felt moments of resistance and have not made perfect choices myself. I've had moments of struggle—some longer than others—but, eventually, I have found a way to reconnect to the singing and to my clients. When I could not reconnect, I knew it was time to move to a new job.

Continuing to stay when not connected to the music leads to burnout, and it is just not worth it. It's like doing eight shows a week of a long-running Broadway musical, but without the fame and fortune. There is also an aspect of guilt over not trying harder to connect to the client. Also, there are ethical considerations: "Should I still be singing this song with this client if I am miserable in doing so?"

You can begin to see how voice—as a primary therapeutic instrument in its connection to self-esteem, psychological makeup, biological history, and understanding of the client can be complicated. Yet, these very complications are the key to meaningful and deep singing.

There is a self-care metaphor that portrays a parent on an airplane flight in a cabin pressure emergency. The message is for the parent to don the oxygen mask first before putting it on a young child. Of course, the parent cannot help his young child breathe if he has fainted. In *The Theory and Practice of Vocal Psychotherapy*, Diane Austin states: "Pianos go out of tune, violin strings can wear out, and drums sometimes need repairing. Being a human instrument requires commitment to self-care" (Austin, 2009, p. 100). Quite simply, the therapist cannot help his clients to sing authentically if he does not know how to use his own authentic voice.

Although the vocal journey may be work, it can also be extremely relaxing, invigorating, and peaceful and can bring the singer a strengthened sense of self.

The following section contains techniques and exercises for exploring and expanding one's voice. They are helpful for students, beginning music therapists, and those with experience in the field as a way to connect and reconnect to one's natural singing voice.

BASIC VOCAL TECHNIQUE EXERCISES

The purpose of vocal exercises is to increase the strength and flexibility of the musculature used to produce sound, including the larynx, the diaphragm, and the lungs.

Exploring Your Own Vocal Range/Limits

Ultimately, the goal is for the singing to be effortless and natural so that the focus can be on the music and the client. In considering basic technique, the four areas that stand out are: breath support, placement (resonance), diction, and range. Here are some basic exercises and their benefits.

Breath Support

Watch a baby or a pet breathe while sleeping. They have a relaxed and natural wave of inhaling/exhaling. Breathing is a function of the autonomic nervous system, yet this seems to be a topic upon which many self-help books have been written. If you would like to see how many, simply do an online search for "books on breathing."

If breathing is automatic, why is it so hard? The answer is stress. Over time, we learn many habits of reaction to stress, such as tensing muscle groups and shallow breathing. For singers, shallow breathing can limit the ability to sing in tune, to sing high notes, and to sing long phrases, and it can even affect cognitive skills (word and melody memory). In endeavoring to perform, to run a session, and to practice a song, stress and shallow breathing happen. Here are a few suggestions:

1. *Hissing out, or swimmer's breath:* Using a steady "S" sound, hiss out all of the air from your lungs, making sure that you are standing with shoulders, neck, and jaw relaxed, chest open, and stomach tucked. As you hiss out, continue to tuck your stomach inward while your chest stays open (stomach tucked, chest open). When you feel that all of the air has been depleted, continue to hiss a little more. Then, simply inhale through your nose, making sure your mouth is closed. From this depleted sensation, your lungs will completely expand, filling to capacity in a natural, relaxed way, and you will help your body to remember the experience of a full inhale. This is such a simple yet important exercise, as we forget all day long to inhale fully. This is also excellent for stress reduction and fear.

2. *Singing long passages:* A standard but very boring go-to exercise for breath endurance is long tones. Because long tones can be like a competition with oneself, these tend to produce muscle

tension and irritation, which defeats the purpose. As a more interesting alternative, choose a song that has long, sustained phrases. Current pop tunes tend to have very short phrases, so a music theater piece, jazz standard, hymn, or classical piece is a good choice.

There is a tendency for singers to take a breath in the middle of a word or to separate sentence phrases with an inhale. This causes the lyric to lose its meaning. For example, "A-*(breath)*-mazing Grace, how sweet the sound" makes no sense. "And grace my fears re-*(breath)*-lieved" sounds quite silly.

So, let's take "Amazing Grace" (Newton, 1779) and put breath marks in the chart or lyric sheet. You can use a big, red apostrophe.

First, speak the words. Read and say the song as though you were talking to someone and communicating its meaning. Notice and mark where you take a breath while speaking. I will use bold opening/closing parentheses.

> Amazing Grace, **()** how sweet the sound **()**
> That saved a wretch, **()** like me. **()**
> I once was lost, **()** but now am found, **()**
> Was blind, **()** but now I see. **()**

Begin the song at a moderate tempo in 3/4, then gradually slow the tempo. Challenge yourself to hold the notes at the ends of phrases. If you feel as though you are running out of breath, support the diaphragm by tucking in the stomach more and allowing the voice to be less than perfect.

Make sure you do NOT pinch your throat. There are so many great songs that can be practiced in this way. This song-breath exercise is more interesting than long tones and will increase your lung capacity and ability to sing through long phrases.

3. *Playing a recorder:* Sometimes people find it easier to think about breath support when vibrating the air through an instrument outside the body. Again, if the phrases are long enough, this will build lung capacity and possibly be fun. It

may also bring new interest to much-used songs. So, purchase a recorder and play.

Therapeutic Considerations for Singing with Support
When I hear singing with less than average breath energy and chopped phrases, I feel disconnected from the music. What I am experiencing is the singer's lack of breath commitment to my song. On the other hand, when I hear someone engaging their breath and supporting my beloved melody (let's say this is a song from my youth, with many memories), I sometimes cry. As the singer works to support their breath through the melody, I feel as though I am being supported.

So, here is a way to connect through music with your client on every single note simply by singing with breath support. Singing correctly is very athletic. If you feel tired and relaxed after you have finished these exercises, you have done them correctly.

Placement and Resonance

A common phrase heard often in voice lessons is "Avoid singing from the throat." In actuality, the voice does resonate primarily in the throat, mouth, and nasal cavity. Yet, it is a chronic issue for vocalists to pinch and push in the throat and neck area. There is also a psychological component in squeezing and pinching in order to sound louder or emulate a popular singer. In very basic terms, voice teachers use exercises that help the student to focus the tone forward in the front of the face (the mask) or, for very high notes, toward the top of the head. This gives the singer much more warmth, volume, and freely vibrating tone. The counterintuitive action of controlling the throat muscles restricts tone. An open throat allows for more sound vibrating in the facial cavities and a more present voice.

1. *Yawn:* When we yawn, the back of the throat opens in a relaxed stretch. Pretend you are yawning. Then, sing vowels from that same open space. With a soft breath, inhale as though you are surprised by something, then sing. This sets up the beginning of the tone with a throat that is already open (soft palate relaxed and raised). This might feel uncomfortable and vulnerable at

first. Try focusing on hearing and feeling the resonance this creates instead of focusing on the discomfort.

2. *Hum:* Making sure to keep the back of the throat open, simply hum. You can hum a five-note descending pattern, a song, or anything you choose. This is a great warm-up for helping you to remember how mask resonance feels. It is also very relaxing. When humming, there is no pressure to project. The breath slows as we take deep inhales and the vibrations are experienced from within the body. As you ascend and descend, you can also easily feel the tone moving up and down the front of the face and to the head. This gives a clear idea of focusing the tone forward.

3. *Straw:* With your mouth closed around a straw, hum into the straw. This will create a pleasant, buzzing sensation that, again, will emphasize resonance in the mask. Vocal slides fit nicely with this exercise. Try singing Do to So and back down in a smooth, connected slide. The slimmer the straw, the more vibration you will feel. Slides also help to smooth out breaks in the voice.

Therapeutic Considerations for Singing with Resonance
When singing in the throat or otherwise blocking, pinching, and/or pushing the sound, the tone takes on an unnatural and inauthentic texture. The presence of the voice is muted and held back. This can feel to a client like the therapist is not completely present in the music. When the voice is vibrating freely and placed forward, it is more likely that the client will feel the therapist's vocal presence as well as human presence.

Diction

Diction is a tricky concept when singing nonclassical, contemporary music. I have had students express to me that because they are singing a pop tune, they don't need to enunciate. It's true that in singing contemporary music, the vowels are not as long as classical vowels. However, they still need to be open. Closed vowels and a half-open mouth will act as a mute for the sound, and vocal production will be taxing. So, it is helpful and healthful to sing with open vowels. I once had an argument with one of my jazz students who loved U2 and insisted that Bono did not sing with open vowels. I challenged him to listen and report back. Of course, Bono sings with open vowels.

1. *Chewing (loosening the jaw):* On one single tone, sing, "Mow, Mow, Mow" (rhyming with "how," not "no"). Sing slowly and notice the smooth opening and closing motion of your jaw. Look in the mirror and make sure that you are dropping your jaw to form a long *ah* shape that moves to a long *ooh* at the end of the W. Take your fingers and massage your jaw while singing to loosen it up more. Move up in half-steps, continuing to open and close the mouth and jaw. The "M" consonant helps to place the sound forward, which can continue into the *ow* vowel. This can create a pleasant, Zen-like sensation, which also contributes to relaxed singing.

2. *Descending vowels:* Using a five-note descending pattern on Sol Fa Mi Re Do, sing the vowels "May, Mee, Mah, Moh, Moo." Continue working the mouth and jaw in the same way as above. If your jaw stays relaxed and you overemphasize the vowels, you are probably doing it right. Look in the mirror to make sure you are opening the vowels. Move the five-note pattern up in half-steps.

3. *Descending words:* Using the same five-note descending pattern, write words and sing. It doesn't matter what you write, as the point of the exercise is to practice singing through various vowel/consonant combinations while enunciating clearly. You could sing "I can sing with ease," "My dog has the fleas," "Take me to the zoo," "I am o-pen now." Notice on which vowels you find it easier to be open and which hold some tension. If you find a specific vowel that needs work, practice singing any motive you like on that vowel. Some singers love this exercise because the warm-up becomes like a chant and helps them to relax not only vocally, but also mentally/emotionally. I use this with clients, as well.

Therapeutic Considerations for Open Diction
Voice is the only instrument that uses words and notes together as the mode of expression. When doing lyric analysis with clients, I am often surprised by which words have meaning. Each word has the possibility of being a window that opens an emotion, a thought, or a memory for your client(s). When a therapist pays attention to the words, this communicates attentiveness to the client. When the voice and vowels are open, the therapist presents as open and able to be with whatever emotions and experiences may come.

Range

As stated earlier, it is not uncommon for both vocal majors and nonvocal majors to feel a greater connection to and take greater pleasure in a specific part of the vocal range. Added to this, singers can experience psychological discomfort and avoidance of certain areas of the range. In a functional voice lesson, a soprano proclaimed, "The lower part of my voice is manly and ugly." Most often, women and men who are not classical singers need encouragement and instruction to sing higher.

A student who sang alto and tenor through high school discovered she could sing to a high A above high C. Pemberton (Pemberton et al., 1998) found that women's speaking voices have lowered considerably from 1945 to 1993. Cheng (Cheng et al., 2016) determined that people speaking with lower voices ranked higher socially and were perceived as more dominant.

In a desire to compete in society, women have lost a whole range of expression. Tenderness, vulnerability, softness, and childlike playfulness have been given up for strength. These issues present themselves in the classroom and for professionals as we work to keep all of the notes with which we were born.

Similarly, baritones and baritone tenors need to strive to gain comfort above a middle C and to find keys that help them reflect and double their clients. The following exercises are not meant to expand the music therapist's range, but instead to increase comfort in the existing range.

Exploring Your Own Vocal Range/Limits

1. *Lip trills:* Lip trills are used for warm-ups, warm-downs, vocal therapy, and rehab before and after surgery. Lip trills vibrate the vocal folds in a naturally relaxed way because during the lip trill, both the lips and the vocal cords are taking the air pressure, as opposed to the vocal cords alone. Also, when lip trilling, the cords do not completely come together (Gaskill & Erickson, 2008).

   Lip trills are difficult to describe, but, basically, a lip trill is like making a bubble sound with your lips while singing. It is best to simply do an online search for "lip trills" and watch a YouTube demonstration.

   In using lip trills to work on range, the singer can execute an ascending/descending motive of a fifth or an octave. It is also helpful to do glissando slides from low to high. In the same way, this exercise can be used to practice singing in the lower range.

   Finally, if a particular song presents an issue or desire to pinch, it may be beneficial to lip trill the entire song even though this may feel rather silly.

2. *Five-note ascending/descending motive:* On any vowel, sing Do Re Mi Fa Sol Fa Mi Re Do. A common phrase used by voice teachers when warming up students is "Let's get you a good stretch." This translates to the action of singing to the top part of the range. When the vocal cords are viewed in action by using a stroboscope (a magnified strobe light placed in the mouth and throat), the vocal cords are seen to move like a rubber band in a beautiful, fluid stretch. Like the strings on a piano, the higher one sings, the thinner the cord becomes. This five-note motive allows the singer to briefly vibrate the top note and then descend again. It is a helpful way to practice comfort in the higher range while staying relaxed. The reverse exercise can be done for low range: Sol Fa Mi Re Do Re Mi Fa Sol.

3. *Transpose songs:* Take simple music therapy songs and practice singing them in different keys. Some suggestions for songs might be "The More We Are Together" (Raffi, 1976), "Twinkle, Twinkle, Little Star" (Taylor, 1806), and "Bingo" (Fox, 2008).

4. *Practice difficult songs:* Sing songs with a note span of an octave or more. Make sure to find a key in which the melody falls within G below middle C to D above high C. Song suggestions include "Somewhere Over the Rainbow" (Arlen & Harburg, 1939), "Let It Be" Lennon & McCartney, 1970), "Moon River" (Mancini & Mercer, 1960), "The Star Spangled Banner" (Smith & Key, 1773/1814), and "What a Wonderful World" (Thiele & Weiss, 1967).

Therapeutic Considerations for Using Full Range
When a singer avoids areas of their natural range, they communicate exactly that: avoidance of experiencing vibration in a specific area of the voice and avoidance of connecting to a part of oneself. When the singer demonstrates a willingness to express and explore range, they are modeling and encouraging clients to do the same. This also can translate into modeling a willingness to explore and expand as an individual.

ONE FINAL NOTE

Vibrato

Too much vibrato is a tricky issue. Ideally, one should be able to sing in a straight tone (no vibrato) and/or with a light, simple vibrato. When a therapist sings with very present, big vibrato, whether intended or not, she can come across as though she is performing rather than reflecting or leading the client(s).

For years, I worked with children and adults with mental, physical, and neurological disabilities. I can honestly say that not one of them sang with vibrato. Even now, in working with trained musicians, if I use too much vibrato, they politely sing more softly or stop singing. It is possible to sing safely with straight tone. It is a matter of adjusting air pressure—specifically, using less air pressure in the epigastric region or the upper region of the stomach as well as focusing the tone in a specific way (Katok, 2016). There can also be an element of nervousness and self-concept involved in too much vibrato.

In practicing straight tone, there are two key considerations: (1) straight tone tends to be a controversial topic among voice teachers, and (2) it is not uncommon for singers to pinch the throat in order to achieve straight tone.

For these reasons, no exercises are listed here. It is highly recommended that a lesson or two with a professional voice teacher be considered to help with this concept.

Chapter 4

IMPROVISATION

As I sat and stared at this blank page titled "Improvisation," I had to laugh. In the beginning of learning to improvise, it felt exactly like staring at this page. My mind and ears were a big, huge question mark. "I can't think of anything." "I don't hear anything." "I don't know what syllables to sing." "I am going to sound really stupid."

I had been singing professionally for about 10 years when I began to be bored by imitating cover tunes, so I ventured into some jazz. Both of my brothers are professional jazz musicians, so I thought I "should" just be able to do it. In fact, helpful people would say, "Just do it."

So, I tried to "Just do it" for a few months and realized that wasn't working.

After studying with several jazz teachers, I found one who knew how to teach vocalists. Joe Federico of the Dennis Sandoli method taught me the difference between vocal improvisation and instrumental improvisation is the inner ear. This is not to say that instrumentalists don't have to hear their ideas, but they can also glean ideas from the many scales and modes highly practiced in their fingers. Because vocalists have no keys or strings, Joe taught me, if it is not in my inner ear, then nothing's coming out.

The Sandoli method was built around composing alternate melodies and solos over jazz tune chords. As I moved into this process, I realized that what was happening was that I was building up an index card catalog of motives in my head and ear. Improvising is simply composing in the moment. I simply had to learn how to piece my index cards together while singing, and I had an improvised solo.

The good news is that music therapists don't have to take complicated jazz solos, don't have to know the many endless derivations of the modes, and don't have to transpose their solos into all 12 keys. In my experience, there was only one client for whom the therapeutic process was in scat-singing jazz. That's exactly one in 36 years of practice.

In fact, music therapy vocal improvisation is often in one key with an occasional shift to a second key. As well, the song structure is usually less complicated than that of jazz tunes, and the chord changes move more slowly. The more complicated the music becomes, the more the client is encouraged to analyze rather than create from the psyche and the body.

There's more good news. As musicians, music therapists have already listened to a lifetime of music. There are many index cards in the ears ready to go, and all that needs to be done is to access them. The library is full of content. Now let's do some research.

Improvisation Exercises

Keep in mind that these exercises are not designed for the purpose of performing technically advanced improvisations, but instead to help the therapist become more comfortable with spontaneous vocal exploration. Improvisation as a therapeutic intervention can help a client to achieve specific goals that will be discussed later. A rule of thumb in improvisation is to try to keep going for at least 32 to 64 measures, even if you are singing only one or two notes. It's important to practice feeling the discomfort of the unknown and continue anyway.

1. *Two- and three-chord progressions:* Using two or three chords, play the progression repeatedly for at least 32 measures and improvise vocally. In order to orient your ear to the chords, play and sing the scale(s) which correspond(s) to the progression. This basically means that Do is the root of the tonic chord. So, if you play a Cmaj7 to an Fmaj7, play and then sing the C major scale over the chord progression. When you feel confident with the scale, begin to improvise. You can start by singing one note per chord, then two notes per chord, then three. If you are having trouble hearing notes, you can improvise simply on piano or guitar and then sing back the notes you have played. As you gain confidence, explore with varied rhythms, range, dynamics, consonance and dissonance, and/or words and no

Improvisation

words (oohs and ahs, ba, doo, la, etc.). For variety, sing to different time signatures and styles or use different instruments. This simple exercise can open you up to a whole world of vocal exploration. [See Table 1 and Figures 1(a)–1(h).]

Table 1
Sample Chord Progressions

Sample chord progressions:	Sample meter/tempo:
C maj7 to Fmaj7	fast/slow
Fmaj7 to Gb7	3/4 4/4 6/8 12/8
Gmin to Gmin/F# to Gmin/F to C7/E	**Sample styles:**
Dmin7 to Eb7	Shuffle
Amin to Emin	Straight ballad
	Swing
Bb7 to Eb7	Latin
Dmin to Amaj	Gospel
Ab to Bbmin/Ab	Funk

Figure 1(a). Sing corresponding scale.

Figure 1(b). Improvise whole notes. Repeat with different notes.

Figure 1(c). Improvise half-notes. Repeat with different notes.

Figure 1(d). Improvise notes and rhythms.

Figure 1(e). Funk chord progression. Corresponding scale, F Lydian (B♮).

Figure 1(f). Gospel. Corresponding scale, B♭ Mixolydian (blues).

Figure 1(g). Reggae. Corresponding scales, E♭ Major to D♭ Major.

Figure 1(h). Waltz swing. Corresponding scale, D Dorian.

2. *Paraphrase a melody:* Improvise a countermelody over the chords of a familiar song. If you have difficulty in letting go of the original melody, you can play a countermelody first on another pitched instrument like piano, guitar, flute, xylophone, and so forth. Again, explore rhythm, dynamics, range, dissonance/ consonance, and words/ no words. Countermelodies can be very simple and still work beautifully to help reach a client's goals. (See Figure 2.)

Figure 2. "Twinkle, Twinkle," with alternate melody.

3. *The blues:* When a musician decides to learn to play jazz, they are instructed to begin with the most basic and original form of jazz: the blues. Play your basic, grassroots 12-bar blues in any key, and preferably in a key that helps you to access the strongest part of your voice (usually midvoice). To orient your ear, play and sing the mixolydian mode or blues scale over the 12-bar form. In the key of C, the blues scale would be C, Eb, F, Gb, G, Bb, C, Bb, G, Gb, F, Eb, C. Then, let go of the scale and improvise a blues melody. You can again sing one note per

chord, and then two, and so on. You can also sing a very simple melody while improvising rhythmically on syllables. The consonants can be used to make percussive sounds.

The blues form is great for improvising with words. One effective method is to sing about a complaint: "I couldn't find my keys," "A car cut me off on the boulevard," "My boss is mean," and elaborate while singing just as if talking to a friend. The blues is very forgiving because you can sing your whole complaint on one note. You can also listen to some blues artists and imitate their phrasing and motives. You might find the dichotomous experience of feeling quite happy after singing the blues. [See Figures 3(a) and 3(b).]

Figure 3(a). The 12-bar blues.

Figure 3(b). Blues (simple melody, improvised rhythm).

4. *Imitation:* When I sang in cover bands, it was necessary to imitate a wide genre of singers. Without even knowing it, I was building a catalog of vocal textures and styles. The same can be done for improvisation. Find singers you like who improvise over the opening introductions or the closing vamp of a song. As closely as you can, copy the notes and inflections of the singer. Try to capture all of the nuances and emotional expression. Keep rewinding and sing over and over until you feel as though you are completely doubling the recorded singer. This will give your "inner ear" brand-new musical ideas for improvising.

5. *Duo singing:* Practice improvising over simple chord progressions with a friend. You can dialogue, harmonize, echo, reflect, engage in ground/figure, or fugue. You can use words and sing a conversation to one another. When practicing improvisation with a friend, you can inspire one another and feed off of each other's ideas. You can also achieve some beautiful musical moments.

6. *Find a teacher:* Take vocal improvisation workshops or continuing education classes. Find someone who teaches vocal improvisation and take some lessons. This type of lesson could even be possible over Skype.

7. *Buy materials:* There are good recorded and written methods available to help you practice. Some of these are:

    a. Jamey Aebersold's *Nothin' But Blues, Vol. 2* (Aebersold, 1981) is a great Music Minus One recording with an instruction book containing chord charts and corresponding scales.

    b. Rhiannon, a former singer in Bobby McFerrin's "Voicestra" has a CD called *Flight—Rhiannon's Interactive Guide to Vocal Improvisation* (1999). She also offers Skype lessons (https://rhiannonmusic.com/home).

c. Bob Stoloff's *SCAT! Vocal Improvisation Techniques* (1999) is jazz-based but simple and helpful for opening up the creative voice. This book has very fun rhythmic ideas, including imitating sounds of different instruments.

d. Another Stoloff book, *Vocal Improvisation* (2012), offers an instru-vocal approach for soloists, groups, and choirs.

e. *Improvisation Games for Singer and Choral Groups* (Agrell & Ward-Steinman, 2014) contains fun games to expand creativity and can be used solo or with groups of two or more.

f. Lisa Sokolov's (2020) duet games are designed from her lifelong journey in and passion for vocal exploration. She developed the method entitled "Embodied VoiceWork." A small sample of duets is located in the Appendix. More detail and an elaborate description of the method can be found in her book of the same name.

g. *Authentic Voices, Authentic Singing* (Uhlig, 2006), chapter 12, contains body warm-ups and exercises for groups and dyads. However, some of these can be practiced individually.

Therapeutic Considerations for Using Improvisation
There are times in music therapy when no precomposed melodies or songs can express the client's experience of self.

When we endeavor to improvise, we are letting go of the fear of making mistakes; we are trusting in the creative process and allowing expression of whatever comes in the moment; we are accepting ourselves as uncensored and real. In the same way, we are modeling for our clients that it is okay to make mistakes, that it is okay to express whatever comes in the moment, and that it is okay to accept ourselves as we are.

Chapter 5

SIMPLIFYING THE VOICE WHEN WORKING WITH CLIENTS

For the purpose of this chapter, simplifying refers to performance voice versus therapist voice. In considering this concept, what comes to light is not only individuals who majored in voice for music degrees but also those individuals who have gained self-esteem through vocal performance. This includes middle school, high school, and community music theater singers; middle school, high school, and community choir singers; singers in cover bands and original bands; church choir singers; and so forth.

Some of the issues that arise include …

1. *Use of vibrato:* This topic was discussed earlier in the basic vocal exercises section.

2. *Use of volume:* **People with particularly powerful voices, such as participants in music theater, gospel choirs, and opera, may need to practice the technique of singing at a medium to soft volume. To find out whether you are someone who needs to practice this skill, record yourself while leading a music therapy session. Of course, sometimes leading vocally is important. However, if your clients are singing and you can hear only yourself, it is most likely the dynamic level needs to be adjusted. This seems counterintuitive, and, at the same time, singing softly requires the same amount of breath support as singing loudly. Singing softly can also encourage the use of throat pinching to mute the sound mechanically rather than healthfully. Throat pinching and lack of breath support do not help the voice to vibrate more softly. In very simple terms, less

air pressure on the vocal folds or subglottal pressure produces softer sounds (Leanderson et al., 1987).

3. *Use of style:* This applies to both rhythm and melody. I have heard music therapists who could not sing the rhythm of a song straight, or as written. For example, when singing "Somewhere Over the Rainbow" (Arlen & Harburg, 1939), they might sing a popular R&B version of the song rather than reproduce the original version. Likewise, I have heard jazz vocalists apply back-phrasing or singing behind the beat rather than singing on the downbeat.

    If the client loves R&B and jazz, these choices in style are appropriate; however, it is important to know the originally composed rhythmic notation of the song. This also applies to melody. There are many artists who "cover" or arrange their own versions of another artist's hit. These covers are readily available on the Internet. To ensure the authenticity of the original song, it is sometimes best to buy the sheet music or borrow it from the library. While this suggestion may seem unorthodox in this age of YouTube and Google, it is the most accurate way to verify the validity of the song. Perhaps your facility has a budget for purchasing supplies that includes sheet music; if you are self-employed, any supply purchases are tax-deductible. In our field, research to prove the effectiveness of music therapy is highly valued. On a clinical level, research to ensure accurate re-creations is equally valuable. It is also beneficial to support the original artist and the perpetuation of published music.

4. *Use of range:* Avoiding parts of your voice in terms of range was discussed earlier; here we are approaching the topic of range from a different angle. Very simply, strive to sing in the range best suited to your client(s). Most clients, including children and adults, will sing in an average range of G below middle C to C above middle C. For sopranos, this means limiting the upper range; for contraltos, baritones, and basses, it would be limiting use of the lower portion of the range. Limiting range, in general, is not recommended. In order to

keep the voice healthy and strong, it is important on a personal level to sing using your full range from bottom to top and back down.

5. *Use of sustain and duration of notes:* In the lesson studio, the traditional singer works diligently on sustaining and connecting a unified tone through a phrase, ending by holding the final note precisely at full value. For some songs and situations, this kind of sustain is appropriate, as in singing "Amazing Grace" (Newton, 1779) or Sarah McLachlan's "Angel" (1998). However, there are many situations that call for more rhythmic singing. This means using a subtle accent and pulse on each note rather than a smooth flow. Two examples of this are "Take Me Out to the Ball Game" (Norworth & Tilzer, 1908) and Queen's "We Will Rock You." Try singing "We Will Rock You" (May, 1977) in a traditional voice. You will probably feel silly, but you might clearly understand that singing the rhythm rather than sustaining tone is often more important.

   Sustained singing has a soothing quality, while rhythmic singing is beneficial for leading, focusing the client's attention on the music, and encouraging energy in withdrawn individuals.

   With rhythmic singing, the last note of a phrase or song does not need to be held at full value. Rhythmic singing still requires continuous breath support for vocal health.

6. *Use of vowels and consonants:* At the risk of contradicting the section on resonance, although it is important for vowels to be open, they do not need to be as elongated as they are in traditional singing. A simple way to understand this concept is to make sure the inside of the mouth and throat are still open with relaxed tongue while the lips are forming the words in a way that is more natural to speaking. Again, for resonance, singing open vowels is still important, but with a little less drop of the jaw. Even though "Amazing Grace" (Newton, 1779) has many open vowels, they would not be sung with the same length as those in an Italian aria like "Caro Mio Ben" (Giordani,

1785). Practice saying the words, then singing. Try to sing in a more conversational style while still staying open.

Conclusion

I am a short, 60-something-year-old woman with an unassuming presence. I often feel invisible or unnoticeable. However, when I open my mouth to sing at a performance level, for the most part, I get attention and respect. I can remember running groups for seniors and looking up to see staff members grimacing at one another in what I thought was a response to my singing. Possibly, they were responding to my middle to mid-high, straight tone "cheerleader voice," which was helpful for waking the seniors up but probably annoying. Or, maybe they were responding to the song choices. They may have even been grimacing about some work issue.

It doesn't matter what they were thinking. I wanted to scream, "I'm a really good singer!"

It's truly uncomfortable for those who identify themselves as singers to give up that part of their self-esteem in order to be a "good enough" music therapist.

For this reason, it's essential to the self-care of music therapists who are singers to have a consistent time and place for expressing the whole vocal self. It could be in your friend's living room, at an open mic, in church as a choir member or soloist, in community or professional music theater, in a cover or party band, in a recording studio, or in a drum and singing circle. It takes work to maintain both your music therapy voice and your personal voice. Yet, this is necessary because if you do not give yourself a place to authentically express vocally, you will begin to resent your clients or you will begin to unconsciously ask your clients to be there for you. This can present itself in song choices and the therapist's desire to be listened to by clients.

On a positive note, if you find a way to nurture both voices, you will have a wealth of vocal experience to share with your clients, and your clients' music will give rich emotions and depth to your personal singing. Your hard work will be rewarded with peak musical moments in both areas of your singing.

Chapter 6

VOCAL IDENTITY AND SELF-EXPRESSION

If someone had told me in high school that I would be making a large part of my living by singing in the years to come, I would have laughed. Often when answering a question to a confused face, my friends would explain, "Oh, she mumbles." I truly did not believe that anyone would be interested in what I had to say, and I thought my church choirmaster gave me solos out of kindness.

As well, I have worked with students who had beautiful voices, but what they heard was not beauty. One particular student had a voice that resembled Josh Groban's, yet he would stop in agony in the middle of songs, unable to continue, proclaiming that he sounded horrible.

Another student had issues in executing correct pitches. This student studied from ages 13 to 18 and did not progress, yet she performed a solo in every single music school performance. Her parents were supportive of her simply maintaining vocally, and it was so clear that she was deriving meaning and joy from sharing her voice with others.

All this is to say that vocal identity and self-expression is a complicated topic entwined from the very beginning of life with self-concept and the world's response to our expressions.

I see young children asking wonderful, curious questions and trying to capture their parent's attention while the parent's face stares expressionless at a cell phone screen. I am not judging. I have been guilty of staring at magazines to "check out" when my son was young. However, imagine this behavior as chronic, and you can see how a child might slowly learn: "No one is interested in what I have to say." Or, "No one is interested in me."

Even for parents who are conscious of the effects of their behaviors on their children, staying present while a very young child wails in pain is heart-wrenching and often goes on much longer than one would think. It takes every ounce of strength to stay present for the pain. Similarly, hearing a teenager screaming in anger about injustice can require ironclad impulse control in order to refrain from screaming back, "I don't want to hear it!"

We've all experienced to one degree or another an "other's" disapproval or discouragement around self-expression, and this affects our vocal identity in speaking as well as singing.

In the case of the Josh Groban–esque singer, the beauty of his voice was irrelevant because somehow the world had taught him that his voice was ugly. In the case of the less-than-perfect singer, the deficiencies of her voice had no effect on her knowing that "it is enjoyable to sing for others."

I know music therapists who have high vocal self-esteem and are comfortable in expressing a range of emotions. I also know music therapists whose histories have affected their connection to their voice in an adverse way. Because this connection to our voices can influence our clients' ability to achieve therapeutic goals, it is important to engage in self-inquiry. It is equally important to flesh out perceived limits as well as to highlight strengths.

In having the courage to be aware of our vocal imperfections, supervision can be sought if a client's vocal needs confront us. It is also possible to choose populations that do not push against these limits but instead allow the therapist time to develop clinical skills. In an ethics master's degree class, Dr. Cheryl Dileo asked with what population we could not ethically work. My son was then two years old, and I knew immediately I could not work in a pediatric hospital, as I would not be able to stay present. As long as you are continuing to grow as a therapist, I believe it is not only acceptable but also ethical to make choices around vocal identity and population.

Alternatively, awareness of strengths can be of great benefit in motivating and modeling vocal expression for clients.

In addition, when we not only accept our weakness but also lean into them, we gain valuable skills as clinicians. I know a wonderful guitarist who has impeccable time. When I commented on this, he told me he had trouble in keeping a consistent beat and had worked diligently on improving this. I would never have known. Acceptance of weaknesses can open a door to growth.

In the same way, I had a student who was struggling to produce pleasant, on-pitch tones. This student persevered through vocal exercises, vocal lessons, and ear training. As she was progressing, it occurred to me that she was going to have so much to offer to clients who really want to sing but struggle with their own voices.

In summary, just as for any other area of music therapy, self-awareness of vocal identity is crucial to using voice for sound, ethical therapy. Our instruments are our power tools, our paint brushes, our co-therapist. If you don't like playing piano, you can play guitar. If you don't like playing your guitar, you can buy another one or play autoharp or ukulele. If you don't like your voice or parts of your voice, what do you do? If you do like your voice or parts of your voice, how do you use that? There are those singers who have a completely natural approach to and acceptance of their voice. More often, regardless of ability level, vocalists have at least one area of their voice that they would like to improve. How do we use our knowledge of these imperfections to sing with clients?

Years back, in a graduate class with Lisa Sokolov, 40 of us sat in a huge circle and improvised vocal solos. This exercise was total improvisation from wherever our bodies and our minds wanted to go, with no structure or direction. One quiet young woman was earnestly exploring when she found a vocal break (a place where the voice shifts from one register to another with a bump in the sound). She began moving back and forth over the break, and, after a few moments, the tears began to flow down her cheeks. It was awe-inspiring to witness. Voice teachers and students work diligently to smooth out the breaks. Yet, here was this woman finding a wealth of emotions in the quarter tone between two half-steps. The sound was so beautiful that I never again thought of breaks as bad.

By the end of her life, Billie Holiday had barely an octave range and was singing on drug-ravaged, damaged vocal cords. Yet, to this day, she is known as one of the greatest jazz singers because of what she expressed for people. I'm not saying it's okay to have damaged cords. I am saying that when a clinician is aware of their positive or negative countertransference and biographical reactions to clients, they can use this awareness to better understand and facilitate the therapeutic process. In the same way, if a clinician is aware of vocal strengths and limits, those qualities that they embrace or avoid in their voices, and past and present influences on their vocal self-expression, they can use this awareness to better understand and guide the client's vocal process.

So, let's do some exploring.

Self-Inquiry Exercises for Vocal Identity

Insights About Your Vocal Identity Through Journaling
Write your answers to the following questions in as much detail as possible. Typed or handwritten is fine; however, keep in mind that writing by hand forces you to slow down and focus more on your internal world (Mueller & Oppenheimer, 2014). Try to be open to the questions. Although they may seem simple or obvious, once you start writing, you may make some new connections.

1. What do you like about your singing voice?
2. What do you dislike about your singing voice?
3. Describe your singing voice.
4. Does your singing voice sound like anyone familiar?
5. Who is your favorite singer? Describe the qualities of this person's voice. Do you have any qualities that are similar?
6. Has anyone ever discouraged you from speaking or singing? If so, write about the first person and situation that comes to mind. If you want to write about more situations, do so.
7. Has anyone ever complimented you on your speaking or singing voice? Describe this person and situation.
8. What was vocal expression like in your home of origin? Describe tempo, rhythm, dynamics. Were there duets, solos, harmony, cacophony?
9. What was (is) vocal expression like for you in elementary school, middle school, high school, college, post-college?

Suggestions for Expanding Your Writing Insights

1. Read what you wrote out loud to yourself.
2. Read what you wrote out loud to a safe friend who is open to exploration or a peer therapist who feels safe. Discuss any new insights that come from this reading.

3. Write together with a friend or peer therapist and read to one another.
4. Read what you wrote to your personal therapist if you have one.
5. Read what you wrote (or the parts that feel safe) to your personal supervisor or peer supervision group.
6. Read what you wrote out loud and circle or write down the words that stand out or cause emotions. Write about these emotions and seek therapeutic supervision.

Insights About Your Vocal Identity Through Mandala
The word "mandala" is Sanskrit for "circle." Basically, the circle represents completeness: the whole self (Tucci, 1961). According to Jung, mandalas symbolize "a safe refuge of inner reconciliation and wholeness" (Jung, 1964). The mandala can be used to explore a deeper insight and experience of oneself or, in this case, one's voice.

Using a plate or a compass, draw a circle 10 inches in diameter on a white sheet of paper. You can use colored pencils, but it is best to use oil or chalk pastels, which can be purchased at an art store. Oils and chalk especially allow for smudging and blending, which creates more textures and colors. Don't think too much. Simply focus on the goal of the mandala and, while looking at the white sheet of paper, allow your hand to pick up the colors to which your hand is drawn. Move your hand to the paper and follow the energy in your hand and body.

1. Draw your relationship to your voice. What color(s) stand out? What shapes call your attention? How do you feel when you look at the mandala? What is the energy of the mandala?
2. Draw mandalas to represent the words or emotions that stand out from item #6 in "Expanding Your Writing Insights" above. Ask the questions from item #1 immediately above.
3. While listening to a recording of yourself singing, draw a mandala. Again, use the questions from item #1 immediately above.

To process this, you can write about what you learned and share it with peer supervision, a colleague, or your therapist.

Singing as Self-Inquiry

1. Using the two- and three-chord exercise from the section on improvisation, close your eyes and sing without any goal other than enjoying your own voice and following the sensations of your body. Record this exercise and then listen and write about what you hear. You can also draw a mandala while listening.
2. Using the duo exercise from the improvisation section, record your duet and write about what you hear. Again, you can also draw a mandala while listening.
3. Find a vocal psychotherapist within traveling distance or take a vocal psychotherapy or Embodied VoiceWork training.
4. Take voice lessons with a voice teacher who is open to some psychological focus or with a music therapist who teaches voice.

Discovering and Allowing Self-Expression

Vocal identity and self-expression are closely related. So, although you may already be working on self-expression from doing the exercises above, here are some ways to parlay the exercises into self-expression work, plus some other ideas.

1. Take the self-inquiry exercises a step further and use them to practice self-expression.
    a. To start with expressing easier emotions, review your answers from item #5 in "Insights About Your Vocal Identity Through Journaling." Based on what you like about this singer, pick one or two songs and, as closely as you can, imitate everything you hear: dynamics, articulation, twists, slides, accents, whispers, growls, and so forth. After you do this a few times, go back over the lyrics and think about what emotions/experiences you are expressing. Now, sing the song with enhanced awareness of what you are expressing. Take away the other singer's voice and sing in this way, accompanying yourself.
    b. Do the same as above using a singer whose voice you do not like.

c. Write item #6 in "Insights About Your Vocal Identity Through Journaling." Circle words that stand out. Write a song using these words. Sing the song, using textures acquired from your favorite singer to express the emotions.
d. Take any mandala that you've drawn from vocal self-inquiry, place it on the keyboard or music stand, pick a short chord progression, and sing to the mandala: "I see you." "I love your orange color." "You look like the long road I've traveled." "I miss my younger voice." If a phrase causes emotion, repeat that phrase and/or expand it into a conversation with yourself. Allow emotions to be expressed.
e. Create your own self-expression exercises from any suggestions in the self-inquiry section.

2. Other ideas
    a. Take a song to which you feel deeply connected. With the sheet music or chord chart/lyric sheet, mark specific dynamics you would like to use when singing the song. Sing with these dynamics and notice any emotional connection to the words. Sing the song again and really bring out these emotions in your voice.
    b. Remember a time of great joy or love in your life. Pick a song or chords and express that emotion through your voice.
    c. Remember a time of sorrow. Pick a song or chords and express that emotion vocally.
    d. Think about an injustice done to you. Pick a song or chords and express your feelings about this time through your voice.
    e. Create your own ways to allow self-expression.

Conclusion

These are only a few suggestions for exploring vocal identity and self-expression. You can, of course, create your own or morph the ones in this book. Add in drumming, singing bowl, improvising on Orff instruments, and combining various techniques. It is important to strive beyond the comfort zone at least a little bit, while also feeling safe. Go for eustress, which is moderate or normal psychological stress interpreted as being beneficial for the experiencer (Mills et al., 2018; Selye, 1956). If you are feeling eustress or positive stress, you are probably striving and learning.

One of the characteristics of burnout is boredom, so if you are experiencing positive stress in your self-inquiry journey, you are doing self-care and acquiring insights that can help with job satisfaction.

In my fascination with vocal improvisation, part of my journey involved singing with no structure with a saxophonist and dancer. We would rehearse in a dance space for about 10 months. The saxophonist and I would create soundscapes and textures for and around the dancer's movements, while attempting to provide a synchronous improvisational piece. At the end of 10 months, we would improvise for a huge audience of performance art devotees.

Having no music save for a few indefinite duo motives, we would improvise for 10 minutes. I can't remember being more nervous for any other performance, and the 10 minutes moved agonizingly slow. Backstage, I was thinking, "Why do I do this to myself?" I'm not even sure that I had fun. But, then, the next time I went to scat-sing over 32 measures of "Take the 'A' Train," the level of comfort and ease was freeing. When we set goals to stretch ourselves vocally, we can feel grounded and calm when our clients are stretching vocally. Without ever saying a word, our clients instinctively know we have walked the walk and are modeling: "It's safe to strive. I know the way. Follow me."

A voice teacher told me that it is ideal if a singer can vocalize two steps higher than any piece of music he will perform. With this practice, the singer's cords become flexible beyond what they are performing. When the singer executes the highest note in the piece, rather than "reaching up" for the note, he is already there and "lifting down."

Likewise, if the therapist's vocal identity is secure and self-expression is flexible, rather than reaching up, the therapist can lift down to meet the client with ease.

PART TWO:

WORKING WITH CLIENTS

Chapter 7

ETHICS OF SELF-AWARENESS FOR VOCALISTS

How many times have you held your breath upon being asked what you do for a living and answered, "I'm a music therapist"?

"Oh! You do music therapy? Oh, that's so cool! That must be so much fun! Whaddya do, like, play drums with 'them'? Have 'them' sing something relaxing? I have a friend who does Sinatra shows in nursing homes. He's doing such good work."

Education with regard to understanding music therapy has been necessary as long as the field has been in existence and will continue to be necessary for untold time to come. We have no control over how fast the general public will comprehend the diversity of methods and the potential of music therapy to effect significant therapeutic change. However, we do have control over our own understanding and level of respect for our field and for the powerful tool of music.

Years back, in my personal therapy, I said, "I want to work on my child's anger." My therapist said, "You want to work on your child's anger? Okay, then. Work on yours." In another moment of feeling invisible in the world, I said, "I want to be seen." And she said, "Kelly, let's work on you seeing you."

> *"You want to work on your child's anger?*
> *Okay, then. Work on yours."*

We want to be taken seriously as a field. We want licensed practitioners, psychologists, social workers, and those seeking therapy to understand the immense number of hours we have spent in learning, maintaining, expanding, and honing our craft. We want them to know that music therapy can be a highly effective tool for many varied therapeutic goals. According to our expertise, we want to be valued at fair and just prices.

In the same way my therapist turned the mirror on me, we can turn the mirror to look at ourselves in the field. We want to be taken seriously, and we also have a responsibility to approach each session with serious focus, to respect the tenderness of the relationship, and to value the trust our clients have placed in us to keep them safe.

In using clinical vocal methods, one of the main ways in which we can meet this responsibility and honor our own individual creative approach to practicing clinically is through self-examination.

When we enter into the client/therapist musical relationship, even when singing words, we are automatically engaging in nonverbal communication. The vibrations we sustain through our instruments—including voice—resonate to cause emotions, memories, physical sensations, images, and so on in clients as well as therapists.

Therapist and client are resonating together on a musical journey, and what happens can sometimes be surprising for both. In an ideal session, the relationship looks like this:

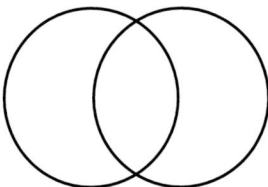

The therapist is using her life experience to connect with and understand the client, without being overwhelmed by or needing attention to that life experience. However, sometimes the therapist's life and the client's life unexpectedly bump together like two pinballs and begin lighting up discomfort. When this discomfort occurs, it is the therapist's ethical responsibility to engage in self-inquiry and/or to seek supervision or therapy in order to maintain safe boundaries, appropriate decision-making, and an unconditionally accepting presence.

I have heard of music therapists saying that supervision is not necessary when working outside of psychotherapy. This simply is not true, as discomfort can occur with any population and setting.

Ethics of Self-Awareness for Vocalists

The wonderful client named Marvin (see "Harmony" in the musical elements section) was a source of discomfort for me. He was highly deformed, with atrophied arms and legs and a misshapen head. He communicated by grunting and groaning, and he salivated on the instruments. I had an amazing supervisor who was also a music therapist. He gently required me to work with Marvin.

> *As I sat in the room with MARVIN early on, my stomach was filled with unease and I was frightened. The feeling was so disturbing that I would have discontinued his therapy had the supervisor not been there. I had no choice but to explore, so I began journaling, and what I discovered was my own sense of powerlessness. I viewed Marvin, with his profound disabilities, as powerless. But, really, Marvin was mirroring my own powerlessness. I found an affordable CBT group and began my work as well as continued to work with Marvin.*
>
> *What I found out was that Marvin was far from powerless. On the contrary, Marvin blossomed in terms of social interaction with another human being and taught me so much about how to connect with very differently abled people as well as how to have a long-term relationship without words.*

At the time, I was 25 years old and working in a special projects division of a school system. I was not working in psychotherapy, yet I still needed help with self-awareness in order to stay present and make ethical decisions.

> *In another situation, JOHN, who had five years' experience and both a bachelor's and master's degree in music therapy, was working with a geriatric group in a psychiatric setting. He kept receiving direction from his supervisor to be more empathetic and, apparently, was coming across as insensitive. When John decided to explore this issue in therapy, it turned out he had not fully mourned the loss of a family member. It had been decided for him that he was too young to visit his dying grandparent. Thus he had not*

> *gotten to say good-bye or attend the funeral. He had suppressed his grief about this loss and, as a result, could not be present for his seniors group.*
>
> *As he continued to do mourning work, including bringing his trumpet to a session and playing his grandparent's favorite song, he began to find joy in working with the geriatric group. Because he had connected to his grief, he could then connect to his clients. In fact, he was able to experience the warm, positive regard that he had with his grandparent and extend this life experience to his clients.*

While paying attention to therapist discomfort is essential to sound practice, awareness of extreme positive regard is of equal importance. Here is an entry from the therapist's journal about the client Gloria (see "Melody" in the musical elements section), who could recall language only when singing Baptist hymns.

> *I began to discover a library of hymns preserved in GLORIA's long-term memory. She would also scat-sing with me in a wonderfully expressive manner and make fun sounds. I started to feel uncomfortable about my enjoyment. I felt very concerned because, beyond singing for a half an hour, Gloria could not verbally give me permission to take her for sessions.*
>
> *I needed to explore the question, "Is Gloria singing because I need her to sing or because she needs to sing?" The self-inquiry included in-depth journaling after each session. It was a relief when I realized I was doing personal work through my voice in music psychotherapy, and I was performing frequently. I was already singing for myself, and I did not need Gloria to sing for me. My conclusion was that even though I enjoyed our sessions, Gloria was deriving a therapeutic benefit from singing. I had no way of knowing whether this were true. However, I could rest easy in the knowledge that I had been willing to ask myself these questions.*

Making ethical decisions within music therapy in general, and specifically in singing with clients, isn't always clear-cut. Sometimes, as with the question "Should I date a client who sings in my outpatient choir?," the answer is very clear. At other times, as in the cases mentioned above, doing the right thing can feel mind-numbingly elusive. These are the times when an objective, trusted, third-party view is needed.

Within the context of seeking professional feedback, the mirror can also be turned. I can hear my therapist saying, "You want people to value you? You value you." I have heard colleagues say, "I can't afford supervision." Then I watch as they take a cruise, bring a $5 cup of coffee to work every day, buy lunch instead of pack it, go to Happy Hour, and purchase expensive concert tickets. The message seems to be, "Treating myself with coffee is more important than my professional growth."

And this message comes through to colleagues and to other fields loudly and clearly. We can't have it both ways. We can't profess the power of music and not respect that power at the same time. It's true. Music is powerful. It can open both therapist and client very quickly. Self-awareness of these "openings" is important to staying present and choosing appropriate interventions.

Some music therapists choose to embrace the archetype of the "wounded healer" by engaging in long-term or short-term therapy. Others contract for six to 10 sessions of personal supervision. Temple University's doctoral program includes a self-awareness study in which the student explores personal history and emotions with a clinician versed in nonverbal techniques. This exploration involves only four sessions. When I completed my undergraduate degree in 1982, the field was very young and there was no such thing as personal supervision. Now, Skype has opened the possibility of seeking supervision with your choice of expert anywhere in the world.

There is no doubt in my mind that had I not paid others to help me, confront me (lovingly), and cheer for me when I got it right, I would be long gone from the field. As music therapists nested in various facilities plugging along in the midst of ignorance, we can find it very lonely without help from someone who has "been there, done that." Yes! You do deserve that coffee, but you also deserve to grow and enjoy the practice of music therapy for years to come. It is our ethical responsibility to respect the difficulty of what we do by seeking constructive feedback from experts in the field.

It is also our ethical responsibility to allow constructive feedback. There are times when it truly is a struggle to pay for supervision, and sometimes this reason masks resistance to having deficiencies brought to light. During one phone supervision session in which I kept arguing with my supervisor, I was asked if I wanted him to supervise me. When I expressed that I was having many emotions around the mistakes I was making, not to mention fear that I might be hurting my clients, my kind-hearted supervisor said, "Receiving supervision is really hard. I think it's harder than therapy."

Peer supervision groups are wonderful for connection with like-minded professionals, but because they are filled with friends, they will not suffice when bold honesty is required. As the peer groups bond, a subconscious collusion to mirror only the "good stuff" happens. To be sure, peer supervision groups offer meaningful benefits, but there are still times when paying someone to point out blind spots, although confrontational, is the only true way to grow.

If you feel an unreasonable dislike or excessive positive feelings for the client or if you dread the therapy session or feel uncomfortable during the session, it is probably time to seek support through supervision or personal therapy.

Chapter 8

METHODS FOR AWARENESS OF THERAPIST/CLIENT DYNAMICS

In 2000, I completed a qualitative research study designed by Kenneth Bruscia. The study used a re-imaging technique to explore transference and countertransference in GIM (Bruscia, 1998). I can recall taking three hours to write one paragraph and tolerating the headache when I had finished for the evening. It felt as though I was trying to turn my eyeballs around and see into the back of my head. It was like exploring in a dark room by myself with only a teeny, tiny beam of light and no eyeglasses. I had to slowly navigate and painstakingly piece together, one by one, the brief abstract images that would come forth from the shadows.

The study worked because there was a very clear step-by-step process. If I reached a step that wasn't making sense, I knew I had to go back and redo the step(s) before that. I knew I had missed something. What I discovered was that I was not listening to my client's fear. Me—supreme listener, intuitive high priestess of the universe, and clairvoyant superwoman—was not listening. What? Ouch! Because of this study, to this day, when I get a strange feeling in the pit of my stomach, I know I am missing something. Sometimes when I journal or talk with a colleague, I can figure it out. Sometimes I can't.

As a supervisor, I work with individuals from entry-level to advanced music therapy. They come to me for help with self-awareness and are consistently surprised when the obvious becomes apparent. No matter how far we come in terms of time, progress, and health, our past will always be our past.

With a final caveat to relying solely on one's own objectivity and a recommendation that highly encourages seeking supervision and/or music psychotherapy, the following are suggestions for self-inquiry methods that can be used for the times in between personal work.

A. Read Kenneth Bruscia's "Techniques for Uncovering and Working with Countertransference" (chapter 6) in *The Dynamics of Music Psychotherapy* (1998). This is an excellent resource of techniques for awareness of client/therapist dynamics. Some of the techniques include:

1. *Improvised music portraits (p. 102):* There are four different approaches to this technique, and while reading this chapter is still recommended, a morphed version is presented here.
   a. On any percussion or melodic instrument you choose (including voice), improvise around your impressions of the individual client or group. Simply think about your client(s), pick an instrument(s), breathe, and play. Notice thoughts and feelings.
   b. Again, on any instrument, think about how you interact with this client(s) and improvise. Notice thoughts and feelings.

   When Jason began working at a special projects division in a school system, one of his clients was highly prone to banging his head against hard objects, including the piano. Jason struggled to connect with this client. In using the improvisation technique, he took a cow bell and began banging it with ferocity. As much as he wanted to stop, he kept going. Finally, when Jason stopped, he felt that he understood.

   He had kinesthetic imagery of many painful thoughts colliding in his head, and the only way to get them to stop was to hit them. Jason did not yet have any idea of how to create interventions, but now he felt compassion for his client and knew he could proceed.

2. *Mandalas:* This idea is taken from Bruscia (1998), but the suggested technique is different. Reread the paragraph on mandalas in chapter 6. Draw three separate circles. In the first, create a mandala representing your client. Then draw a second mandala representing you as the therapist. Finally, draw a third mandala depicting the therapeutic

relationship. How are you connecting or not connecting? What is happening within the relationship? What is your client asking for? What are you providing? Notice insights, thoughts, and feelings.

IZZY sought supervision for a client who kept pushing her away by making annoyed faces, interrupting Izzy, looking bored, and refusing to participate in any activities.

The supervisor guided Izzy to draw a mandala of the session dynamics. Izzy drew two circles within the mandala, with various colors representing therapist and client. Izzy then drew four black lines shooting out from one mandala to another. Izzy intended to draw the black lines as the client's aggression toward her.

When the supervisor said, "Tell me what's happening in the mandala," Izzy's jaw dropped as she began to realize the black strokes that she perceived as hitting her were actually emotional ropes that the client was throwing so Izzy could pull her to safety. Izzy and the supervisor developed a plan of action for the next session.

B. Sing

1. As soon as possible upon completion of a session, sing a song reflecting your client's energy. Close your eyes and picture this client or client group as they look during a session. Now open your eyes and scroll through your playlist, songlist, or sheet music (chord sheets). This exercise almost always brings forth the right song or one that is close enough. Sing this song and notice any words or musical textures that stand out. Close your eyes and think about your client(s) again. What is your client thinking/feeling?

2. Thinking of the same client, sing a song reflecting your experience of a session. What are you communicating to the client? What would you like to say to yourself? Does something need to shift?

More and more, Arlene felt drained at the conclusion of a particularly difficult group in a behavioral health facility. She decided to give herself some singing time immediately after running the group. Even though she felt very tired, she was drawn to an energetic, upbeat song about dancing.

As she sang, she began to see an image of herself dancing and happy. She realized she needed to have fun and that she was carrying too much responsibility while running the group. She planned one self-care activity per week and incorporated group methods in which the clients could have more leadership.

C. Receptive methods

1. Choose a song you used in a particularly difficult session. With a recording of the song, lie down on the floor or a mat, do a brief relaxation technique of choice, and listen to the song. What sensations, thoughts, and feelings come into awareness?
2. Again, choosing a song you used in a difficult or confusing session, record yourself singing it without words. You can use a hum or oohs and ahs. The *Oh* vowel has a beautiful long, open shape and feel to it. Lie down and do a brief relaxation exercise. Breathe and listen. What is happening in this song? What is happening in your voice and body? What is the group or client trying to tell you?

ASHER asked a colleague to sit in an area of the room with good acoustics and record his group session on a hand-held digital recorder.

At a time when Asher felt calm and clear-headed, he listened to the recording. He realized he was talking way too much and allowing the group's resistance to decrease the amount of actual music-making. He decided to write a music therapy goal beyond the official treatment plan in which the group would engage in live music activities for 20 to 30 minutes per session.

D. Body scan (Davis, Eshelman, & McKay, 2008)

1. Just before a session, close your eyes. While focusing on your body from feet to head, notice any tension. When you notice body tension, say to yourself, "I am tensing my neck [or another part of the body]. I am hurting myself" (p. 21). Connect this tension to any life situation of which you may be aware.
2. Engage in a body scan two or three times during a session. Notice any tension. Put this into a brief sentence: "My shoulders are raised. I am hurting myself." Try to breathe and let go of the tension.
3. At a convenient time after the session, think back to any tension you discovered and use a new body scan to explore specific reasons for this tension relating to your client(s). For example, say, "I am raising my shoulders. I am carrying too much [emotion, struggle, responsibility, etc.] during this session."

Further Guidance

Because we spend most of the day with an external focus, this simple body scan can be surprisingly effective in a short period of time. Busy people often comment that upon being given permission to focus internally, they are amazed at how they have been engaging in a hurtful behavior all day long. Also, the more you practice body scans outside of sessions, the more awareness around tension will come during sessions.

Some thoughts on possible connections may be:

1. *Holding breath:* feeling overwhelmed by client's emotions
2. *Shoulders tense:* carrying too much responsibility within the therapeutic relationship
3. *Slumped posture:* lacking confidence
4. *Stomach jitters:* identifying too much with client's fear
5. *Tense feet:* wanting to put the brakes on
6. *Spinning head:* lack of focus

These are just a few to get you started exploring.

> HAROLD's head was spinning during and after his sessions with Samuel, a client on the autistic spectrum who would not stop talking. He felt ineffective and unfocused, so he sought supervision. Much to his surprise, he learned that a therapist can be unconditionally accepting and set gentle, honest boundaries at the same time. He was encouraged to redirect the client calmly and firmly back into the music.

E. Journaling around sessions

1. *Facing reality:* Even in my own personal logs, I often hold back from being my true, authentic self. I refrain from writing, "I had no idea what to say or do." Or "I am so bored with this group." I expect myself to be unconditionally accepting and knowledgeable to such a high degree that I hesitate to commit anything less to writing in black and white. It's as though if I write it, I am signing a contract that states I am a terrible therapist. I also feel resistance to taking a look at it.

    Paradoxically, once I confess to myself, it becomes clear that I am doing my best. It's also relieving to give myself permission to have human emotions and imperfections. When these thoughts are whirring around in my head, there is no space for strategizing. When I release these thoughts by writing and telling the truth, I can objectively make decisions and problem-solve. By the same token, it is also helpful to honestly log about extreme positive feelings. So, write your tell-all log and then delete it, burn it, shred it, or keep it and learn.
2. *Writing fantasy:* Once you have written up your "terrible, horrible, no good, very bad" session, imagine how you would have liked the session to go and write this. Fantasizing can foster creativity, bring self-awareness, provide motivation to try something new, and hold a safe space for exploring possibilities (Lisa T. Schlesinger, "Life," 2016). Even though your clients may never hold hands and sing "Kumbaya" (Baez, 1962) together in three-part

harmony, if you allow yourself this very pleasant mental journey, more practical solutions and shifts in perception may come, as well as an overall increased belief in more positive possibilities.

HANNAH had worked in hospice care for years and was reluctant to admit to herself that she was feeling discomfort in working with a new patient. She attributed this to being off her game, but after three sessions, she still felt an odd foggy sensation behind her eyes and anxiety. She decided it was time to journal about her feelings and her patient.

As she wrote, she realized that her patient was reminding her of her piano teacher of many years. She had studied with this teacher from grade school to high school. The teacher had recently passed away. In life's busyness, Hannah had forgotten how much this teacher had meant to her. She now knew she needed to honor their relationship and somehow say good-bye.

3. *Goals and objectives:* Write your own goals for this group or client. Beyond the facility's requirements for notes, write and keep in mind your own music therapy goals. Often when I have felt lost and ineffective in my work, I have reviewed my goals and realized the sessions were on track.

    In working with clients with physical and intellectual disabilities, the main goal was social interaction with me or others. This goal was essential to moving to any other goal.

    In working with trauma, the goal of feeling safe was first and foremost. Goals are the guideposts that help to ground the journey that clients and therapists take through the abstract world of music. In maintaining awareness of your goals, you may be surprised to find that even though a session may seem chaotic and disorganized, the clients are still growing in their own unique way.

VEN left the session highly frustrated and wondering if he were reaching his client at all. It seemed to Ven that his client, Ray, spent the majority of the session running around the room engaging in his own internal world of self-calming and babbling behaviors.

When Ven looked at his goals, he realized that Ray's initiation of eye contact had increased in terms of frequency and that Ray was connecting to Ven as best he could. Ven felt encouraged.

F. Breathe

Give yourself permission to completely turn your attention to yourself and inhale fully two to three times during a session. As simplistic as this sounds, it is a powerful method. In *Modes of Consciousness in GIM* (Bruscia, 1998, chapter 22), Bruscia describes an intentional shifting of one's awareness from client to self. Much like the body scan's goal of internal/external focus, Bruscia's direction to purposefully engage in self-awareness while in session can bring fruitful information. Breathing in while feeling the expansion of the lungs and the refreshing oxygen entering the body is one of the fastest ways to access self-consciousness in vivo.

After beginning to practice brief breathing exercises, AMY noticed that she held her breath frequently throughout the entire workday. Upon further exploration, Amy found fear and reluctance to engage fully with her clients. She knew she needed to go into personal therapy.

G. Combination techniques

Be creative! Combine your favorite techniques or invent your own. For example, item #2 in "Receptive methods" above is a combination of singing and listening. You can combine:

1. *Body scan and mandala:* Draw how your body feels.
2. *Body scan and improvisation:* Improvise your tension.
3. *Personal logs and improvisation:* Journal with honesty, then improvise, or improvise, then journal.
4. *Sing your fantasy:* After writing your ultimate session, pick

a song that you would love to use with clients but may never be able to, then sing.
5. *Mandala and singing:* Using the mandala suggestions above, draw a mandala of choice, place the mandala on a music stand, pick a song or chords, and sing to the mandala.

Davis, Eshelman, and McKay (2008, p. 111) describe the benefits of combination techniques by noting that (1) "when you put two or more relaxation approaches together, the combination can have a synergistic effect" and (2) "combination techniques are often more powerful because the sequence is set up to draw you deeper into the relaxation experience." The same can apply to awareness techniques.

CARLA was contracted to run a music therapy group for women in a domestic violence safe house. She consistently found herself experiencing anger at the conclusion of the session. When she wrote a fantasy session, she imagined the women standing up with fists in the air and singing the chorus to Katy Perry's "Roar" with strong voices.

Carla realized the women were nowhere near connecting to this type of powerful expression, so she decided to sing the song herself. As she sang, she realized she was feeling angry about a situation in her own life in which she felt taken advantage of and that she needed to seek support in being assertive.

Conclusion

These are only a few ideas for exploring client/therapist relationships. There are so many creative options. For example, there are also psychodrama (Dogan, 2018), mindfulness (McCollum, 2015), and somatic experiencing techniques (Levine, 1997). Every workday, we are creating experiential methods for our clients, and we can do the same for ourselves.

One final encouragement for undergoing the rigors of self-awareness is that it has been linked to the prevention of burnout (Baker, 2002; Harman, 2010; Richards et al., 2010; Urdang, 2010).

In my final year before entering private practice, I was working at a senior daycare center. I had been there about two and a half years when a nearby center closed and we received a huge influx of clients. The morning group was composed of 40 people. My wonderful boss, Phyllis, asked me if I was okay with this. I told her that it was quite effort-intensive and also that it was important to me to have one group where everyone was at least sitting together in a common activity. We agreed that if it became a hardship, I would split the group in half.

Unfortunately, kind Phyllis passed away, and when I went to tell her replacement that I was going to split the group, she said, "We have to keep the numbers up. Oh, and we don't call them 'clients' anymore. We call them 'consumers.'" At this moment, I had an instantaneously intense visceral reaction. I felt nauseous and as though I were being consumed. I stayed another six months, during which time I began to become irritated with some clients, including Sydney, the cabaret singer. I also began tuning the autoharp (which took close to half an hour) during one very withdrawn client's session. I didn't listen to my "nausea," and I kept going.

When I left, not only was I resentful, but also I was exhibiting nontherapeutic behavior in my lack of unconditional acceptance. Had I listened to my body, I could have been assertive or avoided working in burnout for six months.

I often hear "That won't work" or "I don't know what color my tension is" or "I don't like to draw." Although the awareness methods may seem simple, they are effective for an open mind. Like tuning in a distant station on a radio dial or adjusting a prism with the slightest turn, shifting the focus on ourselves in an accepting way can bring about a quantum leap in consciousness. Sometimes it takes only the slightest shift to allow the light to come through and reveal the beautiful colors.

So, engaging in the ethical behavior of self-awareness contributes to a decrease in burnout, increase in client satisfaction, increase in the effectiveness of therapy, and increase in therapist joy.

Chapter 9

GOAL AREAS AND METHODS

ESTABLISHING SAFETY

Establishing and maintaining safety is an ongoing concern for every single session. Just because Jovan was comfortable with the first 10 sessions does not mean that he will be so for the 11th session. Issues of fear and discomfort can arise at any time in the therapeutic relationship, with any and all populations, for any reason.

> *In my first fieldwork experience at Misericordia Hospital, my student partner (an amazing guitarist/singer) was sick and I had to run the group by myself. Because we didn't have enough music therapists in the field yet, my supervisor was an art therapist and we were responsible for running the group by ourselves every week for a year.*
>
> *I can't remember ever feeling more awkward in my life. As I introduced the second song, I suddenly had to bear an entire cup of cold grape juice thrown in my face. I was the object of a client's intense discomfort.*
>
> *My amazing supervisor, Maru, lovingly got me a clean shirt, calmed me down, and highly encouraged me to run the group, which I did.*
>
> *The young woman apologized to me, and the clients were so grateful that the music continued. It was the best group I ever ran in my fieldwork.*

I am not saying it's okay to be abused. I am saying that although the client's choice of communication was inappropriate, her discomfort was real. She was having a panic attack, and my extreme performance anxiety was not helping her. Of course, Maru made sure it was safe for me to continue and, because we did so, we validated the client's feelings. We communicated "Yes—being in a psych hospital is upsetting." In that we made room for this client's discomfort, the group members vicariously felt allowance of their emotions, as well.

For this one group, the sense of safety and dynamic energy of unconditional acceptance was rich. When you feel as though your client(s) are throwing grape juice in your face (refusing to sing, saying, "This song is stupid!"), remembering how it feels to be in their shoes will go a long way toward creating safety.

Here are some ways to establish and maintain safety while using vocal methods:

1. *Maintain unconditional acceptance of your client's voice.*
   A client's vocal expressions are beautiful! They are sharing with you as much as they can. Whether they sing with a scratchy voice, off-pitch, or in a monotone, it is uniquely personal and is such an honor to witness. Treat it like an honor and reflect to them this understanding. Listen and watch intently, smile, and/or show delight. If appropriate, say, "I really enjoy your singing." Or cheer them on with a well-placed, "Yeah!" This may seem obvious, but I have caught myself looking very serious when trying to keep the music flowing and be aware of methods, interventions, and therapy process at the same time. When I catch myself and remember to engage with facial presence, my clients' faces relax immediately. I have seen individuals glow from singing when they believe that their voices are not judged and are heard and received with gratitude.

2. *Remember that singing is scary.*
   I remember being gently brought to awareness about my lack of empathy for a client by my supervisor. The supervisor had observed a session in which my young ego was highly involved in pushing an adolescent girl to "produce" vocals so that I could feel better about myself as a therapist. When I look back, I feel compassion for my client and for me. I was so frightened

and felt I had no idea what I was doing. And she was forced to protect herself from me by withdrawing.

Because we are highly trained, it's so easy to forget how frightening it can be for some to sing yet so important to remember. The client is connecting directly from their internal experience to the outside world in sound. They are so vulnerable and so brave!

3. *Don't ask clients to sing emotions that you are not ready to hold.*
Be able to sing sad, angry, happy, scared, soothing, pain, empowered, silly, and so forth. In this way, if your client needs to express these emotions, you can guide them, or double, or sing for them.

4. *Go first.*
I was at a presentation when one of the leaders introduced a toning exercise, put us in a circle with our backs facing and proceeded to sit there doing nothing. The total silence that ensued was very uncomfortable. The group was not established and cohesive so, there was no therapeutic benefit from this silence.

In my opinion, beginning singing from no singing is scary every single time. In fact, the more I know about my clients and how important it is for them to sing, the scarier it is. It is a sacred, intimate, personal space, and the therapist must go first and model "It's safe to sing" or "Feel the fear and sing anyway." One exception would be if there is a specific goal (such as assertiveness) in encouraging the client to sing first or the client wants to sing first.

5. *Be willing to keep singing.*
Sometimes there will be a chorus of singers for the entire session. Sometimes you will be the only one singing. In working with adolescent boys, it was a really good day if they sang for two minutes. Yet, if I had stopped singing, the goal of initiating a positive expression through voice would not have been met. They needed 40 minutes of me singing while they drummed. But what a sense of accomplishment when they

finally sang! It's also okay to introduce new material and keep singing while allowing time for familiarity and acceptance.

6. *Be willing to stop singing.*
   If you take in a singing activity and two sessions later there's no response, put it away. It's okay to accept defeat and also helpful for clients to observe how we handle defeat and disappointment.

   But, how do you tell the difference between a client's healthy communication of disinterest and reluctance to stretch? Of course, this is easier to determine when a client can communicate discomfort or when we know the client's distress signs from experience.

   This is tricky. Signs of shutting down and checking out will be discussed below.

7. *Allow silence.*
   From the profoundly disabled client who wants to be still in order to process sound to the highly verbal client who takes a long pause after singing to breathe into the pleasant sensations in her body, silence is golden. Allow these measured rests to happen even if they are longer than you like.

8. *Stop or change vocal interventions when the client checks out.*
   Sometimes clients can't tell you that they are scared or in emotional pain and discomfort. They may be taking care of the therapist's feelings, they may be afraid of the therapist's anger, or they may be disassociated and unable to communicate. In this way, the cues are the same for both verbal and nonverbal clients.

   Watch for:
   a. *Facial expressions:* flat affect, tension, or color gone from the face
   b. *Body posture:* feet tapping, arms wrapped around the body, slumped over, or turned away
   c. *Breath:* holding breath, shallow breathing
   d. *Tension:* nervous hand movements, shoulders hunched, jaw clenching

e. *Eye contact:* avoiding or looking down, eyes glazed over
f. *Presence:* leaning away from the therapist's presence

Of course, some clients will clearly communicate discomfort by throwing the maraca across the room, hitting a group member, or other disruptive behaviors. Other clients will be able to verbally express a need to pause.

Important Considerations: Words vs. No Words
There are moments when words are placeholders for experiences, markers of insights, vehicles for connection, and instruments of expression both deep and light. And there are those times when only vibrations are needed.

1. In choosing between verbal and nonverbal vocal methods, do so consciously. Endeavor to know why you are making a choice and what objective it is reaching in the moment. It can be appropriate to sing words with nonverbal clients because this is how we communicate and it helps clients with prelinguistic or beginning linguistic skills. It can also be viable to echo and double a client's nonverbal vocals atonally or within a key structure for self-expression and a more immediate connection.

    The use of words when singing with verbal clients can be powerfully effective in achieving many different goals. Yet there are times—as with extreme trauma or confusion—when words do not help at all. At these times, the language center of the brain is minimally engaged (Van Der Kolk, 2014) and an individual's body needs only the vibrations of a human voice for comfort.

2. When you introduce a song to a group or individual, be aware of all of the lyrics and the meaning of each phrase. In choosing songs, maintain focus on your clients' issues and of possible contraindications with regard to the interpretation of lyrics.

    There are some great songs that are lyrically inappropriate for use in music therapy. You can rewrite the words on your own or with clients. For example, there is a beautiful Austrian Christmas carol called "Still, Still, Still" (Süß, 1865). It is a lullaby that can be used for grounding, but it has religious content. I am no Leonard Cohen, but I rewrote the words well enough that for me this became an important song for client-calming and stress reduction. Of course, this leads into the lyric-writing method used when clients take familiar songs and compose their own lyrics.

Finally, when the therapist sings with an understanding of what the lyrics mean to him and maintains awareness of the client(s) while singing these lyrics, the therapeutic relationship can be strengthened and goals reached on so many levels.

> *Twenty-year-old JACKSON was singing "Fly Me to the Moon" (Howard, 1954) in his clinical voice class. All of the details of the music were present, but expression was missing. He was asked to read the words. As he read, he spontaneously stopped and said, "Whoa! These words are beautiful!" The class then discussed that even though it seemed a little corny now, this was a pop tune and a love song in the 1950s. Jackson sang the song again with emotion, and the class agreed this might help a senior client feel some joy in the moment.*

LEVELS OF UTILIZING METHODS

When I finished my internship, my clinical supervisor, an outstanding music therapist, moved on to another job and I took his place. My job was working within a special projects division of a school system. The population was clients with severe/profound developmental, intellectual, and physical disabilities.

Psychologically, I was holding on to my supervisor's ankles as he walked out the door because I felt as though I had no idea what I was doing. To me, it felt like trying to learn how to communicate with someone from Mars. Luckily, my supervisor kept copious notes, and I pored over them every week.

This was helpful, except for the fact that I kept trying to produce the same results as my supervisor. Instead of me being in the room as a beginner, I kept trying to be someone else. In so doing, I was missing out on an authentic relationship with my clients, on being allowed to be green, and on allowing them to teach me.

With this being said, use the methods in the way that is best for you. Below is a suggestion for thinking about the methods. An analogy of studying jazz will be used for examples.

Here are some thoughts:

Level 1
Completely imitating and reproducing the exact method as written. Playing the chord progression and melody exactly as composed.

Level 2
Using the method as written while changing a few or many elements. Playing the chord progression with a few changes in the melody or rewriting the melody completely.

Level 3
Using only the skeleton of the method to create a different method. Soloing over the chord changes.

Level 4
Getting an idea from reading the method and creating a brand-new method. Free improvisational jazz.

All these years later, I've learned that there is no shame in imitating. I hope I will always find myself on Level 1, because this means I am learning something new.

I am also consistently amazed at the level of creativity among music therapists and highly encourage you to explore each level.

Of course, it is not possible to cover every conceivable vocal method. This book is just a place to start and a point in a direction.

Chapter 10

MAINTAINING GOALS AS THE FOCUS

Using these methods, even in direct imitation, works best when the reason for utilizing them is front-and-center. In other words, when the method is not the goal. The method is simply the way to get to the goal.

In my work with a three-year-old boy with severe autism, I sought on-site supervision due to feeling completely helpless and confused. After observing, the supervisor asked me what the goals were. As I read through the goals, I realized that even though the sessions looked like mayhem, we were reaching every single goal within each session.

Sessions can be wildly spontaneous and improvisational, or they can be so passive that we feel that nothing is happening. In working with clients with profound disabilities, a goal might be "Jeffrey will engage in 20 secs of eye contact three or four times per session." If the therapist forgets this goal and focuses only on Jeffrey's initiation of percussing the drum, which often does not happen, discouragement can easily follow. Likewise, in remembering how difficult it is for Jeffrey to look directly into another person's eyes, these moments of visual connection are seen and felt as triumphs.

The concept has changed from "nothing is happening" to "Jeffrey is learning to reach out and interact with the therapist." Not only does this completely change the ongoing diagnostic assessment, but also it highly encourages the therapist and helps them to feel effective and keep striving.

Let's look at the method of call-and-response. The therapist could take the Ella Jenkins song "Long John" (Jenkins, 1998) and use it for many different goals, including to increase attention span (cognitive behavior), to improve receptive and expressive skills (communication), to help with impulse control in encouraging the client to wait her turn (social interaction), to increase assertiveness skills by having clients take the lead solo (self-expression), to promote stress reduction through humor and silliness (physical well-being), to help a group to bond (group cohesion), and on and on.

Although this is a re-creative method, the song would be arranged and introduced differently, depending on the goal.

Not maintaining the goal is like having a big ship with no compass. The ship has a wheel, a sail, and an anchor, yet without the compass, it could be sailing in circles. In music therapy, we have beautiful drums, amazing songs, and jamming music skills, yet without the goal, all of this is meaningless.

For this reason, the following methods are organized by goal areas. However, each technique can be adapted to any population and any goal. All techniques can be varied to serve groups and individuals, as well.

Finally, since some of the methods appear within more than one goal, a Toolbox section was created to provide further description.

GROUNDING AND EMPOWERMENT

While the preceding section is on establishing a sense of safety in general, in this section, methods used to help clients to connect directly to their bodies in a safe way and ground themselves in the moment will be discussed, as well as methods for empowerment. Empowerment is "the process of becoming stronger and more confident, especially in controlling one's life and claiming one's rights" (Oxford Online Dictionary, 2020).

The world is filled with experiences big and small, situational and long-term, which teach us that in order to survive or to avoid perceivably unresolvable pain, we must disconnect from our bodies. Shapiro (1995) calls these big and small experiences "Large-T trauma" and "Little-t trauma."

With individuals who have had "good enough" childhoods, the disconnects are more subtle and related to relationships outside the circle of loved ones.

For example, "When I was 6, we were in a car accident and my sister was taken in the ambulance." Or "My fourth-grade teacher never called on me in class."

Then there are individuals who have experienced long-term stress: "My father left when I was two." "My brother died when he was 12." "My mother has OCD." "I was born with a cleft palate." And, of course, the unthinkable traumas of direct sexual, physical, and emotional abuse.

There is a tendency to forget that "differently abled" individuals have these same difficult life experiences: the child with autism who is asked to suppress his energy all day in school and exhibit "in-seat" behavior; Marvin, whose mother abandoned him at 8 months old; Doris, who was abused in her group home; and so forth.

Whether related directly to voice or not, these disconnects present themselves in the music therapy room and will affect the singing relationship.

This is by no means an invitation to verbally process these disconnects or abuses. In fact, if the therapist does not have advanced training in trauma, verbal processing is not recommended. Furthermore, some clients will have no conscious awareness of big or little traumas, so talking about them is out of the question.

This goal area is about encouraging the therapist to acknowledge that whether documented or not, anyone can have a background that has caused them to experience a lack of safety. Whether you are working directly with clearly diagnosed trauma or in other settings, the following methods can be used to promote safety, resourcing through grounding, and empowerment.

The methods can be used as the sessions open, throughout the session, and/or to close.

> *MARY was being prepped for surgery to repair a heart valve. She was feeling very frightened, and her mind was racing. She was thinking about all of the possibilities of something going wrong and worrying about her family. Mary had been working with a music therapist to prepare for this moment, and she began singing the phrase "Everything's gonna be all right" repeatedly. Some of the medical staff joined in, and, after surgery, Mary reported being able to let go and feel total safety.*

TONING

This refers to sustained tones being sung by the therapist alone or therapist and client together to promote deeper inhalation and comfort through vocal vibrations.

Toning for Highly Stressed Clients (Need for Immediate Safety)
When a client is highly stressed, words will not help them to calm down. When we are in fight-or-flight mode, the diaphragm locks to prepare for battle (being struck), and an individual can feel as though it is not possible to inhale. Singing can remind the body to breathe.

1. *Playing an instrument and humming:* Use any instrument that does not block your body, such as autoharp (in the lap), singing bowl, finger piano, ocean drum, and so on. Sit or stand as close to the client as possible. Say to the client, "I'm just going to play for a minute while you listen." As per the exercises in the Therapist Training section, use the parts of your range and dynamics that most express a soothing sound. Keeping in mind the information about breath support and resonance, hum or sing on open vowels. A song melody is fine, but improvisation provides more freedom to respond to the client's cues. By monitoring presence, you will be able to tell when your voice is reaching your client. When you notice this connection, utilize these specific notes. Some clients experience validation and relief when singing dissonance/consonance. It can feel to them as though the music understands the stress and also provides a subconscious reminder to release.

2. *Client singing along:* If your client seems receptive, invite them to hum along. Begin by holding unison to help the client feel "doubled"; then choose a harmony below the client's note and hold the ground for the client to explore or join you. Often, clients will intuitively respond to this invitation to explore, and giving the client the choice to separate or connect with you can provide for the client the beginnings of practicing empowerment ("I have a choice").

Some groups will find this intervention too adventuresome, so introducing humming on a familiar song can work just as well. A very slow version of "Twinkle, Twinkle, Little Star" with suspended 2nds and 4ths in the accompaniment works well because it is immediately familiar to most people, easy to sing, has a lullaby quality, and can sound quite beautiful at a slow tempo. You can also tell the group that you are introducing a vocal warm-up and hum a scale.

Vocal Exercises for Toning
Because toning can sometimes feel too unstructured to nonmusicians (and musicians), using vocal exercises for toning works beautifully. I call this method "biopsychosocial" (Engel, 1981) warm-ups. The goal is not to exercise the vocal cords but instead to calm the body, calm the mind, and promote well-being within the self and the environment.

1. *Mow, Mow, Mow:* Using this exercise from the section on diction in Therapist Training, encourage the client to take deep inhales in between each motive and just enjoy the feeling of their own voice. Play the chord pattern below and move up and down in half-steps. The client may find a part of their voice to be particularly resonant, and you can maneuver the exercise around this note. Add harmony, if appropriate (remembering doubling and separating from "client singing along").

   Add a crescendo/decrescendo or play with dynamics. This one, simple exercise can provide five minutes of continuous, sustained singing. This can lower blood pressure and increase oxygen to the brain as well as promote entrainment. [See Figure 4(a).]

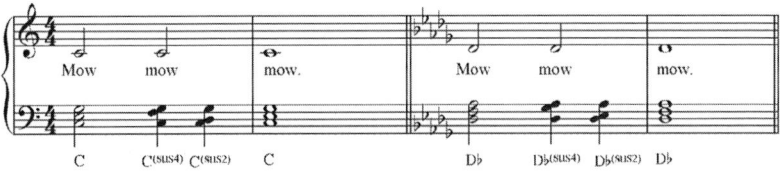

Figure 4(a). Voice exercises for toning. Continue in half-steps.

2. *May, Mee, Mah, Moh, Moo:* Using the same concept as above, sing the exercise below. Clients and students often express experiencing extreme comfort due to the major and minor 7th chords that offer a musical tension/release. [See Figure 4(a).]

Figure 4(b). Exercises for toning, continued. Continue in half-steps.

Word Toning
Once the clients are entrained or breathing naturally, you can begin to add words so that the relaxed state from the toning can be connected to cognition (mind/body). This method is the opposite of affirmations. Affirmations begin with the left brain using words to calm the body. With word toning, the right brain (intuitive, emotional) is induced with music to calm the body and then words are used to engage the left brain (rational, logical) and describe the feeling which already exists.

At this point in toning, the words can be so simple because they are only bookmarking the actual experience, and the simpler the words, the more likely the client will be able to access this word toning in times of stress. Brain-imaging studies have shown that traumatic events tend to activate the right hemisphere of the brain and deactivate the left (Bremner, 2006; Hartley & Phelps, 2009; Van Der Kolk, 2000).

Groups or client and therapist can write the words together. The "Mow, Mow, Mow" exercise could become "All is well," "Let it be," "I am well," or "We see you." The "May, Mee, Mah" exercise could be "I will choose to set more boundaries," "I can learn to live my life with ease," or "I feel safe when I can learn to breathe."

This doesn't have to make sense to anyone but the client; it doesn't have to be fancy poetry or Grammy award–winning lyrics. It can be silly, sad, or angry. When simple words are written together in the moment from a synchronous, internal experience, each member of the group is validating the experience, and this can feel grounding as well as empowering.

The sky is the limit as to how many simple melody and word phrases can be written in the moment. Use the two-chord exercise from Figure 1 to generate ideas.

Word Toning and Positive Goals
This method can work well at the end of a session. Ask the client(s) to share a word or phrase expressing what they would like to bring into their lives or what they would like to take from the session. Using an "Amen" cadence (IV, I) or another progression, tone the phrase. In an individual session, the phrase may expand or change. This is particularly powerful when a group sings each member's phrase. A group of people (or one other person) taking the time to double an individual's personal experience through singing can establish a sense of belonging.

Imagine a roomful of people singing the "Happy Birthday" song to you. At first, you feel uncomfortable, but when they get to the part where they sing your name, you have to admit that being celebrated and paid attention to feels pretty nice.

Keyes (1973, p. 59) also suggests actually toning a person's name on a C chord. She is talking about toning as a form of physical healing, but singing someone's name can also be highly validating. [See Figure 4(c).]

Figure 4(c). Word toning and positive goals.

Toning and Imagery
If your client is responding to any of the above toning exercises, you can stop and introduce imagery along with the singing.

Here are just a few examples:

1. *Unstructured toning:* Using unstructured toning, guide the client(s) to imagine sending their own voice to any part of the body that is feeling emotional or physical discomfort. The imagery can be based simply on the felt vibrations, or visual imagery can be used. For example, imagine that the vibrations of the voice are creating golden light that is warming the part of the body in question. Imagine a relaxing color created by the singing and expanding to create well-being.

2. *Grounding and running energy:* Using a technique from Shakti Gawain's *Creative Visualization* (Gawain & Shimoff, 2016), have your clients sing a one-octave vocal slide slowly ascending from Do to Do and then descending. Instruct the clients to focus on the spine and feel the connection for each vertebra as the voice slowly moves up the scale and back down. On the lowest note, feel the body connected to the earth. On the highest note, feel the energy running off the top of the head to the world and back down to ground again. Move up in half-steps, being careful not to move above C5 unless the singers are comfortable singing higher. This exercise can facilitate a sense of integration and awareness of the body in the present. [See Figure 4(d).]

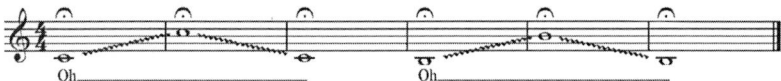

Figure 4(d). Grounding and running energy.

3. *Word toning with imagery:* Using a word phrase that has either developed organically from the toning or has been initiated by the therapist, tone the phrase in unison or in harmonies. Before beginning toning, instruct the clients to close their eyes and picture a time in the past day or so when they had felt discouraged or upset. Tell them to see themselves, what they were wearing, where they were, who was there. Then sing the phrase, having the clients send their voices directly to the image of themselves. The phrase "All is well" from word toning works beautifully. Using this chord progression in repetition can communicate comfort due to the soothing 3/4 tempo, the

plagal cadence which provides tension/release, and the consistent movement from IV to I.

Many different types of images can be used with word toning (e.g., pink bubble, radiating energy, radiating light, toning to a loved one, etc.). [See Figures 4(e) and 4(f).]

Figure 4(e). Word toning with imagery. Add harmonies or improvise over group singing.

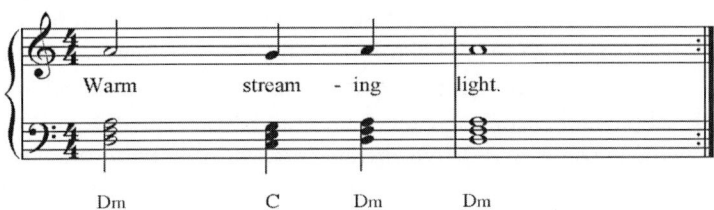

Figure 4(f). Word toning with imagery, continued.

Once a sense of safety through grounding has been established, the therapist can choose to stay with this goal or move to another goal (e.g., empowerment, self-expression, problem-solving, etc.). The therapist can also choose to stay with vocal methods or move to any other method of choice. Be careful not to move from grounding too soon. While this may sound like advice for the beginner, it took me years to learn the compassion of consistently moving at the client's pace no matter how slow or boring it felt to me.

My child took years to learn how to tie his shoes. I had to use every ounce of willpower not to grab his laces and tie them for him when we were trying to get out the door and be on time.

He didn't learn to tie his shoes at a pace that was comfortable for me. As therapists, we often have to deal with our own discomfort when companioning a client's process. Some clients will need to be held in consistent safety for many sessions until expanding the goal is warranted. Some will not be capable of growing into other goals.

Remember that some clients' entire therapeutic process will be repairing the long-term absence of safety, so even though the goal may seem "not good enough," these clients' lives can be changed by learning that "Sometimes some places and some people can be safe enough."

CALL-AND-RESPONSE

When using call-and-response for grounding and empowerment, stay with safety first. If the clients feel receptive, then move gently into introducing more emotional topics or topics that express client goals.

1. *Toning to imitation call-and-response:* An easy way to introduce call-and-response is to take the word toning exercise using two chords and add other phrases on one note. You can sing "I will live in peace," "I am standing strong," and so on. The therapist sings the phrase over the two-chord exercise in any meter, and then the client(s) can echo the phrase. Although authentic call-and-response uses two different phrases, for the purpose of encouraging shy singers, this method uses direct imitation.

    Again, words can be created by the therapist or clients, and the words do not have to make sense to anyone else. As the client becomes more comfortable with this, phrases for empowerment can be added (e.g., "My body is my body," "I will not be broken," "I can choose," "I have a right to my anger").

    Additions: (1) Once the client(s) is/are familiar with call-and-response, you can use any chord progression to create this method. (2) Add drums as an accompaniment to the singing.

2. *Client as leader for imitation call-and-response:* When the client is ready, encourage them to take the lead role. The client can write words ahead of time or sing one line repeatedly. I have had voice students imitate my phrasing to generate ideas. It is incredibly satisfying to have someone listen intently while you sing and endeavor to re-create the idea accurately. In the

echoing, the leader is being doubled, which can increase a sense of confidence.

In our day-to-day lives, deep listening has become hard to find. When the singer calls and the group or therapist responds every single time, this can strengthen the sense of self and connect the singers to a further belief in the power of the words. [See Figure 5(a).]

Figure 5(a). Imitation call-and-response.

3. *Authentic call-and-response:* Write your own call-and-response song or use one of the many already in existence. Here are just a few to get you started: Ella Jenkins, "Barreling On Down the Highway" (Jenkins, 1974); "A Train's A-Coming" (Jenkins, 1974); "Swing Low, Sweet Chariot" (James, 2002); "Angels Watching Over Me" (Grove, 2007); "Iko, Iko" (Crawford et al., 1965); "Minnie the Moocher" (Calloway, 1931); "Banana Boat Song (Day O)" (Belafonte, 1956); "Shout!" (The Isley Brothers, 1959); "It Don't Mean a Thing" (Ellington & Mills, 1932); "Ho Hey" (Schultz & Fraites, 2012); "Da Doo Ron Ron" (Spector et al., 1963). [See Figure 5(b).]

Figure 5(b). Authentic call-and-response.

SONGS OF EMPOWERMENT

Empowerment can be misunderstood to mean anger, aggression, and/or intense emotions. While an individual's journey to empowerment may include expressing anger and using a bataka bat, in my experience, the therapeutic process toward empowerment is much gentler and takes longer than a moment of sublimation. Empowerment will be described here as the process of becoming stronger—a gradual shifting of one's self-concept from being a victim to an awareness of having a choice. Even if you have a client for a brief hospital stay, they can still experience moments of empowerment through singing in a group or individually. Symptoms of fight, flight, freeze (Barlow, 2002) include a tendency to hold one's breath, feeling stuck in a part of the body, and feeling frozen or numb. Teaching an individual that they have a choice to inhale and exhale even when they are scared (as in a new setting) or that they have a choice to feel the pleasant sensation of their own voices rather than feeling numb is certainly a good beginning. These small moments of clarity can feel like water in the desert to clients. And, if you can see the client long-term, this is even better.

So, although they can be such, singing songs for empowerment is not necessarily cursing someone out in song or even singing loudly. Instead, it is the musical experience of connecting to one's own body through resonating, breathing, and letting the voice out first in the music therapy room and then, hopefully, in life. The words are important, but only as a vehicle to be used toward the goal of a solid connection to oneself.

When working in a group setting, it can be tricky to find a song that works for all group members. If the clients are connected first through toning warm-ups, the possibility of clients being open to connecting to a common song increases.

As long as the goals of empowerment are kept in mind, the therapist will guide the song in the moment. Songs that tend to work consistently will become clear; portions of songs, bridges, or choruses will be repeated because they generate the desired feeling.

It is not necessary to engage in a lengthy lyric analysis or verbal discussion. A few words can ground and bookmark the experience for clients, but too much thinking can pull a client away from resourcing the body. I have often witnessed clients overthink in a desire to communicate, which moves them to shallow breathing and body tension.

A great way to process without words is to have the clients draw a mandala representing what it felt like to sing the song. Then ask them to say a few words describing the mandala.

Just a very few ideas for songs to include: "We Shall Overcome" (gospel/folk, 1900s); "Firework" (K. Perry et al., 2010); "No One" (Keys et al., 2007); "Blackbird" (Lennon & McCartney, 1968); "Amazing Grace" (Newton, 1779); "I Shall Be Released" (Dylan, 1968); "Singing for Our Lives" (Near, 1979); "Beautiful" (L. Perry, 2002); "Song of Good Hope" (Hansard, 2012); "Shake It Out" (Welch & Epworth, 2011); "Carry On" (Bhasker et al., 2012); "I'll Stand by You" (Hynde et al., 1994).

SINGING AND RHYTHM

The goal here is to help the client to achieve the physical experience of grounding oneself and one's own voice. A chordal instrument may be used if it will motivate the clients to play with energy, but the focus is on the sound and feel of percussion supporting the voice. It is fine to percuss simple quarter notes, as any drumming will have the same effect.

1. *Call-and-response:* Using a cappella call-and-response technique, add drums.
2. *Songs:* Use any song that has worked for empowerment and add drums. With this technique, the song (especially the chorus) can be used like an anthem and can connect the client(s) to grounding in stressful times. You can also write a chant based on an empowering song.
3. *Beats and grooves:* Reproduce rhythms or chord grooves from familiar songs, including hip-hop, rock, reggae, African, and so forth and sing with these beats. Sing positive phrases that emerged from the word toning exercise, sing free-form over two chords with words or no words, sing a familiar call-and-response, or sing a familiar chant. Use well-known rhythms like the "We Will Rock You" (May, 1977) beat or "Yellow Submarine" (Lennon & McCartney, 1966). Look up beats on YouTube and replicate them on drums. [See Figures 6(a) and 6(b).]

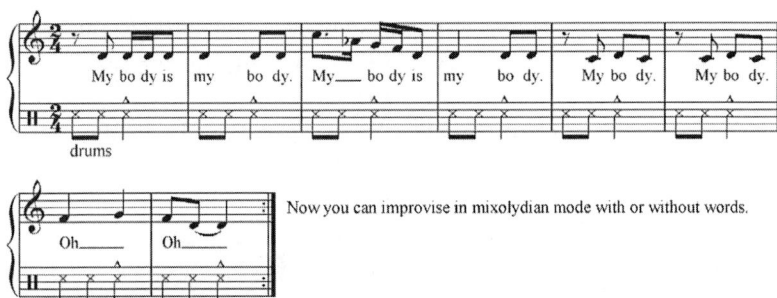

Figure 6(a). Singing and rhythm ("We Will Rock You" drum pattern). Can be done as a call-and-response or with solo singer improvising an answer.

Figure 6(b). Chant with rhythm written from a familiar and empowering song.

THE BLUES

Prewritten blues can be used for creating feelings of safety and empowerment in many ways. If someone is ready to express anger, by all means, the blues is a ready tool with which to improvise emotional melodies and words. Precomposed blues tunes are more contained, with a defined number of verses written by someone else. The individual can cover one of the many established tunes without having to connect the meaning to themselves. In so doing, the individual can still sustain a feeling of release.

Finally, there are many blues tunes written for comedic purposes. Not all clients will want to laugh, but some clients respond positively to ending with humor. After hard work, a silly song can help an individual to let go of the work and shift their body into a lighter place with the resource of laughter.

Some funny blues tunes are: "Oreo Cookie Blues" (Mack & Wilkerson, 1985); "Cordon Chicken Blues" (Goodman, 1989); "Steamroller Blues" (Taylor, 1970); "Straighten Up and Fly Right" (Cole & Mills, 1943). (See Figure 7.)

Figure 7. Blues ("Hello Blues").

FINAL THOUGHTS

While singing for or singing with your clients, be aware of their breathing. Help them to belly breathe by:

1. Introducing the hiss out exercise from teacher training.
2. Asking them to inhale while raising their arms in an arc to each side. (This encourages the natural motion of the diaphragm.)

3. Reminding them to feel their feet on the floor. When stressed, individuals can become disconnected from the lower body.
    a. Initiate stamping or tapping your feet, especially alternately, as this emulates bilateral stimulation for self-regulation (Grant, 2019).
    b. Instruct them to feel the oxygen moving all the way down to the bottoms of their feet. This imagery encourages connection to the lower body, feet feeling grounded, and deeper breathing.

Chapter 11

SENSE OF UNITY (GROUP COHESION, INDIVIDUAL CONNECTION)

Closely related to empowerment is the goal of unity or group cohesion. Vickhoff (Vickhoff et al., 2013) found a distinct propensity toward heart rate entrainment when individuals sing structured music in unison. This means that their heart rate not only is synchronized, but also accelerates and decelerates during entrainment. There is a theory that oxytocin, the feel-good hormone associated with emotions of love, increases during pleasurable singing (Grape et al., 2002).

In researching the psychological effects of choral singing, Kreutz's (2014) results suggested that singing "… induces a socio-biological bonding response."

While hearts are beating together, singers are inhaling and exhaling together, and oxytocin is being released, an increased atmosphere of trust and understanding is being created. In a study done by Oxford's Department of Experimental Psychology, adult educational classes were observed for seven months. Dr Eiluned Pearce concluded that the singing groups bonded more quickly than creative writing or craft classes. She said, "It's been suggested that singing is one of the ways we build social cohesion when there isn't enough time to establish one-to-one connections between everyone in a group" (Pearce et al., 2015). Thus, singing together provides an opportunity for individuals to experience a sense of unity and a decrease in feelings of loneliness and isolation.

> *The music therapist led a women's singing group in the senior daycare center once a week. Most of the women were connected with a Baptist church, and the group became a hymn-sing. Due to neurological issues as well as emotional withdrawal, very little conversation and interaction took*

place in the multipurpose room where they spent the day. Even during lunch at a common table, the women were shut down and unaware of one another.

In the music therapy room, the hymns requested were "Deep River," "By 'n' By," "Take My Hand, Precious Lord," "Amazing Grace," "Standing in the Need of Prayer," and so on.

Although the music therapist would set a tempo, the women would consistently adjust the tempo slower, finding a common time without any discussion. They would draw out each note with great emphasis and expression, filling the spaces with slides which bordered sometimes on low sighs of having lived. It was one of the most soulful sounds that the music therapist had ever heard.

This was also a time when the women connected through singing about their diseases, the end of their lives, their loneliness, and their many losses.

SINGING SONGS IN UNISON

The main goal here is to motivate the client(s) to sing consistently for a 20- to 30-minute length of time. Even though it doesn't matter what song material is used, choosing songs which will hold the clients' attention takes diagnostic skill, a willingness to explore and take chances, and a willingness to fail momentarily. I have a long-running singing for stress reduction group (over 10 years), and I still introduce songs that fall to the floor with a resounding thud. When this happened in my first years of practice, I felt mortified. It's still slightly uncomfortable, but I now know that it is as inspiring for the clients to see me take chances as it is for them to see me fail and just move on.

So, if singing "Dead Skunk" (Wainwright, 1972) creates unity, by all means use it.

Otherwise, do research and planning behind the scenes and more research and evaluating during the session. Try to be like a good track coach and keep the singing momentum going. Some clients will want to digress and talk too much in between songs. Verbal processing is okay, but for this method, keep the comments to a minimum and keep therapy in the songs until the end. This allows a more visceral rather than cerebral connection to happen.

One way to know you have achieved your goal is by the silence and stillness when the singing stops. If individuals have reached entrainment, they will sit quietly for a few moments because the focus has become experiential and not verbal. You can use a directive like, "Just sit and breathe and enjoy the sensations of your singing for a few more moments." Encourage them to not pull themselves out of this experience too quickly. Give them permission to take their time (a rare occurrence in life).

SINGING HARMONY

Once again, some clients will find great pleasure in singing in unison and will not need to move beyond this technique. However, if your individual client is able and/or the group is firmly established, use of harmony can enhance a sense of unity. Using any of the ideas in the Toolbox section, introduce five minutes or so of harmony and then move back to unison. Through this method, the clients can know a sense of separating and coming back together. In the coming home, or returning to unison, clients can feel anew this sense of connection to the therapist and one another.

SINGING FUN, SILLY SONGS

Singing songs that promote laughter or lighthearted fun, if placed within a session correctly, can help an individual client and/or group of clients to bond. The experience of connecting in a group or as an individual client with others can bring a wonderful feeling of security, inclusion, and belonging. At the same time, it can feel quite unfamiliar and vulnerable. Similar to eating too much sugar, one can feel a need to stop. Clients can tolerate only so much connection and then may want to shut down and distance themselves to stay safe.

Of course, at this point, the therapist can shift to other interventions. However, if it is desirable to keep clients singing, introduce playful songs. The humorous songs suggested in the Toolbox section not only create silly scenarios but also use cumbersome, difficult word combinations that encourage calisthenics with the tongue and mouth. Oftentimes, people make mistakes while trying to enunciate, especially if the tempo gradually increases. Not only does this allow a space for laughter and less "serious" work, but also it allows for permission to be imperfect and still have fun.

If you notice clients shutting down by not singing, looking down, slumping, and so forth, check in and see if you feel it is time to shift energy. Silly fun can be effective at any point in the session.

VOWELS

Purposefully planning a few songs with obvious open vowels can increase vocal resonance, allowing voices to be heard and felt more by each participant in the session and thus creating connection through voices openly vibrating together.

Chapter 12

STRESS REDUCTION AND RELAXATION

This chapter is not about stress due to a traumatic event (PTSD) or anxiety disorder.

Stress can be chronic (sitting in traffic jams every day while traveling to work) or momentary (losing your house keys for five minutes). It can be severe (divorce) or fairly benign (spilling tomato sauce on a new dress). Regardless of the situation or severity, stress can be defined as the body's fight-or-flight reaction to perceived pressure or danger (Davis et al., 2008). For example, losing one orchestral audition can be consciously or subconsciously perceived by the musician as a sign that he will never get a paying gig. Thus, losing the audition feels like a threat to his survival, and although he is not in imminent danger, his body reacts by releasing hormones to prepare for fight-or-flight.

Stress that continues over a long term can lead to physical and psychological issues.

Below is some science about how singing can help.

The vagus nerve is the longest running cranial nerve in the body. It connects from the brain to the throat, the lungs, the heart, and the gut, as well as to other organs. Stimulating the vagus nerve activates the parasympathetic nervous system and increases relaxation (Fallis, 2019). "The vagal response reduces stress. It reduces our heart rate and blood pressure. It changes the function of certain parts of the brain, stimulates digestion, all those things that happen when we are relaxed" (Golubic, in Fallis, 2019, p. 1).

There are many activities that stimulate the vagus nerve, one of which is singing—specifically, humming, chanting, singing in unison, and upbeat, energetic singing.

In a study done in South Wales with five separate groups, singing was found to decrease the stress hormone cortisol as well as modulate mood and stress positively (Fancourt et al., 2016).

Of course, the most obvious benefit of singing is that it forces the singer to inhale more deeply for an ongoing period of time, thus increasing oxygen to the brain and lowering blood pressure.

When the body is in fight-or-flight mode, the brain does not respond to commands of "Relax!" and "Calm down!" Instead, it needs tools that are nonverbal ("Understanding the Stress Response", Harvard Health, 2011).

> *PAM is a retired water company secretary who began attending a community music therapy singing group focused on stress reduction. She had been experiencing increased stress while driving in city traffic. She had found lip trill warm-ups to be calming, and she had begun lip trilling when someone cut her off in traffic or drove too close. Pam reported to the group feeling more relaxed and confident while driving, which had increased her sense of safety and overall enjoyment of her life in retirement.*

Vocal Exercises

With empowerment, vocal exercises are being used to facilitate and maintain a safe connection to one's body, so the goal has a deep inner focus.

When working on stress reduction, the interventions are teaching the body how to move out of fight-or-flight in response to outside stimuli. There is a didactic component, as well, in that once the relaxation response has been engaged, cognition is used to: (1) Problem-solve—for example, "Rather than tensing my muscles on my drive to work, I can listen to music" or "My stress is coming from holding in my emotions about the divorce—maybe I need to find a support group." (2) Research and plan—for example, "This stress reduction technique works sometimes, but this one doesn't work at all" or "My goal is to remember to sing a C scale three times in one hour of doing homework."

With this in mind, any vocal exercise can be used as long as the mind connects it to the goal. So, if an individual sings a C scale rapidly with barely any breath support, this probably won't help.

Conversely, singing a C scale slowly with purposeful pauses for each inhale increases the possibility of relaxation.

Therefore:

1. Choose and sing any vocal exercises from the Therapist Training or chapter 10 or make up your own.
2. Discuss each client's symptoms.
3. During the session, practice 10 to 20 minutes of vocal exercises that encourage the release of tension. (You will need to be creative so that boredom doesn't promote stress—change tempos, sing a harmony, etc.).
4. Ask each client to pick one stressful situation with which to practice during the week.
5. Instruct clients to use any vocal exercise with a goal of decreasing stress/tension during their specific stressful situation.
6. Check in on efficacy the following session and brainstorm as a group to help each client to tweak their approach to increase effectiveness.

CHANT

Chants have a triple benefit when used for stress reduction. Chants help to slow the breath and relax the body, while focusing the mind as well as replacing negative thoughts with calming thoughts. Try not to stop chanting before clients have become entrained. This works in individual sessions as well as for groups.

Ideas for chant:

1. Use resources given in the Toolbox section.
2. Write your own chants from phrases that arise in the session.
3. Take short phrases or choruses from popular songs and use them as a chant.
4. If you find a song you would like to use for chant, but the words are inappropriate, rewrite the words. For example, there is an Austrian Christmas Carol called "Still, Still, Still" (Süß, 1865). The first line reads, "Sleep, sleep, sleep, / 'Tis the eve of the Savior's birth." Below is an example of the re-created text:

Still, still, still,
I will let my heart be still.
When trouble assails me, physical ails me,
Friends won't avail me, in time of need,
Still, still, still,
I will let my heart (breath, mind, etc.) be still.

Another idea for alternate lyrics is to take the "Battle Hymn of the Republic" and sing:

We are gathered here together now to lift our voice in song.
As we sing, we come together and we know our hearts are strong.
We will let our voices freely ring, our journey won't be long.
Our truth is marching on …

5. Sing through an entire song once or twice, then turn the last line into a chant.
6. Sing chants at different tempos.
   While singing "This Little Light of Mine," change the tempo from a gospel-rhythm 150 bpm to a flowing 80 bpm with suspended chords to an even slower a cappella. This is especially calming when repeating "Let It Shine" as a shorter chant.

SINGING AND IMAGERY

Connect imagery to any one of the vocal methods in this goal section with a brief verbal narrative.

Here is one example:

After singing a few repetitions of "This Little Light of Mine" (Loes, 1920), pause the singing and, while continuing to play simple chords, briefly introduce your imagery, speaking slowly and fluidly:

"Let's just take one moment to connect to the lyrics. Close your eyes and imagine light in any way you choose. Imagine the light in you, with you, near you. Now, as we sing, continue to see the light and allow the light to shine wherever you need it to be [a person, a struggle, a geographical area, a body part, etc.]."

Continue to sing, and when the song is finished, encourage clients to continue breathing and hold the image for a few more moments before opening their eyes. Honor the stillness until one of the clients breaks the silence.

Sometimes individuals just want to indulge in the imagery without having to explain, so allow as much or as little verbal sharing as happens to occur. Some people do not have visual images. Reassure them by explaining that this is normal and that they can still derive benefits from the exercise.

There are so many creative ways to use imagery with songs and vocal exercises and readily available imagery scripts online. Be careful to keep the script very short so as to maintain the benefits of singing.

A few more ideas include a 1960s David Van Ronk song called "River Come Down (Bamboo)" (Van Ronk, 1961), along with a "letting go" imagery. Place your worries on the stick and let it float down the river. Also, try singing the chorus to James Taylor's "Shower the People" (Taylor, 1976), with an image of singing from the heart to a loved one.

SINGING AND MANDALA

After singing for a time, and once the group's energy has shifted to a more relaxed state, you can pause at any point and have clients draw the experience of singing or the experience of relaxation or any directive which seems à propos.

These mandalas can be kept and used throughout sessions to refocus clients on relaxation before singing. Clients can also draw intermittently in order to view their own stress reduction progress.

Fun, Silly Songs

I used to work in a wedding band at the Atlantic City casinos. This may sound like fun, but the bandleader was being paid a lot of money, and the gig was a high-pressure, high-energy performance. On Saturdays, we would play one party in the afternoon and one in the evening. Around about the seventh hour of continuous music, we were undoubtedly miserable.

On one particular gig, the piano player, who was always trying to make us laugh, did some hilarious dance move. We all lost it. There were tears streaming down our faces, and we could not stop laughing. The shift from intense stress to total release of tension was instantaneous.

Laughter and/or silliness can relieve stress. Use the ideas from the Toolbox or create your own.

Chapter 13

COGNITIVE BEHAVIOR, RATIONAL THINKING, AND EMOTIONAL REGULATION

Cognitive behavior therapy (CBT) focuses on becoming aware of negative, disruptive thoughts and learning to change one's perception by rewriting statements that are realistic, rational, and probable. It holds to the idea that depressive/anxious thinking goes hand-in-hand with irrational, unrealistic, self-talk and uses labels like "mind-reading," "fortune-telling," "catastrophizing," "black-and-white thinking," and "overgeneralization" to encourage awareness of this thinking. (Burns, 1999). Sentences with "should," "must," "ought to," "have to," "always," and "never" are red flags for absolute thinking that causes distress. The premise is that with correct thinking, client distress decreases (Beck, 1979).

Self-regulation or emotional regulation is closely related to the concept of CBT, as it involves the ability to control behaviors, impulses, and emotions. In its most basic form, it is the ability to stop and think before acting. It is also being able to balance oneself out and bring oneself back to center after disappointments and upsets (Cuncic, 2019). As in the vignette below, assertiveness is a CBT skill.

> *LEE is a 48-year-old woman, married with two children. She is a gifted writer who came to therapeutic voice lessons to work on the strength in her voice and receive support for anxiety related to achieving her career goals, which she had put on hold to have children. Her voice was very quiet, and early on, the therapist began to realize that her quiet voice was connected to her family dynamics. Lee did not want to work biographically. She chose to stay with support work.*

Lee was working in a somewhat abusive and hurtful work environment, and slowly she began to connect to and allow anger to be expressed through lyrics. One day, she discovered that she loved singing "Don't Rain on My Parade." Lee and the therapist worked with this song repeatedly to help her to move it further into her body. Lee ended her therapy after quitting her job, applying for writing jobs, and taking college music courses.

Through singing these words, Lee was able to use her voice assertively and begin to move toward her goals.

SINGING SONGS FOR CORE BELIEFS

In *The Relaxation and Stress Reduction Workbook* (Davis et al., 2008), there is an inventory with 50 questions (p. 130). This inventory helps the individual to hone in on negative core beliefs such as "I must have love and approval from friends," "I must be perfect in every way," and "Things should be exactly the way I want them to be." The inventory is illuminating even for those who deem themselves to be self-aware because the core beliefs are clearly irrational and to the point, so it is a good way to uncover and work with these thoughts. Often, irrational concepts were formed preverbally or subconsciously and never put into words, so finding these sentences first is critical to changing thinking. As with Lee, once the client is aware of negative thinking, songs can be an effective tool for replacing the harmful voice with the more positive voice of the singer/composer.

At first, just as in a meditation practice, it can seem as though the song isn't working, but reconnecting neuroreceptors takes practice and perseverance. "Our brains do not contain fixed hard-wiring; the neural pathways and circuits can, in fact, change with learning and with mental exercises" (Krishnakumar et al., 2015, in "Conclusion"). Building new muscle takes time, so the client needs to be diligent about singing the song. With this practice, eventually, the song can become louder than the core belief sentence and can be sung or audiated in times of stress.

Here are some ideas for using songs to refute irrational core beliefs and the thoughts that follow:

Core belief 1. "Things should be the way I want them to be." *Thought:* "People should stop at Stop signs!" *Emotion:* anger. *Song:* "Let It Be" (Lennon & McCartney, 1970).

Core belief 2. "I must have approval from friends and family." *Thought:* "Sally must be mad at me because she hasn't called me back! She's never calling me back." *Emotion:* agitated fear. *Song:* "Beautiful," performed by Christina Aguilera (Perry, 2002).

Core belief 3. "Outside events have caused my misery." *Thought:* "I would be way more successful if my parents hadn't constantly criticized me." *Emotion:* anger, disappointment. *Song:* "We Shall Overcome" (folk song, 1900s).

Core belief 4. "I must be perfect." *Thought:* "I sounded horrible when I missed that note. I should just throw my horn out!" *Emotion:* intense frustration. *Song:* "If You Want to Sing Out" (Stevens, 1971).

Core belief 5. "I am afraid of the unknown." *Thought:* "Why are they late?! They must have been in a bad accident!" *Emotion:* fear. *Song:* "Peace Like a River" (Mormon Tabernacle Choir, 2004).

Core belief 6. "It is easier to avoid difficulties than to face them." *Thought:* "I can't tell my boss that she's giving me too much work. She'll fire me." *Emotion:* fear. *Song:* "No One," performed by Alicia Keys (Keys et al., 2007).

Core belief 7. "Some people are evil and should receive punishment." *Thought:* "I go to sleep at night trying to figure out how to hurt him like he hurt me." *Emotion:* resentment. *Song:* "Down by the Riverside" (Nelson & Marsalis, 2008).

Core belief 8. "Happiness can be achieved by having passive leisure time." *Thought:* "If I could just win the lottery, I would be a happy person." *Emotion:* discontent. *Song:* "What a Wonderful World" (Thiele & Weiss, 1967).

Core belief 9. "I need something stronger than myself to rely upon." *Thought:* "It is horrible for me when my partner goes on business trips" *Emotion:* depression, fear. *Song:* "This Little Light of Mine" (Loes, 1920).

SIMPLE LYRIC WRITING

As stated above, becoming aware of specific negative thoughts is only the beginning. Like a phonograph needle settling again and again into a well-worn groove, our distracted, tired minds can return to the habit of a familiar thought over and over. Through our developmental years, our parents showered us with well-meant phrases like "If you don't get up off the ground, you'll get sick" or "If you don't comb your hair, everyone will laugh at you." Often, the phrases were more subtle or implied, but the motivator still was avoiding negative consequences and fear.

These phrases were learned by rote over many years. There is a technique called "thought-stopping" with which, upon awareness of a negative thought, the individual shouts "Stop!" in order to let go or redirect the thought (Davis et al., 1995, pp. 127–133).

In times of great distress, a quick, direct method like this might be of better use than singing through an entire song.

Take only a portion of a favorite song, write a thought-redirecting sentence from it, and then simplify the sentence for singing:

1. "If I don't finish this now, I'm never going to finish it." *Rational thought:* "Although I have more to do, if I stop and take a break now, I will feel refreshed and probably do better work." *Sing:* "It's okay to stop right now" repeatedly through the first eight measures of "It's Only a Paper Moon" (Arlen et al., 1933).
2. "I'm a terrible musician." *Rational thought:* "Even though my pitch was off, I have had good performances in the past, and if I keep practicing, it's possible that I will play this in tune." *Sing:* "You can do this" to "Good Day, Sunshine" (Lennon & McCartney, 1966).
3. "I said that stupid thing right in front of everybody." *Rational thought:* "I am embarrassed by what I said, and if I accept my human flaws, I can probably forgive myself." *Sing:* "I forgive myself for saying that, I'm human after all" to the "Battle Hymn of the Republic" (Steffe & Howe, 1861).
4. "I'm afraid something terrible is going to happen." *Rational thought:* "Even though I was taught by my family to worry, if I keep working on my thoughts, I will probably learn to feel safer." *Sing:* "I am in a safe place now" to "We Shall Overcome" (Seeger, 1963).
5. "Oh, no! I lost my wallet." *Rational thought:* "If I breathe and remain as calm as I can, I will probably be able to better

problem-solve how to find my wallet." *Sing:* "I can calm down" to the chorus of "Hallelujah" (Cohen, 1984).
6. "My partner broke up with me. I am lost." *Rational thought:* "Even though I am in a lot of pain, I have been through struggles before. If I keep working on myself, I will probably be stronger than before." *Sing:* "I know I'll be all right" to "My Lord, What a Morning" (Belafonte, 1960).
7. "If my daughter moves away, I'll just die." *Rational thought:* "Even though I would miss her very much, I could use my tools and not only be okay, but also be proud of myself for letting go." *Sing:* "I can use my tools" to The Rembrandts' "I'll Be There for You" (Sōlem et al., 1995).

A thought-changing statement cannot be a lavender sparkle platitude. In true cognitive behavior style, the statement must be probable and rational as well as positive, because if the client does not believe the statement, it will not work to decrease distress. The therapeutic work also lies in fleshing out negative thoughts and feelings resulting from the thoughts, writing new thoughts, and supporting the client in using the new thoughts in practice. There are excellent cognitive behavior worksheets easily downloaded from the Internet.

The lyrics do not have to match the melody like poetry but can be awkward like some of the statements above and still be effective. Trimmer et al. (2016) used lyric writing in a CBT group for the goal of behavioral activation, or engaging in positive activities. This was done by rewriting the lyrics to Bob Dylan's "Like a Rolling Stone" (Dylan, 1965). With consistent support in learning the techniques, rational thinking can increase (Ezegbe et al., 2018).

SONGWRITING

Songwriting can be used to enhance the practice of replacing cognitive distortions (negative thinking) with reframing thoughts (rational thinking) (Beck, 1976). As in all songwriting, this can be approached in different ways. Each verse of the song can contain one negative thought that shifts to a rational thought by the end of the verse. Or, as in the case of the example below, the verse has an AB form that changes tonality as the thought becomes reframed. Musical shifts of minor to major, meter or key changes, and changes in tempo can possibly increase the effectiveness in awareness of cognitive distortions and the ability to remember how to reframe these thoughts. (See Figure 8.)

Cognitive Behavior, Rational Thinking, and Emotional Regulation

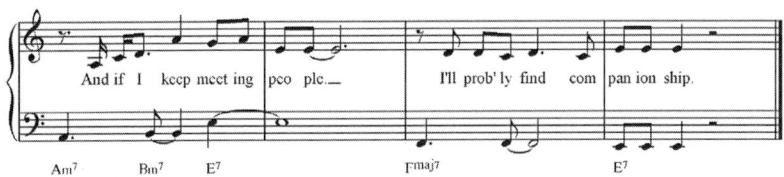

Figure 8. Rational thinking song.

MINDFUL SINGING

"Mindfulness is the basic human ability to be fully present, aware of where we are and what we're doing, and not overly reactive to what is going on around us" (Mindful.org, 2020).

In research conducted by Lesiak (2017) using DBT (Dialectical Behavioral Therapy) mindfulness and music therapy, DBT mindfulness skills were discussed and incorporated into each session.

These skills included wise mind (balance between logic and emotion), observe (pay attention to the music), describe (talk about what you observed, just facts), participate (engage completely in the activity), nonjudgmental (neither good nor bad), one-mindful (present in the moment), and effective (building healthy relationships).

More detailed descriptions of these skills can be found in the book *DBT Skills Manual Training* (Linehan, 2015). You can also find detailed descriptions of each skill simply by searching online for them by name.

Mindful singing can be done with any and all vocal methods, including toning, vocal exercises, chant, song-singing, and improvisation.

To introduce clients to the concept of mindfulness, begin with awareness of breathing.

You can direct your client(s) to feel the air moving through the nasal passage and throat and into the lungs, as well as bring attention to the expansion of the chest, back, and sides.

Then you might possibly use a slide vocal exercise and encourage focused awareness of where in the body each note resonates.

At this point, mindfulness can be finished, or you can use any of the vocal methods to work on skills such as wise mind, participate, and effective. Remember to help clients to describe what they have observed.

From here, design brief homework assignments for incorporating Mindful Singing into day-to-day situations.

SINGING WITH BILATERAL STIMULATION AND GROUNDING TECHNIQUES

I am one of those unique individuals who loved marching band in high school—especially when they handed me a piccolo and I suddenly became louder than the trumpets. It is common for many music therapists to describe a powerful connection to music as a way to get through their developmental years. What I recently realized was that every day after school and for a week in the summer, I was rigorously practicing bilateral stimulation and thus grounding myself.

Bilateral stimulation is a left–right pattern of any stimuli. This concept began as EMDR (Eye Movement Desensitization Reprocessing), which is solely based in visual stimulation (Shapiro, 1995), and has expanded to include auditory and tactile stimulation (Wikipedia, 2019).

According to Shapiro, bilateral stimulation may work because it improves the processing of emotions and can decrease physiological stress, increase flexible thinking, increase objectivity, and decrease worry (Grant, 2019).

A study using an EEG after EMDR found a significant functioning shift from the limbic regions of the brain with high emotional activity to the corticol regions with higher cognitive activity (Pagani et al., 2012). Basically, the right side of the brain is largely responsible for activating fight-or-flight, which engages in response to perceived situations of danger. Bilateral stimulation allows for a more even conversation between left and right so that issues and problems can be viewed more objectively. With this objective view, the body calms down, and from this calmer place, rational thinking can occur.

Bilateral stimulation techniques include …

1. Drumming with an alternating left-right pattern and singing.
2. *Butterfly hugs and singing:* Cross one hand over the other at chest level and, in a medium slow tempo or tempo of choice, pat near the collarbone or pat the arms.
3. *Alternating hand clasps and singing:* Clasp the hands together, intertwining fingers with the left forefinger on the outside of the hand. Hold this clasp while singing a measure or two and then move the hands to a closed prayer position. Now clasp hands with the right forefinger on the outside of the hand. Hold this position for a measure or two. Continue alternating the clasp.
4. Walking or marching while singing.
5. Alternating left–right tapping of legs while singing.
6. *Playing piano with an alternating left–right pattern while singing:* This can be done with one note in each hand an octave apart or the same triad in each hand. Although this may not be aesthetically pleasing, it can be very effective for a client to

experience holding the ground on piano while expressing vocally.

7. *Chest rub:* Although this technique is not bilateral, it is grounding. Take your right hand and make slow, gentle circular motions over your heart while singing.

Chapter 14

SELF-EXPRESSION AND COMMUNICATION

I'll never forget the shock I felt when I was dialogue-cooing with my six-month-old son and heard him reach a goal that my profoundly mentally disabled clients had not been able to reach. I heard him attempt to imitate my cooing. Once I thought about it, this made sense, as most of these clients were diagnosed at a mental age of five months. They didn't have the receptive and expressive pre-linguistic language skills to process and reproduce my vocal sounds. While I felt happy for my son, I also felt a peculiar unease, for imagining my son being unable to surpass the expressive skills of a five-month-old was the closest I had come to identifying with what it must be like to live 18, 20, 21 years in a verbal world with such limited abilities.

Very young (and older) human beings need to be held or treated with care, need to see someone see them, and need to be heard by someone listening and responding consistently in order to feel safe and to thrive.

Whether our clients are limited verbally, completely nonverbal, or highly well-spoken, they need the same elements present in order to express sounds, experiences, beliefs, concepts, and emotions.

"Self-expression allows individuals to distinguish themselves from others, to reflect their own beliefs and needs, and to validate their own self-concepts" (Kim & Ko, 2006, p. 4).

In Ackerman (2019, p. 1), Judith Glazer, CEO of Benchmark Communications, Inc., is paraphrased as saying, "When we open up and express ourselves, we move from what she calls a state of protection (coddling our ego and manning our inner walls to protect ourselves) to a state of partnering (being open to sharing yourself with others and vice versa)."

In expressing as well as listening, the prefrontal cortex is activated to access higher-level thinking, which includes new thinking, thinking together, and co-creating possibilities (Glazer, 2016).

> *At the time of treatment, ELLY was a 21-year-old woman with Down syndrome who was in the process of being diagnosed with a psychological disorder (possibly schizophrenia). Elly was not able to put her thoughts and feelings about this into words, and often her communications did not make sense. It was clear that she was frightened. We began writing songs about the positive aspects of Elly's life. Elly decided she wanted to sing one of her songs at a concert designed for this purpose. During the performance, Elly completely forgot every single word to her song, yet she continued to sing in gibberish. Elly's eyes were shining with tears as she sang, and she was smiling from ear to ear. It appeared that Elly was having a peak experience. The audience reported having goose bumps and feeling Elly's utter joy and bliss even though they could not understand a single word. It's unclear what this experience meant to her. Perhaps it was important to Elly to know that she could still express herself to others even when the words no longer made sense as she moved into dealing with her difficult diagnoses.*

LISTENING

Sometimes clients need to be listened to in order to express vocally: at other times, they need to listen to others express and model how to communicate before they can summon the courage to do so.

For some, the need to have their voices listened to is strong, but the fear of connecting is stronger (clients with autism, issues of abuse, etc.). These clients need to be held with attention, consistent presence, and patience. The goal for all is to be able to hear themselves.

Here are some ways to listen:

1. Sing together in unison slightly softer than the client (both verbal and nonverbal), so that the client(s) is supported but hearing their own expression.

2. Sing together in unison slightly louder, allowing the client (both verbal and nonverbal) to feel their voice but not hear their voice.
3. Using vocal exercises, chants, or call-and-response, have the client directly imitate you or directly imitate the client (in this way, you are listening for a finite period of time).
4. When singing in a group, project with leadership, and when the group is vocally cohesive, lower your dynamic so that each member can hear one another.
5. Listen to each tone, word, dynamic, and emotion while your client sings a solo (accompanied or a cappella) and then reflect in words what you heard, making sure that your statement is about the music, not the client—for example, "When you sang 'I will remember you,' those words sounded so important."
6. Listen to prerecorded singers together (allowing someone else to express for the client when they can't). Ask your client questions about the singer's voice, the lyrics, the final chord, and so forth, and if your client shares, reflect back what was said with interest.
7. Listen with awe to your client's silence. From profoundly disabled clients pausing to enjoy vibrations to highly verbal clients finding a place of quiet calm, silence truly is golden. Allowing silence communicates: "You don't have to take care of me or explain to me or connect to me right now. We can just sit here and breathe together while you allow this experience to be." When you listen to your client's silence, you are allowing them space to listen to and hear themselves. If you are uncomfortable with silence, focus your mind on breathing exercises or do some personal work.

DIALOGUE

Dialogue with Nonverbal Clients
In using dialogue with disorders of consciousness and intellectual disabilities (unless the client objects), it is important to be close in proximity, as often the client is being encouraged to work on awareness of self and others as well as self-expression.

Even though it is not necessary, having a chordal instrument can be grounding, especially for the therapist. A client's vocals can be quite wild and random (atonal, arrhythmic). In order to connect but not get lost in the client's world, it's important to have some connection to a tonal center, even if it is only one note. If possible, allow the client to explore instruments tactilely while you play (sometimes the vibrations from instruments can elicit a vocal response). While guitar and piano give great texture, some clients will benefit from the therapist's body not being blocked so that they can be stimulated to express vocally not only through sound but also through body vibrations. For this purpose, try a steel tongue drum, a shruti box, finger cymbals, a kalimba, or an autoharp laid flat between client and therapist. Ukulele gives more flexibility for close proximity, as well.

When ready, simply vocalize on a simple song or chord pattern, inserting the client's name often. When the client responds, imitate their tone and rhythmic quality. If the client's vocalizations are pitched, transpose the key of your accompaniment to support their tonal center. You can take breaks from the dialogue by singing simple songs. For some clients, this exercise can continue for an entire half-hour session. For others, you will need to shift activities. A nonverbal client's singing can be truly unique and exotic ... like singing with someone from another world. They can also help us to expand our own vocal textures and gain expressive freedom. This can be facilitated in a group by moving slowly from one individual to another and then introducing a group activity. This vertical–horizontal method can stimulate brief moments of cohesion, even with very withdrawn individuals.

Dialogue with Verbal Clients
Diane Austin developed a method called the Vocal Holding Technique (Austin, 2008). This involves using two or three chords to access hidden parts of the self that have been fragmented due to trauma. This is a depth psychology method that requires advanced training. Therefore the dialogue method described here is not connected to Diane's depth method. It is highly recommended that when this method is being used, the singing be limited to expressing in the present. Also, because the hypnotic, rocking sensation of two chords can be regressive, if the exercise moves too deeply, switch to three or

more chords for this dialogue. Finally, no matter how well the exercise is going, stop after 5 minutes and check in. If all is well, continue.

Extract a chord progression, feel (style), tempo, meter, and rhythm from a song that you or your client likes or one that you've written. Finding chord progressions in different styles can really change the way you sing. Then, improvise a conversation. You can use vowels, syllables, scat-sing, or words. The client can sing about current struggles and issues or goals and dreams. You can have a conversation ahead of time about what to sing. You can also take the first line to a song and start there.

Let's look at John Mayer's "Gravity" (2006). The opening chords are G to C in slow 3/4 with a blues quality. The opening lyrics are "Gravity is workin' against me. / And gravity wants to bring me down." Sing this a few times in unison, pause and listen to the chords, then ask the client in melody what's bringing them down or introduce your own theme.

Client: "Oh! I am out of cigarettes."
Therapist: "Oh, it's bringing you down."
Client: "And I feel like I won't make it without a smoke."
Therapist: "Oh, oh, that must feel so bad." [See Figure 9(a).]

Figure 9(a). Dialogue. Chords to "Gravity" by John Mayer.

After a couple of rounds of this, for variety or to prevent someone from regressing, you can move to the outro and sing in unison "Keep me where the light is."

When I sing like this with clients, sometimes I'm thinking, "I have no idea what to sing back. In these times, I just sing "Oh" or "Oh, no" or I repeat what the client sang.

This particular song can work well with a group by alternating between each person taking a solo and the group singing the phrase "bring me down." Then end with a chant on "Keep me where the light is." When used with a group or individual, a singer can take the opportunity to "stretch out" or just sing on one note. You can alternate singers every four to eight measures or as seems right. If clients feel more comfortable starting with or remaining with nonword singing, that's okay.

This method is not meant to sound like a polished duet. It will sound raw and at times awkward because our clients have rarely been given an opportunity to create vocally in the moment.

If the technique is creating fear rather than supporting expression, you will see signs of distress like those listed in "Establishing Safety."

If clients are quiet but not in distress, you may be confronted to hold the tension and keep offering the opportunity to dialogue.

You can do this by:

1. Repeating the chord progression and allowing time for clients to process the request.

Self-Expression and Communication

2. Asking clients what they might like to sing about and singing it for them.
3. Singing your own day-to-day concerns, dreams, and so forth.

When I feel compelled to give in to my fears that I am causing clients discomfort and they won't return to music therapy, I do an objective diagnostic and usually see that they are earnestly engaging. At this point, I realize that being supported to explore with no judgment is very effective and can reach to many different developmental stages.

Those clients who did have a vocal repartee with an adult as young children can tap into that sense of holding and bring it forward into the present singing experience, while those who did not have this relationship can come to know a slight shift in understanding their own voices: "I am allowed to express myself. Sometimes I will be listened to."

Another song to use for dialogue is "I Can See Clearly Now" (Nash, 1972), which has a completely different feel and message. Sing the first line in repetition and then introduce singing about positive resources in each person's life. [See Figure 9(b).]

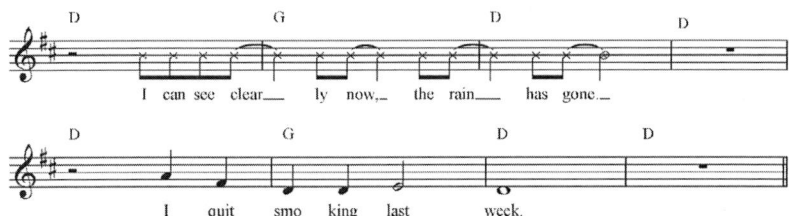

Figure 9(b). Dialogue. "I Can See Clearly Now."

There is also a beautiful chord progression in the opening of K. T. Tunstall's "Heal Over" (2004) that could be used for open dialogue. [See Figure 9(c).]

Figure 9(c). Dialogue. Chords to "Heal Over" by K. T. Tunstall.

There are so many song structures available for opening into dialogue improvisation. I also highly recommend that you buy the sheet music (Sheetmusic.com or Musicnotes.com), as the original chord voicings can inspire and ellicit emotions.

Assignment: Go through your music (sheet or chart), pick out a song or two, and practice playing and singing a structure of your choice for dialogue or use some of the two-chord progressions from the teacher training. It's not necessary to use this exact technique for your sessions. If you practice this technique, you will be more likely to create one of your own, but you can also just use this one. That's the beauty of music. It opens up the creative mind.

FILL-INS AND ONE-WORD PHRASES

Vocal self-expression takes courage, but in my experience I have found that, deep down, our clients want to sing. Fill-ins are great for providing high levels of containment and lowering the risk factor with the goal of singing one note. The following methods can be adapted for any population. I have used "Bingo" (Fox, 2008) with successful high achievers in a music-as-therapy community-based group, and it brings much joy, allowing the concept of "play" for adults.

"She'll Be Coming 'Round the Mountain" (Hudspeth, 2017) was originally a spiritual, and "I've Been Working on the Railroad" (Raffi, 1977) is a folk song (be careful with this one, as the lyrics are controversial).

With a little YouTube research, you can find very creative versions of folk songs, such as "She'll Be Coming 'Round the Mountain" as a rock tune (Neil Young has a gritty version on the album *Americana*, 2012) and "Old MacDonald" (B. Crosby, 1959) as either gospel or funk. Ella Fitzgerald sings a jazz version of "Old MacDonald" on her album *Whisper Not* (1967). With this type of treatment, these songs are no longer just for children.

Admittedly, the population that seems most resistant to singing is adolescents. Some adolescents will sing some of the time, but no one will sing if space and encouragement are not initiated.

To use fill-ins:

1. Take any song you like and stop when you would like the client to sing. Some clients will respond to musical cues, while others will need much verbal cueing (calling their name and repeating what you want) and still others will even need physical touching, such as tapping, hand-holding, and so on, if this is allowed.

2. Use a song prompting each client to sing the same word or phrase. For example, take "Hello, Dolly!" (Herman, 1964) and change the words a bit to:

    Hello, Dolly, well, Hello, Dolly, it's so nice to have you back where you belong.
    Hello, Dolly, Hello, Dolly, you're still growing, you're still glowing, you're still going strong.
    Hello, Dolly, Hello, Dolly, playing your old favorite songs from way back when
    (finish the song as originally written and repeat)

3. The fill-in can happen anywhere in the phrase with any song. Basically, anyplace in the phrase that you stop can be a place for filling in.

    a. Beginning: "Ho Hey" (Schultz & Fraites, 2012)
    b. Middle: "Bingo" (Fox, 2008) (Have client sing the letter "I")
    c. End: "She'll Be Coming 'Round the Mountain" (Hudspeth, 2017) (Yee-ha!)

4. Call-and-response songs or repetitive songs can be used for longer fill-ins.

    a. "Down by the Riverside" (Nelson & Marsalis, 2008)
    b. "Amen" (J. Hairston, 1964)
    c. "It Don't Mean a Thing" (Ellington & Mills, 1932)

5. The client(s) can create the word phrases and in so doing express by singing and by sharing thoughts.

    a. "This Little Light of Mine" (Loes, 1920) (Ask "Where do you want the light to shine?" e.g., "All around my heart")
    b. "We Shall Overcome" (Seeger, 1963) ("What do you want to overcome?")
    c. "Open Your Eyes" (Corea & Potter, 1973) (Covered by Lizz Wright on *Salt,* 2003) (Fill in "Never be afraid to …")
    d. "Everybody Loves Saturday Night" (The New Christy Minstrels, 1963) "What do you love?"

6. Here are a few "hipper" ideas:

    a. "Ho Hey" (Schultz & Fraites, 2012)
    b. "The Sweet Escape" (Stefani, 2006)
    c. "Get Up, Stand Up" (Marley & Tosh), 1973)
    d. "Happy," Pharrell Williams (Williams, 2013)
    e. "Shout!," The Isley Brother (Isley et al., 1959)
    f. "Werewolves of London," Warren Zevon (Mannell et al., 1977)

Fill-ins work with individuals and groups. To facilitate with groups, you may need to walk to each person in the group in order to motivate singing. You can do this with guitar or you can record the song into an electronic keyboard and have your hands free when moving to each person. Although the recorded song is less flexible in terms of giving clients time to respond, it is workable. You can wait for the fill-in portion of the song to come back around again or walk to the keyboard and reset so that the song begins anew.

It may be helpful to have a portable voice amplifier (available online for $25 to $140) so that all group members can hear you.

Although there is no specific rap material suggested, expressing vocally through the spoken word is connecting with the outside world through voice and definitely counts as self-expression.

Dynamics and Tempo

When my son was in elementary school, he had a friend who was in therapy. This dear soul, upon learning that I was a therapist, brought me a chart with feelings faces on it so I could use it with my clients.

Therapists use these with children to help them to understand what they are feeling and express it in words.

We can help clients to explore expressing feelings by using dynamics and tempo.

Singing Songs
Take a client's favorite song and sing it with different dynamic levels. Choose to discuss this experience or not.

Short Songs
Sing together through short songs with fairly benign lyrics (meaning not heavy or provocative) to give clients of all levels exposure to how different dynamics feel in their own voice. With clients who are capable of processing, you can talk about which dynamics they like and don't like. For example: "What other dynamics would you like to try?" "Do you want to sing another song like that?" "How does that feel in your voice?" Make sure you compliment strengths: "You really brought that word out!" "It sounds like you really liked that part." Or, just keep singing.

By focusing on the music and not the individual, the client is allowed to do the same. Meditation teachers consistently profess that even when the mind wanders and the meditation feels unfocused, an individual can still end the practice feeling refreshed.

So, even though a client may not be able to or want to make the connection between dynamics and self-expression, the kinesthetic learning is still happening.

Singing Songs and Planned Dynamics
Introduce a song or pick a song with your client and sing it through. Choose a song that contains lyrics relevant to the client. Preferably using the sheet music (chord chart or lyric sheet, if you must), read through the words, decide together which dynamics to use in each portion of the song, and mark the dynamics.

Sing together in unison or listen to your client. When running a group, direct the dynamics vocally and instrumentally. Facilitate the group in discussing and planning which dynamics to use next, making sure that everyone has a voice in the planning.

Discuss: "What was that like?" "Did that bring out the words differently?" "Would you like to change any dynamics?"

Allow the discussion to move on from these questions or any questions that seem appropriate.

Continue singing the song as many times as seems relevant or ground the singing with a method from chapter 10. Remember to compliment—for instance, "I really enjoy hearing your choices. You are all so creative!"

Singing Songs at Different Tempos
As part of our musicianship skills, we know it is important to be able to play songs, scales, arpeggios, études, and so on at different tempos. We also know, as music therapists, to apply the use of tempo in order to reach specific therapeutic goals.

For this technique, as for the technique above, plan varied tempos with the client(s) within a given song for the purpose of vocal expression.

Larghissimo is 20 to 40 bpm (wow! that is slow!), and *prestissimo* logs in at around a "mellow" 200 bpm.

Of course, because we are not striving for extreme musicianship with our clients, the tempos we use are going to be much more modest.

Also, keep in mind expression markings for tempo changes, such as accelerando (speeding up), piu mosso (more movement), ritardando (slowing down), and rubato (free tempo).

Gloria Gaynor sings the opening verse to "I Will Survive" (Perren & Fekaris, 1978) dramatically with rubato, and it is so effective in telling them off!

Try it!

> At first I was afraid, I was petrified
> Kept thinking I could never live without you by my side
> But then I spent so many nights thinking how you did me wrong
> And I grew strong
> And I learned how to get along

SHARING SONGS, RECEPTIVE TO SINGING

Listening to prerecorded songs may seem nonthreatening for clients, but this can move people deeply. Sharing the name of a song to be listened to by others is a very personal risk and a form of self-expression. Someone might laugh or think it's stupid or be bored.

Then again, someone might actually get it and have a view into vulnerable thoughts and feelings.

A connection with another human being might be made, and this can be really scary. On top of this, the listening is ongoing for a whole song. When this method is at its best, it can feel as though the individual is being held in listening for three to five continuous minutes. How often in life does that happen?

So, pick a theme like "What song represents where you are in life right now?" or "What song sounds like future goals?" or "What is your favorite song?" and listen to each client's song.

Then, encourage them to sing even if it is only one line of the song.

SHARING SONGS IN INDIVIDUAL SESSIONS

Sometimes clients really need to connect to their journey through voice but simply do not have the ken to do so. Often, this inability to let the voice connect to the body and be heard pertains to some kind of trauma, whether this is from not being given a chance to express or being told with direct threats of harm not to express or any variance of that nature.

At these times, it is most kind to acknowledge the fear and help the client to find one or more singers who can express for them. Sometimes the words to a song are the determining factor, but this can also be the vocal textures or the sound of the singing voice.

Glen Hansard's voice and Bonnie Raitt's voice, for me, hold such a quality of strength and fortitude in the face of adversity. Their voices say, "I will be heard." Yet, they sing with compassion rather than anger. They get me through life.

Usually, when clients are asked if they would like to listen to music together (with the therapist), they say, "I don't know. I guess."

Just persist: "Okay. Let's try it." The next hurdle is, "Who would you like to listen to?" At this point, clients will frequently insist that they do not know. Have them take out their phones and go through their library. If they can't or don't have a phone, have your phone or iPad ready and search online for their favorite artists. Have them do research or help them. You may hear a lot of "I don't know."

Hold their "I don't know" with unconditional acceptance by waiting patiently (do some breathing exercises and be still) and occasionally saying, "It's okay. No hurry. You'll find it." With this basic interaction, you are not only facilitating a re-educative experience by modeling patience (McWilliams, 2003), but also already listening together.

"I don't know" is a place of growth. Clients don't know the answers to these questions because no one's ever asked. And, if someone has asked, they may not have deeply listened to the answer.

So, when you ask, you are teaching the client that some people really do want to get to know their authentic selves, and when you listen while they search for the answer, you are teaching them to listen to themselves.

Once the recording is playing, listen deeply. Sometimes I read the lyrics on my iPad because I don't want to miss any words. Get still and quiet. Think about your client while listening and be as "receptive" as you can. When the recording is finished, you can ask, "What is important about this song?" Or just say, "Thank you for sharing that with me" and allow the shared listening experience to speak for itself. You can also listen again, listen to another song, or, as suggested above, do some singing.

SHARING SONGS IN A GROUP

This same procedure can be done in an ongoing group. Pulling numbers out of a bowl can be used to avoid issues around who shares when. Clients can also negotiate through trading numbers, which promotes group process. When a song is finished, ask the client if they want to share anything about their song or if they want feedback. If not, move on to the next client's share. It's okay if a client does not want feedback, as this is a moment to work on boundaries and impulse control for other group members. If the client does want feedback, this gives a good opportunity to help clients to learn how to give feedback in a positive way.

Once again, see if you can incorporate singing within this method.

Receptive Listening and Mandala

After a sharing and listening experience can be a perfect time for mandala-drawing, especially if clients do not want to talk. If you have enough paper and a few boxes of colors (instructions for mandala setup are in the Therapist Training section), this can be done in a group as well as individually.

You can say, "Draw your experience of listening to the music together." Or just say, "Draw whatever shapes and colors you like on the paper." It's also helpful to sit and draw a mandala with the clients.

If asked "Why the circle?," instead of talking about Jungian archetypes (Jung, 1964; Kellogg, 1992), you can just give a simple reason such as that the mandala has to do with the circle of life and the belief that everything is connected. Further, in drawing after listening, the art can be about their connection with the music.

Often, after some resistance (worries about doing it right) and reassurance (there is no right or wrong), clients find this method focusing and calming. You may notice that they get very relaxed and breathe more deeply. Also, because drawing with "colors" can be regressive, sometimes groups get talkative and silly—which is a great way to end a listening experience.

If a client has a positive connection to their mandala, this can be carried forth into other sessions as a resource image and further explored through more music. If a client does not want to take their mandala, you can hold it for them or they can take a photo on their phone (if applicable).

Singing for Clients

Sometimes our clients can't sing and don't have the capability of picking a song.

These clients include populations such as those with brain injury, dementia, stroke, coma states, profound intellectual disabilities, and catatonia and those in hospice and palliative care. If you know from a family member some favorite songs or see in their history that they used to sing in a choir or musicals, it may be highly beneficial to sing for your client.

It's really difficult to gauge when there is therapeutic value in singing for someone who is unresponsive and when it is time to stop. Sometimes, even though the individual cannot respond, you will feel a resonance and a sense that you are connecting or you will see deeper breathing and a more relaxed demeanor. Sometimes no response is perceived.

The best you can do is to sit close to the individual, sing, and use your intuition.

Chapter 15

SUPPORT FOR EMOTIONAL PAIN

It is difficult for me to be objective about the strength of music to support, ease, companion, provide an avenue for expression of, and heal emotional pain. As many music therapists say, I don't know where I would be without music in my life. For me, this began with singing in Sunday school and has continued on up through higher levels of music-making and GIM classical music recordings in which the music holds me like a loving parent.

When I remember to sing (even just vocal exercises) during times of stress, I am aware of the thoughts in my head changing from gloom and doom to possibilities. My work as a client in GIM and vocal psychotherapy has also taken me to levels of emotional depth and healing I never knew possible.

Can we truly explain in research the phenomena of music connecting so completely with human emotions?

Hazrat Inayat Khan says, "There is no magic like music for making an affect upon the human soul" (1993). About the singing voice, Khan writes, "However perfect strings may be, they cannot make the same impression on the listener as the voice which comes direct from the soul as the breath."

Studies on music and emotion using neuroimaging show that music can modulate activity in brain structures responsible for emotion (Schaefer, 2017). This modulating and regulating is the amygdala's job. The amygdala receives input from the auditory and sensory systems. Through various channels, it effects the release of hormones like dopamine, serotonin, cortisol, and endorphins (Kraus & Canlon, 2012).

In a controlled clinical study, 70 patients with mild to moderate depression were given either music therapy or psychotherapy every day. At the end of eight weeks, the music therapy group had fewer depressive symptoms than the psychotherapy group (Castillo-Perez et al., 2010). There are also studies citing the effectiveness of music therapy in reducing anxiety before and after surgeries and procedures (Kahloul et al., 2015; Palmer et al., 2017).

Music therapy has been found to be effective in various stages of grief and bereavement (Dalton & Krout, 2005; Hilliard, 2001; Hudgins, 2007; Iliya, 2015; Lindenfeiser et al., 2008), particularly as a vehicle for expressing emotions related to grief and in feeling connection to others in a bereavement group. In a study analyzing the effectiveness of different interventions for grief, including psychotherapy, expressive arts therapy, and the normalizing of grief, music therapy was found to have the most promising outcomes for relief (Rosner et al., 2010).

Joanne Loewy (Loewy, 2013) found that music therapy in the NICU has a strong possibility of improving sleep and decreasing infant and parent stress. In a meta-analysis of music therapy in the NICU, Bieleninik (Bieleninik et al., 2016) found overarching evidence of music therapy's positive effect on parent stress.

> *When CARL arrived for his session, he was having a panic attack and truly believed he could not breathe. Carl and the therapist had been working on deep breathing through a V7–I cadence. The therapist immediately began playing and singing a soothing sigh on So Mi. After a few moments, Carl was able to mechanically inhale on V7 and exhale on I. As the oxygen entered Carl's body, he began to calm down and find a natural breathing rhythm.*
>
> *The music continued in this way for five more minutes to give Carl time to fully entrain his breathing to the chordal rhythm and to trust that his body could and would be able to breathe.*
>
> *At the same time, Carl was becoming aware of the trigger for his anxiety attack and preparing to put into words what had happened.*

TONING

When an individual is in intense emotional pain, even too much aural stimulation can feel opposing rather than supportive.

Words make no sense and serve only to provide a platitude. Yet, the presence of a very simplified human voice can reach to and express pain beyond words. "Toning is a very positive, consciously directed identification with the inner power of life and the full awareness of the release of it at will. Rather than being submissive or losing consciousness, the toner is extremely alert and the feeling is one of new control" (Keyes, 1973).

As in the method description in chapter 10, the therapist can sing alone, the client and therapist can sing together, or the singing can be done a cappella or with instruments such as singing bowls, ocean drum, finger piano, and so forth. Harmony or unison can be used. A specific technique for sounding the pain is to sing dissonant and consonant intervals with the singing bowl. On occasion, clients have verbalized that this felt very validating and helped them to breathe.

Also, imagery and relaxation techniques can be used with the toning. At these times, elements of nature can provide a sense of belief in something bigger than oneself and an inner knowing that growth will happen.

One important consideration is that the therapist needs to be comfortable with their own emotional pain in order to be with the client in sound.

SINGING SONGS

A grassroots folk singer–songwriter named Bryan Bowers wrote a beautiful song called "Friend for Life" (2000). The lyrics include:

When ya learn a song, ya got a friend for life
That ya can call on, in the still of the night.
When you're down and out on a two-way road,
Your friend the song will be there to ease your load,
will be there to ease your load.

Find the song online and listen to it. It's quite poignant in its simplicity and truth.

One of my clients has been coming for seven years. A song that has been her staple for the duration is "I Dreamed a Dream." Initially, it connected her to high school years and a joy in singing. It has gone through many incarnations, and most recently she sang and cried while mourning the fact that her family lives across the country and cannot be in her day-to-day life to help in raising her daughter. This woman has a powerful connection to this song as a life companion.

Songs as containers for emotion are quite versatile in their ability to hold a plethora of subtle and complicated textures, which can stay constant or shift like the tide.

For some, the song will change many times. For others such as my client above, one song will return again and again over time.

Sometimes, the song is my good co-therapist, and sometimes the client trusts the song more than me to listen and to hold. At these times, I stay out of the way and let the song do its magic.

Here are some ways to use songs for emotional pain:

1. *In bereavement:* Songs for reminiscing, life review, and coping. Oftentimes, only the therapist sings, allowing a grieving space for the loved ones.
2. *In the NICU:* Very simple, consistent, rocking melodies with a small range emulating the parents' soothing voice for self-regulation. Songs can be sung with or without words
3. *In end-of-life care:* Singing a favorite song with or to the patient. The song can be sung on words, while humming, or on syllables like "oo." Also, the family can choose to sing to the patient. Songs for reminiscing, life review, and coping can be used to support the patient's grief.
4. *For anxiety:* Using the chorus of a song to promote deep breathing and self-regulation.
5. *For depression:* Singing for or with the client songs that aid in expressing underlying emotions. This works well with lyric analysis. Many times, I hear clients say, "I have no idea why I've been listening to this song all week"—and when we sing it, it turns out that the composer has put into words what the client could not. In these moments, the client usually feels relief because if someone has taken the time to put this into words, they can't be the only one experiencing it. They are no longer alone.

VOCAL IMPROVISATION

Vocal improvisation for emotional pain is often very simple melodically. The therapist's voice can soothe or reflect the pain of the client in sound. Two or three chords are used, with a finger-picking or arpeggiating style that emphasizes a low, tonic tone on the downbeat for grounding. On piano, A min provides flexibility and ease of maneuvering through consonance and dissonance without needing to analyze chord structure. A I–IV chord pattern is commonly used, as it allows a circular flow that encourages rhythmic breathing. In the NICU and in hospice care with those actively dying, the monitors are closely watched, as sometimes even a soft voice can be too stimulating. At these times, the therapist moves to instrumental music (Summers, 2019).

In terms of vocal range, the therapist can match the pitch and tempo of the sound the client is making or sing in lower tones for grounding. (See Figure 10.)

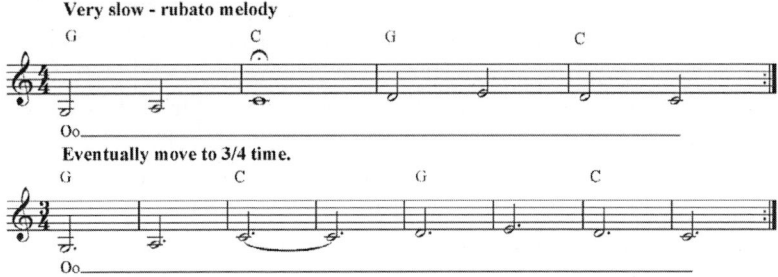

Figure 10. Emotional pain. Soothing, simple, vocal improv, courtesy of Molly Hicks.

1. Sing on vowel sounds matching heartbeat and breath patterns for entrainment.
2. Reflect any moans or sounds the client is making. For example, a grieving client may call out "Why me?" or "Why, God?!"
3. Create a music meditation by singing on vowel sounds for the purpose of sending the therapist's presence in energy and vibration to the client who cannot sing or respond. Add occasional words to reinforce this intention.

4. Look around the room and incorporate into the improvisation singing about personal affects or photos.
5. Engage in any of the above in dialogue with the client if they are able to sing.
6. Ask loved ones what they would like to say to the client and write these sentiments into your improvisation.

SONGWRITING WITH A GOAL OF SINGING

When my father died, my mother kept his wristwatch on the bedroom bureau for many years because it kept ticking. It signified something very comforting for her ... that he had existed. In our present world, we move on so quickly. Someone passes and a group adapts for survival, but the one grieving is very much alone. A song is temporal. It exists in time. If a song is written specifically for or about someone's life, family, joys, accomplishments, or humor, for the moment the song is being sung or listened to, that someone is very much alive in the music.

To re-iterate the versatility of songs as containers (see above), a song really does become like a presence to which an individual can turn to feel less alone and to remember having been validated in the therapy session. So, depression, anxiety, trauma, fear—all of these—can be crafted into music that is designed for the client's personal connection to aesthetics and provides comfort for emotional pain.

1. Write a song with the family or the patient in hospice care to be recorded for loved ones. This can focus on life review and how the patient wants to be remembered or on whatever is important to express.
2. Music therapists in NICU and child end-of-life care write and record a lullaby for the parents to keep after the child has passed.
3. Write songs about depression and anxiety with a few words of hope so that the client can listen and feel less alone during the week.
4. When the client is ready, write a song about gratitude and the progress that has been made.

Support for Emotional Pain

One of the easiest ways to do an alternative to songwriting is lyric substitution. This is simply taking a favorite song and completely rewriting the lyrics with the client or for the client.

Although my style tends toward active music-making/-listening as opposed to "thinking" pursuits like writing chord structures and lyrics, the benefits of songwriting as a therapy are many. Of course, the end goal would be to sing the song and express it in the moment. More on positive therapeutic outcomes is given in the Toolbox section, along with simple songwriting suggestions.

Specific self-care considerations for emotional pain can be seen below the physical pain section. (See Figure 11.)

Figure 11. "Remember Me"—original song.

VOCAL PSYCHOTHERAPY (AUSTIN)

Austin Vocal Psychotherapy is a method developed by Dr. Diane Austin that combines Jungian theory with vocal improvisation using words or no words over a simple chord structure (simple or altered voicings). The client can tap into an altered state and regress back to different developmental stages. For example, the client can sing about age three, or to age three, or even from the voice of themselves at three. In viewing depression and anxiety as suppressed and/or undifferentiated emotions (Tull, 2019), this method of singing can uncover deep past experiences and allow release.

In trauma related to abuse, survivors are often taught—sometimes with brutality—not to "tell," so the act of telling by singing can be highly effective for healing.

This method requires a master's degree and Austin Vocal Psychotherapy training. For more information go to www.dianeaustin.com. You can also read about the techniques in *The Theory and Practice of Vocal Psychotherapy: Songs of the Self* (Austin, 2008).

Chapter 16

SUPPORT FOR PHYSICAL PAIN

Years ago, I had to drive about two hours from Philadelphia to Lancaster, Pennsylvania, for a gig. My lower back was in pain, and as I loaded my equipment into the car, I pictured being stranded on the turnpike, unable to drive my stick shift. When I got to the job, waiters helped me to load in my equipment, and as the gig began, the strangest phenomenon occurred.

On a jazz gig, the vocalist sings a few choruses and then allows space for the instrumentalists to improvise. As I sang, I started to think that I was being dramatic and imagining the pain, but every time I stopped singing, my back felt so tight that I had to go sit down. After about an hour of this consistent pattern—accompanied by my great incredulity—I remembered a communication given in a music and medicine class. We were told that the stimuli for both music and pain run along the same neural pathways, so if one stimulus is stronger, the brain will process only that one.

In this in vivo, unplanned experiment, every time I sang, there was absolutely no pain, and every time I stopped, the pain returned. I must admit that if someone else had told me this story, I would have thought they were seeking attention. I don't have any quantitative research other than the reaction of my pain-wracked body to the singing.

Actual data show that "[t]he neural signature of pain ... overlaps with areas consistently modulated by music." There is also "... evidence suggesting mechanisms through which music could ameliorate pain, including its impact on the mesolimbic system and cortical and limbic/paralimbic brain structures involved in the affective and cognitive modulation of pain" (Cheever et al., 2018).

Finally, Hsieh theorizes that because music stimulates the release of dopamine, serotonin, and endorphins in the brain, the pleasureful experience of this release may be a distraction from pain (Hsieh et al., 2019).

If this is so, the challenge lies in determining which individuals have a strong enough connection to music; whether their connection is strong; what method of music works to override pain for that individual; whether if a method works one time, it will work the next; and for how long and against what intensity of pain will the music work?

Beyond eliminating pain, it is also valid to set a goal of decreasing pain.

In a study using music therapy for cancer patients with musculoskeletal conditions and advanced organ failure, positive outcomes in pain management were found in that 100% of the patients reported pain relief after only one session (Kwan & Seah, 2013).

Krout (2001) found music therapy to be highly successful in providing pain control, physical comfort, and relaxation with hospice patients after one session, using both passive and active music therapy methods, including singing.

In a study on pain and music (Dunbar et al., 2012), participants were asked to hold their hands in extremely cold water until they could no longer tolerate it. Those listening to music of their own choice were able to withstand the discomfort longer than those listening to prechosen "relaxing" music.

> *One of the students in a music therapy grad class, MICHELLE, had been living with chronic back pain so severe that she was considered to be disabled. This particular class was covering entrainment, and Michelle was invited to be the "patient" for the experiential. Michelle was instructed to pick out instruments that sounded like her pain and instruments that sounded relaxing. Great care was taken in picking sounds that matched.*
>
> *A few members of the class played pain just long enough to establish the connection of sound to body and then gradually shifted to relaxed. The shift was clearly visible in Michelle's body. When she sat up, to her delight, her pain was gone, and it did not return for the remainder of the class.*

TONING

Elizabeth Keyes (1973) was a firm believer in the power of toning to heal. While it would certainly be contraindicated to imply to patients that they are going to be healed, given the research above, toning is a viable option in support for and possible relief of pain. In chapter 7 of *Toning* (1973), Keyes talks about singing from A below middle C to A above middle C with a specific purpose to each note, including creative force for A, vitality for D, and gratitude for G (p. 57).

When toning for others, Keyes also suggests, we should tone the individual's name on a C chord, thinking of C for purity, E for healing, and G for gratitude (acceptance).

Particular attention can be given to the lungs (*ah* sound) and stomach (*oo* vowel) when toning for babies in the NICU (Loewy et al., 2013; Summers, 2019).

Hospice care music therapists (Hicks, 2019; Summers, 2011) must first find the resonance within themselves and then send this presence to the patient through sound. This is much like holding and comforting a colicky infant. Although the singing may not alleviate the pain, the therapist is holding, comforting, and staying present with sound. Like an intense meditation practice, this takes strength of purpose, utmost focus, and endurance, so the music therapist must be centered and grounded when engaging in this method, especially if the client cannot tone along.

There are many books on approaches to toning, yet what remains most important is intention.

SINGING FOR ENTRAINMENT

As described briefly in the Toolbox section, music therapy entrainment (MTE) can be implemented using voice for pain management.

Music therapists (Dileo, 2011; Hicks, Ismail, & Westle, 2019; Summers, 2011) describe meeting the client through singing in rhythm with breath and matching vocal expressions of pain. These two methods of using voice for MTE stand out, whether working in the NICU, where the goals are to keep the infant from physically clamping down and to increase positive feeding behaviors (Loewy et al., 2013);

in hospice care, where the goal is a peaceful end-of-life; or with chronic pain, when the focus is on quality of life.

1. For singing to slow heart rate and breathing either with or without an accompanying instrument, sing a very simple song or melody completely matching the rhythm of the client's breath. In hospital care, monitors can be watched for heart rate. Very gradually begin to slow the tempo of your singing. You may need to move back and forth from the client's tempo to the desired tempo for an hour or more in order to achieve entrainment and a shift. Here is where vocal care and self-care is essential to endure this long, extended practice of singing in a safe way. Not only do the vocal cords need to be vibrating freely (sometimes at a very soft dynamic), but also the therapist needs to be centered and grounded as in a long meditation practice. There is a case example of breath entrainment singing on E major and A major 7 explained beautifully by Summers (Summers, 2011).

    Regardless of whether the client can communicate, shallow, fast, and arrhythmic breathing presents as distress. The goal in slowing breathing/heart rate is to increase relaxation and decrease pain.

2. Dimaio (2010) describes an hourlong session in which she matches the moans of a dementia patient with expression and pitch. In the key center of D Dorian on piano, she reflects the client's pain sounds by using the same vowels and resonance. She then begins to move to a D major on harp sound (which she explains takes 15 minutes of moving back and forth), as the music becomes very simple and repetitive, entraining to the patient's breathing. In my experience in singing nonverbal pain, I most often use D minor or A minor, and the vocal part feels very much like a loose, unstructured blues with slides, siren sounds, groans, and sometimes intensity. It is then easy to take the third out and slowly shift to a more soothing, pentatonic singing in a slower tempo.

    Anya Ismail (2019) speaks of playing a C and G drone on a shruti box, which provides a steady ground for soothing vocals.

The following elements can be used to promote entrainment while singing:

a. Minor to major key
b. 4/4 to 3/4
c. Pain vocals to soothing, softer volume
   Vowel sounds to simple words or chants, such as: "You are safe." "Peace." "Breathe." When singing vowels, be aware that sometimes *ah* can be too intense. The *oo* vowel and humming are recommended.
d. Singing songs in the rhythm of the client's breathing as they become entrained and the breathing slows

Modified Forms of Singing for Entrainment

1. *The synchronized voice (Dileo, 2011):* In order to help a patient slow her breathing, Dileo sings an elongated Mi–So–Mi phrase, shifting to So according to the patient's breathing. She begins by shifting to So for every third exhale. Then she shifts for every two exhales. Finally, as she shifts for every exhale, the patient's breathing has effectively slowed.

2. *Adding imagery to singing for entrainment:* Once the patient and therapist are entrained, the therapist can continue to play with supportive chords or in a drone while adding imagery. In the same way that a therapist might verbally introduce an imagery exercise, the words can be sung. Long, flowing vocal lines can be used to encourage fluid imagery of light, water, angels, trees, and so forth. (See Figure 12.)

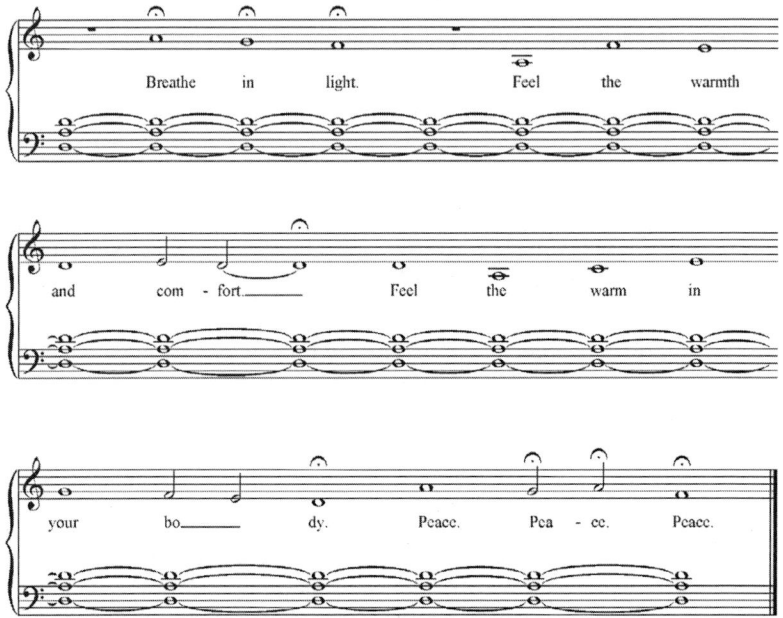

Figure 12. Entrainment with imagery. Singing in the rhythm of the client's breath.

SONGWRITING AND SINGING

Bernhard (2015) writes about four techniques to help with chronic pain:

1. Focus on and description of the pain
2. Noticing a part of the body that is pain-free
3. Being aware of pleasant sensations like the breeze on the face or the scent of a candle
4. Using imagery

   Songwriting and singing can accomplish every one of these tasks. While writing lyrics, the individual can describe the pain in detail as well as create prose describing captivating imagery that redirects the mind. And, of course, while singing, it is possible to notice parts of the body that are pain-free as well as to feel pleasant sensations from calming breathing and vocal vibrations.

Songwriting also fits the idea of mindfulness, which is "a mental state achieved by focusing on the present moment while calmly acknowledging and accepting one's feelings, thoughts, and bodily sensations, used as a therapeutic technique" (Oxford Online Dictionary, 2020).

When writing a song, your mind is focused on creativity and flow. You are in the moment and not projecting into the future how long the pain will last or increasing tension with emotional responses to pain. This redirects the focus away from the pain and onto a pleasant pursuit.

SINGING SONGS

As we saw in the Bryan Bowers lyrics in the emotional support section ("Friend for Life," 2000), and the concept of a song as a friend, songs can be a container and a redirection for physical pain as well as emotional pain.

A song can be used for entrainment, for expressing pain, for focusing on pleasant sensations in the body like vocal vibrations, and for redirecting the mind to beautiful memories and imagery. Lamaze breathing during labor (Karmel, 1959) is designed to reduce heart rate, anxiety, and pain perception. Singing a favorite song or song designed for a specific pain issue can accomplish this goal as well.

Here is an example of using a song with lyric substitution to describe and express pain. Use the melody to John Fogerty's "Have You Ever Seen the Rain?" (1970).

> Yesterday was wild and free
> Now I live in misery
> I know, this may last a lifetime
> I can't even tie my shoes
> Sometimes I think I'm gonna lose
> My mind, I can't stop this feelin'
> I wanna know, have you ever felt the pain?
> I wanna know, have you ever felt the pain?
> I wanna know, have you ever felt the pain
> Comin' down on a sunny day?

When picking songs to express pain, a good technique is to find a singer whose voice leads the way. Not only does John Fogerty's voice sound agonized, but also the lyrics and melody have specific, brief moments that literally sound like a howl of pain. "I wanna know" opens into a wide vowel sound that stretches out the strained note and gives space for the singer to emote. When a client really needs to let out an emotion but is uncomfortable in doing so, imitation can be a welcome motivator.

Turn the recording up loud or play drums and guitar/piano loudly and wail away.

When choosing songs for redirecting focus from the pain, any loved or favorite song in any genre can work.

There are many beautiful jazz tunes with imagery, such as "I Wish You Love" (Chauliac et al., 1957), "Feeling Good" (Newley & Bricusse, 1964), and "Quiet Nights of Quiet Stars (Corcovado)" (Jobim & Lees, 1965); Beatles songs like "The Long and Winding Road" (Lennon & McCartney, 1970) and "Blackbird" (Lennon & McCartney, 1968); and more current tunes like "Chasing the Sun" (Bareilles, Antonoff, & Anderson, 2013) and "Falling Slowly" (Hansard & Irglová, 2006).

Self-Care Specific to End-of-Life and Bereavement
Therapists working in hospice care and bereavement (Hicks, Ismail, Summers, & Westle, 2019) report collaboration in that a consistent schedule for self-care needs to be maintained for biopsychosocial health. Self-care is such an individual pursuit. They use meditation, exercise, Quaker meetings, songwriting, performing in musicals, yoga, eating healthfully, adequate sleep, and so on.

Chapter 17

SOCIAL INTERACTION AND RELATIONSHIP-BUILDING

I remember going through a particularly difficult time during midlife transition. I had always been self-employed and had very little contact with colleagues. My only son had moved away to go to college, and an empty nest was not agreeing with me. My husband and I worked opposite schedules. On one particular day, I was feeling very low. I had to go to the grocery store, and in the checkout line I came face-to-face with a friendly cashier. When he smiled and welcomed me ("Hi! How are you today?"), he mirrored to me a much different self than I felt inside and instantly my mood lifted slightly. I felt seen, and I had the thought that everything was going to be okay.

In our work, it is so important to use our skills in order to connect with people and pull them out from their inner processes to a supportive atmosphere.

Whether it's with the individual who takes over the session by excessive nervous talking or drumming too loudly or the client who is intellectually impaired and extremely withdrawn, working on social skills can decrease loneliness, which is connected to physical and emotional well-being.

Studies have shown that social relationships contribute to self-esteem and the development of trust, empathy, and a sense of right and wrong at all stages of life. At birth, social interactions begin to occur with caregivers; beginning at around age two, children are exposed to early childhood lessons of sharing and non-aggressive play (Kington, Gates, & Sammons, 2013); adolescence brings deeper connection to and more time spent with peers involving sharing worries and dreams (Burnett & Blakemore, 2009); in adulthood, as we face careers, marriages, parenthood, financial issues, success, and struggles, our social structure remains essential.

Social isolation can lead to anxiety, depression, substance abuse, and suicide, as well as a higher risk for heart disease and stroke (Ladden, 2019). There is a particular concern connected to older adults (Cornwell & Waite, 2009) and to excessive Internet use (Amichai-Hamburger & Schneider, 2014).

Although social interaction might be effortful for some clients and seem simplistic for others, the underlying goal is decreasing loneliness—and this is significant.

> *JORDY, a 10-year-old boy with Profound Pervasive Developmental Disabilities, had highly limited social interaction skills. Jordy's language level was age-appropriate, however, he was completely echolalic and unable to engage in conversation. Jordy would come into the music therapy room and proceed to run around banging percussion instruments for the entire half hour while the music therapist attempted to synchronize with him on piano a la Nordoff and Robbins (Nordoff, P. & Robbins, C., 1971).*
>
> *One day, while changing Jordy's socks, his mother said, "I think Jordy has some stinky toes." This became Jordy's repetitive phrase for the day. When Jordy arrived for his session, the music therapist seized upon the golden moment and the "Stinky Toes" march came to be. During the song, Jordy would sing the phrase in unison with the music therapist while simultaneously drumming in time.*
>
> *So as not to overuse the song, the therapist would transition to drumming only and then re-introduce the song for two to three minutes. Each time, Jordy returned to singing with the therapist.*
>
> *There was no eye contact or visual acknowledgment, however, through singing, Jordy connected with the therapist in the moment.*
>
> *Though, in following sessions the phrase lost its charm, from this one session, the therapist knew that Jordy was aware of her presence and could initiate some social interaction.*

SING-ALONGS

Recently, a woman from my yoga class who really annoys me with unsolicited advice started talking with me about how she loves jazz. Somehow, we found ourselves singing Charlie Chaplin's "Smile" while looking into each other's eyes and beaming with joy. To add more contradictory elements, she is six feet tall and I am five feet two inches. She and I had a spontaneous sing-along right there in the yoga studio without a care of disapproval.

It is safe to say every music therapist has witnessed this positive change from detached behavior to animated connection in individuals and groups.

Gibbons (small apes) sing together as couples and with their babies (Fan et al., 2009; Koda et al., 2013); not only do birds sing together, but also their brains synchronize when doing so (Hoffman et al., 2019; Planck-Gesellschaft, 2019); mice (Arriaga et al., 2012), bats (Prat et al., 2016), and whales (Mercado et al., 2010) sing to communicate with one another.

Researchers hypothesize that very early in human history, singing encouraged positive social behavior (Brown, 2000), beginning with mother and infant communications (Malloch, 1999).

If you have a group or individual with whom you would like to facilitate 20 minutes or more of ongoing singing, I encourage you to make your list as suggested in the Toolbox section and go bravely forth.

If necessary for the sake of making this more appealing, you can call it senior choir, outpatient choir, singing lessons, and so on.

Sing-Along Variations

1. Divide the group in half and alternate each line of the song between halves. So, group A sings one line and group B sings the next line. You can also alternate every two lines or every verse. This will create an antiphonal effect as well as a space for listening and a space for singing. This technique also involves impulse control and attention to task, which is necessary for positive social interaction.

    In another variation, every other person is assigned to group A and every other person to group B, making the singing and listening experience a little more personal.

This technique can also be used in an individual session. Back in the '80s, trading stanzas was a popular duet technique (e.g., Sheena Easton and Kenny Rogers, Jennifer Warnes and Joe Cocker, Billy Preston and Syreeta Wright). Of course, it goes without saying not to sing a love duet with your client. Just use the technique.

2. If you have solo singers, have each group member sing a line or two. If competition and comparisons begin to happen, steer away from this or take a moment to teach the importance of supporting one another and the beauty of each unique voice.

3. Sing songs in different tempos and dynamics. It's also fun to play with meter and groove.

4. With more savvy musicians, have each person in the group sing only one note, as in "Twin-kle, twin-kle, lit-tle star." This is just a fun singing game for interacting. It can become quite humorous the faster it goes. [See Figures 13(a) through 13(e).]

Figure 13(a). Sing-along variations. "Amazing Grace" (Newton, 1779) in 4/4 (12/8) time.

Social Interaction and Relationship-Building

Figure 13(b). Sing-along variations. "Three Little Birds" by Bob Marley (1977) as a funk groove.

Figure 13(c). Sing-along variations. "I'll Fly Away" by Albert E. Brumley (1932) in a reggae beat.

Figure 13(d). Sing-along variations. "Daisy Bell" by Harry Dacre (1932) as a bossa nova style in 4/4.

Sing-along variations. "Fly Me to the Moon" by Bart Howard (1954) as a slow swing ballad.

CLIENT'S CHOICE

Much like the receptive methods technique under self-expression, with this approach each client shares a request for a song, except that rather than being listened to, the song is to be sung by the group or the client and therapist together.

Almost everyone has had an experience of feeling as though they don't belong—some for extended periods of time as in middle school and high school and some for even longer periods of time.

Hearing others (especially in a group) sing a meaningful song such as Jeanette's "Take Me Out to the Ball Game" (1908), Harold's first dance song at his wedding, or, a song that helped Kara in a time of struggle can create positive regard and social connections.

It takes courage to share a song choice: "This is my favorite song—what if everyone hates it?!" Even in individual sessions, clients often express feeling vulnerable or apologize for the genre of the song. They may need encouragement or help to feel safe in making a song choice. Before the music even starts, the client is already working on social interaction by putting themselves out there authentically.

Other group members can also learn social tolerance through the understanding and acceptance of other's choices.

Family members or care workers can sometimes provide information for those clients who can't choose a song.

FILL-INS

There are many ideas for fill-in singing in chapter 14. The goals of self-expression and social interaction are closely related, as both focus on the bridge between self and other. There is one slight difference to note in introducing the same activities for different goal areas. For self-expression, the focus is on the individual communicating the experience of self, while for social interaction, the goal is to connect outwardly to another human being.

There are no specific instructions for introducing fill-ins within these two different goals, other than remembering your goal and facilitating it accordingly. For example, eyes being open or group members knowing one another's names may be more important with social interaction than with self-expression.

With Higher-Functioning Populations

Take the method ideas given in the self-expression section and use these for social interaction. Keep in mind that attention to task, impulse control (taking turns), and appropriate behavior are all part of social interaction skills. Sometimes, I still have to remind myself to stop talking and listen, so even I can benefit from fill-ins.

With Populations with Profound to Moderate Delays

We are social creatures. For many reasons, including survival, our brains are wired to connect (Lieberman, 2014). There is no research on whether highly delayed populations need social engagement to thrive and decrease loneliness. Indeed, all I have to go on is in vivo observations and years of documenting behavior changes that looked to me (and others) to be positive responses to social interaction goals.

In working with highly withdrawn populations, it can be difficult to realize benefits. Follow your intuition. If Horace initiates one fill-in vocal in an entire session, this may be a highly successful session.

The main objective under social interaction is awareness of self and others. If a client is locked in an isolated world and becomes aware of self as existing in the environment with but one second of vocals, this is significant for individuals who have no social interaction skills. It is the client throwing you a line that can be used for more possible interactions. That a client would reach out at all communicates, "I want to connect."

Here are some techniques to stimulate fill-in vocals:

1. Use simple five- to six-note song structures with minimal words.
2. Use energetic visual and verbal prompts to encourage the client to vocalize, stopping the pulse of the song and giving extra time for the client to process your request.
3. Use any vocal response the client gives within the song, no matter how wild or amusical. Change the melody if necessary.
4. Use repetition. Be prepared to keep singing.

As stated in the chapter 14, fill-ins can be done in groups as well as with individuals.

CALL-AND-RESPONSE

Call-and-response is a great tool for implementing social interaction and creating a musical duet (Oesch, 2019). Engaging in this type of exercise emulates the receptive and expressive language skills needed for conversation in social settings and also helps group members to tune in to one another (Wollner, 2018).

Use the call-and-response and dialogue ideas from previous sections. If you would like to work on higher-level social skills like eye contact and face-to-face communication, arrange your clients in two facing lines, in a circle (sing to the person across the circle), with one or more individuals in the middle, and so on. Be creative or be simple. If your clientele is adventurous, you can use more complicated material like Rhiannon's "Call and Response" (track 6) from the recording *Flight* (1999). The book *Sing After Me* by Brian Kane (2007) has fun echo songs for young voices. If these song lyrics are inappropriate, you can rewrite the lyrics to fit the clients' needs.

Call-and-response can be done with anywhere from one client on up.

Tempo and Dynamic Changes

Using the ideas from chapter 14 or creating your own, modify tempos and dynamics not as a way to explore self-expression but instead as a way to generate interaction.

Tempo changes can be especially motivating to sing for those who like a challenge. You can keep speeding a song up faster and faster and see who wins.

There is a particularly funny vintage song called "What I Want Is a Proper Cup of Coffee," written by R. P. Weston and Bert Lee (1926) for an adult musical comedy. It is a tongue twister that creates lots of attention to task when sped up (listen to it at "Trout Fishing in America" on YouTube). For additional silliness, you can use a British accent.

Be careful to promote vocal health when using dynamics.

Singing a song softer with each verse and then medium loud for the last verse is a way to use dynamics as a social tool.

Occasionally, when clients are very loud, you can create a game of "Who Can Sing or Play the Softest?" Whoever wins gets to pick the next activity.

However, use tempo and dynamics changes with caution, as these take higher-level music skills and, for this reason, can pull the clients out of the process.

Silly Songs

Humor is a great social motivator (Chadwick & Platt, 2018; Chapman, 1983). If you think your client(s) would respond to humor, take some initial ideas from the Toolbox section and give it a try. Remember, there are some funny blues tunes you can use, as well.

SONGS TO PROMOTE FUNCTIONAL SKILLS

While functional skills at first glance may not seem to come under the goal of social interaction, they are, in fact, connected.

I have a dear friend whose son is extremely bright and on the spectrum. When he was three years old, it was important that he begin preschool, but he was not yet toilet-trained and had no interest in it. The school would not take him unless he was trained. During the months preceding the start of school, my friend, in desperation, introduced a toilet-training program that included the child being made to clean his own underwear following an accident. At one point during a meltdown, the child cried, "Why are you being so mean to me?" Of course, my friend felt frightened and riddled with guilt, but she had to continue.

Had this child not been toilet-trained, he would have been behind educationally as well as socially. Social skills can be difficult for children on the spectrum, and finding gentle ways to help them to learn how to socialize can greatly affect their sense of self and sense of belonging.

For this child, learning to go to the potty was pertinent to his entire educational and social future.

In a case study written by Kern, Wakeford, and Aldridge (2007), the importance of self-care tasks in fostering independence and inclusion in social groups, as well as for cleanliness, appearance, and health, is discussed in detail. Familiar songs as well as an original song were used to teach "Andy" to go to the toilet, wash his hands, and pick up his toys.

They used "The Clean Up Song" from Barney and Friends (1992), lyric writing to "Row, Row, Row Your Boat" (1961), and an original song by Petra Kern called "Let's Go Potty!"

Suggestions for song material:

1. Use a client's song preferences and rewrite the lyrics to communicate step-by-step instructions for the functional skill goal.

    For example, it is a common practice to take "Here We Go 'Round the Mulberry Bush" (2009) and use it for functional morning skills. In using the song for one skill, it might sound like this:

This is the way we wash our hands
Wash our hands (2x)
This is the way we wash our hands early in the morning.

Now we walk to the sink
To the sink (2x)
Now we walk to the sink early in the morning.

Turn the faucet to the right
To the right (2x)
Turn the faucet to the right, early in the morning.

Run the water on your hands, front and back
Front and back (2x)
Run the water on your hands, early in the morning.

Be careful to be very specific, repeat verses if the client so needs, and sing the song in the rhythm of the client's movements.

2. Write your own song around the client's needs and musical preferences (e.g., brushing teeth, getting dressed, picking up trash, blowing your nose, combing hair, etc.).
3. There are many online resources written by music therapists and music teachers for facilitating routine skills, appropriate behavior, transitions, having manners, waiting, and so forth. The extensive website www.songsforteaching.com has the work of many different special needs composers.
4. There are also useful songs written by famous artists, such as "Put Your Finger in the Air," by Woody Guthrie (1954); "Brush Your Teeth," by Raffi (1976); and "Don't Put Your Finger in Your Nose," Barry Louis Polisar (1978).

SINGING TO PROMOTE SOCIAL SKILLS

I worked with a young man in his 30s who had Asperger's Syndrome. He was a wonderful saxophone player who was lonely and very much wanted to have a relationship, but he could not engage in social conversation. Over the years, we listened to music together, sang, and talked. Josh was building his social self-esteem through his passion for music. He was able to overcome his social anxiety enough to begin a conversation with a woman at an event, marry her, and have two children.

To say that music therapy changed this man's life is a valid statement.

I write about this now not to brag or preach to the choir about the power of music therapy but to again bring up the idea that we still minimize our trade in our minds (e.g., "I'm just singing with them") and to encourage music therapists to know that just singing can be quite effective for developing social skills.

In the words of Amy Murphy, a mother of two with autism, "Music is one of those mood stabilizers, a grounding force that helps me to bring my mind back into focus. … It's akin to being scattered from one end of the room to the other, and the music brings all of the pieces back into one cohesive moment. It allows me to focus and function. It is the background noise that provides rhythm and pace and gives my restless mind something to grab onto" (Bergman, in Edwards, 2016).

Thoughts for organizing singing groups for social interaction skills:

1. Start a community music therapy "Singing for Stress Reduction," "Singing for Fun," or "Community Chorus" for those on the spectrum or those dealing with social anxiety and friendship challenges. Advertise that this is providing a fun, low-pressure atmosphere for socializing through music. In big cities, this can be done with community night schools. Night schools are required to provide space, and often churches will give space as part of the community. You can charge a standard fee per week.

    If you live in a small town, put the word out through the grapevine, with notices in local places or in the local news-

paper. If you really have no idea where to begin, just start making calls and asking people for advice. Although it may seem "old school," this actually still works.
2. Start a group of this same nature or work with individuals at a private music therapy agency.
3. Of course, if you are working in an autism center or a facility that includes clients with autism, you can design sessions specific to social interaction.

Thoughts for activities:

1. For those with moderate autism, singing hello songs and other social skills songs while engaging in handshaking or any movement that seems appropriate (waving, high fives, etc.). In a small group, this can be done while each individual goes around to group members one at a time or be done in pairs.
2. For those with moderate autism, singing songs with spaces for expressing likes, dislikes, interests, favorite foods, and so on, such as "I Like Me" (Hap Palmer, 1973):

   I Like Me
   I Like Me, I Like Me, Because I_____
   I Like Me, I Like Me, Because I _____
   I Like Myself Because _____
   I Like Myself Because I _____

   Other group members can help the client to fill these in and sing along or the group can focus on each member and write an "I Like You" verse for them.
3. There are many resources for songs about manners, empathy, respect, and so forth; www.songsforteaching.com is a good place to start.

It is slightly more difficult to plan singing activities for those more highly functioning on the spectrum or those dealing with social anxiety in terms of having the activity be effective without being patronizing. It's important to note that there are so many different levels of social skills and desire for social skills among this group that they are "lumped together" in this section only for the purpose of suggesting a few methods and not for the purpose of stereotyping. It is also important to allow room for emotions that come up around society's expectations to adapt to social "norms" (Macleod, 2013).

Using any of the methods from any previous section, including sense of unity, stress reduction, and self-expression, adapt them for subtly encouraging interaction, allowing for the thought that some groups will be able to acknowledge deficits and others will not. For example, in viewing #1 below, facilitating this will depend upon the level of safety and confidence in the group. Some groups may be immediately highly uncomfortable with facing one another and resistant to talking about it. If so, change plans. Some may engage and be willing to process any related feelings. It really just depends on the group personality. But here is where your creative, flexible, and intuitive skills will help.

Examples:

1. Using round technique for two parts (from Toolbox, under harmony), arrange the group in two lines so that one part is facing the other. In this way, clients can work on looking in the direction of a person's face while focusing on the music rather than eye contact. If using round in an individual session, sit or stand facing one another.
2. Have each client conduct the group in a familiar song using dynamics and tempo.
3. Engage in song-sharing (each client suggests a favorite song) and have a list of specific questions to promote conversation after each song.
4. Just sing and allow any methods to be created spontaneously from the clients. As in Amy Murphy's writing above, this population can be so articulate, intuitive, and highly intelligent. Why not use those skills to move the process forward?

Chapter 18

COGNITIVE DEVELOPMENT

In research involving clients with mild to severe dementia, singing was found to be an effective tool in enhancing memory and language skills (Lyu et al., 2018).

Singing has proven to be highly effective for patients with traumatic brain injury and stroke in recovering expressive speech skills. Although language is held in the left side of the brain, music is located in both the left and right. Singing songs and MIT (melodic intonation therapy; Thaut et al., 2015) help patients to rebuild language using the right side of the brain through what is called neuroplasticity, which allows the brain to form new neural pathways. Often patients who cannot speak sentences can sing familiar songs. Singing can also help patients to regain a more natural vocal sound as opposed to a monotone.

Gabrielle Gifford's recovery of speech after a gunshot head wound is well-known.

In a study involving children with autism at the University of Roehampton (Reece, 2015), singing was found to improve not only speech but also understanding and memory of language in the classroom as well as in everyday life.

For those with intellectual disabilities, research also "supports connections between speech and singing," in that music is effective as a prompt and reinforcer to increase verbal response in pre–school age children with limited verbal communication" (Agheana, 2017).

> *After sustaining a brain injury from a car accident, BILL, a man in his 30s, came to the aphasia center to work on his expressive language skills through melodic intonation therapy. Bill was a particularly outgoing person who enjoyed meeting new people. However, what would begin*

> with Bill enthusiastically initiating social connection would quickly dissolve into the onlooker uncomfortably witnessing Bill's intense frustration at not making any sense.
>
> Essentially, Bill would exhibit emphatic garbled vowel sounds, become highly irritated, and walk away. This was quite awkward for all involved. As Bill's aphasia was chronic, he could learn only basic functional phrases. The most important phrases to Bill were "My name is Bill," as with this phrase he could begin a conversation with someone, and "I have two kids," whom he of course loved dearly. Because Bill was so charming, from a few simple phrases, Bill and his conversation partner could figure out a way to communicate. For Bill, learning four or five functional phrases was life-changing (Wade, 2019).

SINGING FOR REMINISCING

I was driving on a back road in my home area that went from my first college to my first house when a Led Zeppelin tune came on the radio and, suddenly, I had strong memories of being 21 again. Not only did I remember things I had not thought about in years, but also I physically felt the sensations of being 21. We know from GIM the power of music to transport us back to an earlier time not just as a memory but as a full sensory experience.

When music that evokes a memory is played, the medial prefrontal cortex, one of the last parts of the brain to succumb to Alzheimer's disease, lights up and allows the individual to remember songs from the past. This is one of those very simple yet highly effective music therapy tools that can help clients to continue to access remaining cognitive functions (Yen & Lin, 2018).

In planning songs for reminiscing:

1. Speak directly with the client with regard to their favorite songs.
2. Ask staff and family members for song ideas.
3. Do research on popular songs during the client's teenage and young adult years and make a list.
    a. Encourage the clients to choose from the list.

b. If the clients can't choose a song, pick some songs and do in vivo research, noting responses.
4. Be aware that some clients' cherished songs will not be from their own era but may be from their parents' or children's era. For example, I love jazz, which was popular in my parents' youth. Songs from the early 1900s are still being sung in nursing homes. "By the Light of the Silvery Moon" was written in 1909 (Edwards) but sung by Doris Day in a film in 1953. The same can be said for songs like "If You Knew Susie (Like I Know Susie!)" (DeSylva & Meyer, 1925) and "Five Foot Two, Eyes of Blue" (Henderson et al., 1925).

   Keep in mind that these were really sexy songs when they were written and used in the films.
5. Encourage clients to share memories or thoughts that arise from the music. In a study by Fang (Fang et al., 2017), sad songs were found to stimulate the most past recall.

SINGING FOR LABEL AND OBJECT RECOGNITION

Adding music or movement to cognitive memory tasks stimulates multiple parts of the brain, making retention of information easier (Turner, 2014).

There is a wealth of creative and simple children's songs geared to teaching language and memory skills readily available with the click of your finger.

1. *Counting:* "The Ants Go Marching" (Gilmore, 1863), "Five Little Ducks" (Raffi, 1982)
2. *Colors:* "I Can Sing a Rainbow" (Hamilton, 1955)
3. *Body parts:* "Head and Shoulders, Knees and Toes" (2018)
4. *Articles of clothing:* "What Are You Wearing?" (Palmer, 1969)
5. *Days of the week:* "Days of the Week" (Greg and Steve, 1980)
6. *Months of the year:* "Months of the Year" (Greg and Steve, 1978)

Of course, use patience and repetition and repeat a verse or a phrase as long as needed before moving on.

Also, use visual cues for colors, telling time, body parts, clothing, and so on.

MELODIC INTONATION THERAPY

Employed by music therapists and speech/language therapists, melodic intonation therapy is a method developed in 1973 (Norton et al., 2009) that uses both rhythm and melody to rehabilitate language skills for individuals who have suffered damage to the language center of the brain (typically, the left hemisphere). The condition caused by this damage, which can be sustained from stroke or traumatic brain injury, is called aphasia (American Speech–Language–Hearing Association, 2019). The method has been proven effective: "[S]ubacute aphasia patients receiving MIT improved considerably on language tasks measuring connected speech and daily life communication" (Van Der Meulen et al., 2016).

However, this is a highly formalized, repetitive method that may be more suitable for those music therapists who enjoy structure and precision.

MIT varies considerably among therapists. Some use only two notes a fourth or fifth apart, some write different melodies for each language phrase with up to eight notes, and others use familiar songs. Most therapists sing a cappella, while some accompany on piano. Often, the individual is cued to tap their left arm with their right hand in the rhythm of the phrase. Regardless of the method variance, the phrase must be repeated many times with and without the melody, and progress is best when sessions are held two or three times a week.

Some specific examples:

1. *My name is Joe:* So Do Do So (with two pitches)
2. *How are you?* Do So Mi (with three pitches)
3. *I am fine:* So Do So (with two pitches)
4. *Hello:* So Do (with two pitches)

Some clients can progress to longer phrases. Those individuals who cannot progress are considered to have chronic aphasia, and although their improvement is limited, MIT can still make a difference. "Although the effect is small, its impact should not be underestimated: Being able to say the name of one's partner or to ask for a drink can represent a considerable improvement in the quality of life of someone who, before MIT, was unable to utter any intelligible words" (Van Der Meulen et al., 2016).

For more detail on specific MIT steps, see *Melodic Intonation Therapy: Shared Insights on How It Is Done and Why It Might Help* (Norton et al., 2009).

Neurologic Music Therapy
"Neurologic music therapy is a research-based system of 20 standardized clinical techniques for sensorimotor training, speech and language training, and cognitive training" (Thaut et al., 2015).

This is a formalized mode of study involving a four-day intensive at sites all over the world. For in-depth information on the techniques and trainings go to the Neurologic Music Therapy website (www.nmtacademy.com).

Chapter 19

PHYSICAL DEVELOPMENT

DYLAN, a rock bassist who had suffered a brain injury from a fall at work, came to music therapy to rehabilitate his singing. Dylan had spent months in learning how to walk again, but after returning to band rehearsals, he realized that he could not keep up vocally with the tempo of his bandmates. As Dylan and the music therapist worked together, it became clear that the musculature in his tongue was sluggish and that he could not articulate the words as fast as the rock tunes required.

The music therapist designed vocal exercises using alternating B's and D's in order to exercise Dylan's tongue. After some time, they moved on to working on N's and L's and then to singing song material.

With some five-minute breaks, Dylan would sing for the entire hour. By using singing to physically exercise his tongue, Dylan was able to increase his articulation tempo and enjoy singing with his band once again.

VOCAL EXERCISES FOR SPEECH ARTICULATION

Vocal exercises are a great tool for working on speech/language issues. To use vocal exercises, begin a melodic motive and move up in half-steps. It's really helpful to be able to play the melody on piano or guitar for pitch accuracy. If you can't play the motive in its entirety, at least play the first note of the exercise. Begin on a comfortable low note such as A3 (lower for male voices) and move up at a tempo in which the client can work on forming the vowels and consonants. If possible, gradually (over weeks and months) speed up the tempo. Keep in mind

that this is physical rehabilitation and—just as with lifting weights—
allow for slow, consistent progress.

Some exercises:

1. On a five-note ascending/descending motive, sing *bi di, bi di, bi di, bi di, ba* in order to work B's and D's. Create a variety of B and D exercises. For example, you can also sing the words *bibbidi bobbidi boo* on an arpeggiated chord.
2. On a five-note ascending/descending pattern, sing *la ni la ni la ni la ni loo* to work L's and N's. Make up any variation of syllables that would be helpful for your client.
3. The Bob Stoloff *SCAT!* book (1999) has both rhythmic and melodic scat exercises ranging from easy to difficult.
4. "Singing Tongue Twisters A–Z" by Brian Kane (2005) has fun tongue twister vocal warm-ups like "Betty Better Butter Brad's Bread," "Mommy Made Me Mash My M&M's," and "Lovely Lemon Liniment."

MONOTONE AND ARRHYTHMIC SPEAKING (DYSARTHRIA)

Vocal exercises, songs, and rhythmic patterns can be used to rehabilitate those with slow, slurred, or monotone speech (Baker & Wigram, 2004; Tamplin & Grocke, 2008) due to stroke, brain injury, brain tumors, and conditions which cause facial, tongue, or throat muscle weakness, such as Parkinson's disease (American Speech–Language–Hearing Association, 2019).

For improvement in vocal intonation (monotone):

1. Baker and Wigram (2004) describe using vocal exercises and songs with a particular emphasis on posture, muscular tension, and improving tone. The recommendation for familiar songs is given.

    Vocal slides are excellent for improving intonation. The therapist can conduct a slow slide on any vowel, moving from the bottom of the client's range up and back down, or introduce short chromatic slides (C, C#, D, D#, E, D#, D, C#, C), moving up in half-steps. Intervals of thirds, fourths, and fifths work for slides, as well. Basically, any vocal exercise taken from this book or others that motivates the client to sing will increase posture, diaphragmatic tone, and lung capacity, as well as exercise the larynx for improved vocal intonation.

2. Specific musical patterns that emulate the rise and fall of natural speech can be played on an instrument or sung and repeated by the client. These may include sliding up or down at the end of sentences and/or using louder dynamics for excitement and enthusiasm. The Tamplin and Grocke article titled "A Music Therapy Treatment Protocol for Acquired Dysarthria Rehabilitation" (2008) contains many detailed exercises in the appendix.

For improvement with arrhythmic speaking:

1. Repeating spoken or sung sentence phrases many times while the therapist keeps a consistent pulse and stresses a different word with each repeated sentence. "Rhythmic speech cueing (RSC) is based on research suggesting that rhythm stimulates the arousal of the motor speech system and organizes motor behavior" (Tamplin & Grocke, 2008).

2. In using song material for rhythmic fluency, Tamplin and Grocke (2008) suggest staying away from complex lyrics and patterns, wide pitch range, difficult melodic lines, fast tempos, and negative lyrics. They also suggest initially using songs with shorter phrases so that clients with weak diaphragmatic support can work without tiring too quickly.

For more specific detail and clear protocols for facilitating exercises for dysarthria, refer to the aforementioned Tamplin and Grocke article in *Music Therapy Perspectives* (January, 2008).

Singing for Diaphragmatic Strength, Lung Capacity, and Fluid Speech

Parkinson's choirs have become a fairly new phenomenon in communities across the world and have gained the interest of researchers. In a study completed at Iowa State University (Stegemoller et al., 2018), singing was found to improve respiratory control and the musculature needed for swallowing as well as mood and stress levels in people with Parkinson's disease.

Along with music therapists, Jaye Budd (2020), executive director of the Alchemy Sky Foundation, developed a grant-funded Parkinson's choir group. Although no research is available, Budd believes singing helps to mitigate decline in rhythm and fluency of the speaking voice.

Frank Russo (2020) of Ryerson University is also conducting research highlighting the ability of singing to improve facial expression, which is helpful for social connections.

Parkinson's choirs can be funded through grant writing or possibly a generous benefactor. Although group choir experiences are currently popular, clients can achieve the same benefits from singing solo, in duos, in small groups, and so on.

Chapter 20

PSYCHOTHERAPY

TRAINING REQUIREMENTS

If you endeavor to utilize vocal psychotherapy techniques, it is essential to undertake an advanced music psychotherapy training—preferably vocal psychotherapy—that involves case supervision and to engage in your own music psychotherapy with an individual trained to do so.

I recently saw an ad for someone offering a course for music therapists consisting of six sessions of hypnotherapy online or over the phone. These six sessions offered the possibility of reparenting and rescuing one's inner child from past trauma as well as finally healing.

As a therapist who has witnessed the trauma journey of many clients as well as having been and continuing to be on my own journey, I can tell you without reservation that this is not possible. First of all, reparenting one's inner child is a depth work reparative experience that involves more than six sessions. A human physical presence modeling utmost consistency and unconditional acceptance while companioning memories and emotions over time is needed for repair. The therapist models a good enough parent by staying present over time even during very difficult struggles, and eventually the client becomes able to gradually shift from unhealthy parent introjects to internalize the model of positive regard.

If an individual moves back to their past without a human being present in the room and becomes stuck or in crisis, this individual can become retraumatized and/or relearn that others will hurt them, are not safe, or are not paying attention and suffer the consequences.

My point? If you want to do vocal psychotherapy with clients, do not take a shortcut on your therapeutic work. Do not Skype or phone in your music psychotherapy experience. It's too easy to hide that way, and it's not safe.

If you can't find a music psychotherapist near you and you don't want to travel, I highly recommend you refrain from practicing vocal psychotherapy.

Austin Vocal Psychotherapy training is now offered in various places around the world and new teachers are being trained, so it will be expanding even more. When I was in GIM training, people would travel from Mexico, California, Wisconsin, Australia, and so forth to study.

So, again, I highly recommend training and therapy as a precursor to using vocal psychotherapy techniques.

Contraindications (using the technique without sufficient knowledge of method and self):

1. Uncovering memories or feelings that the client is not prepared to process.
2. Moving to a place of vulnerable intimacy before a safe therapeutic relationship has been established.
3. Client moving into deep grief and pain with a therapist who has not worked through their own grief.
4. Therapist inability to breathe through countertransference and discomfort during session. Countertransference will occur for the duration of one's professional life.
5. Therapist colluding with client's denial due to undifferentiated countertransference.
6. Therapist's ego unable to sustain unconditional acceptance for client's negative transference. A negative transference can present itself with passive-aggressive behavior and/or client's direct anger at therapist.
7. In depth work, a client's struggle can last for years. Supervision is needed for objectivity so that the therapist can determine whether the technique is not working or the struggle is a necessary part of the therapeutic relationship. If the therapist is not in supervision, they can become frightened by the struggle and potentially communicate to the client "You are too much" and/or "You are not healing fast enough." This can retraumatize a client.

8. Inattention to the therapist's own creative process can lead to boredom when using the holding chords. This can develop into the therapist exploring creatively rather than grounding, holding, doubling, and reflecting the client. Because clients are expressing something that has never been listened to, they may need to sing it many times.

Those in our field are consistently bemoaning the therapeutic world not taking us seriously. We can't change legislation (immediately) and other's minds, but we can take our own field seriously by paying respect to the elders and pioneers of this field (e.g., Dr. Helen Bonny, GIM; Dr. Diane Austin, AVPT; the late Dr. Benedikte Scheiby, AMT; Dr. Kenneth Bruscia, qualitative research designs; Lisa Sokolov, Embodied VoiceWork, to name only a few). We can take on the rigors of their training, be willing to be confronted by supervisors versed in their knowledge, and undergo therapy within those trainings that we seek to utilize.

GRIEVING

After vocal surgery, Liz had originally come to music psychotherapy to reconnect to her new voice. Her voice had sustained damage due to a vocal cord nodule that Liz had chosen not to remove for 10 years, from ages 18 to 28. Neither the therapist nor Liz understood why it took her so long to remove the nodule. However, it gradually became clear that Liz's voice held many painful emotions and she had not been ready to hear and feel these emotions until age 28.

In the first session, Liz sang a C5 and expressed a feeling of power. As Liz reconnected to her range, she also reconnected to feelings that had not been safe to express while growing up.

While speaking about her voice at age 13, which she described as loud and rebellious, she began to cry and talk about her sister who at age nine had died of cancer after a long battle. Liz had been 11. Liz exclaimed, "I thought I was over this."

Using holding chords (Austin, 2009) and meaningful songs, Liz began a four-year journey of expressing grief and loss. She expressed the loss of her sister, the loss of her voice, the loss of her childhood, the loss of her parents' support (parents hurting so badly that she did not want to burden them), the loss of her grandmother, and the loss of a three-year relationship that ended during therapy.

In an early session, Liz described an image of being away from the shore in an ocean and feeling afraid that she was going to drown. With this image, she and the therapist gently improvised vocally light, airy melodies floating in and out of one another as Liz explored. When finished, Liz shared that this felt as though someone had been on the shore and thrown her a line. She added that she could still feel the line in her hand even after the singing had finished.

Liz expressed her grief by singing Sarah McLachlan's "Angel" (1998) to her sister and "In the Garden" (Miles, 1912) for her grandmother; she expressed her anger by singing songs like "Rolling in the Deep" by Adele (Adkins & Epworth, 2010) and "Love Song" (Bareilles, 2007) and improvising over gospel holding chords (Cm7 to Fm7); she resourced and rested by scat-singing over jazz tunes like "It Don't Mean a Thing" (Ellington, 1932).

In one particularly sublime session, the texture of Liz's emotion shifted from anger to pleading to prayerful to self-compassion.

She was grieving her boyfriend by singing Neil Young's (1970) "Helpless." After singing through the song, Liz began to sing "You were supposed to help me!," which flowed into expressing a demand and then an acceptance in the phrase "Help me." The therapist and Liz ended with "Nobody Knows the Trouble I've Seen," in which Liz was able to connect to a deep sense of grace.

As Liz continued to express her grief, she was able to open herself more to receiving and allowing herself to be taken care of.

HEALING DEEP WOUNDS

Lauri, a musician in her 50s, initially came to music psychotherapy reporting occurrences of panic attacks and pain/tightness in her chest. Lauri's job was highly stressful, and she wanted to learn relaxation techniques.

We began doing breathing and vocal exercises into peaceful songs; then, drawing a mandala of this experience. On the sixth session, Lauri came in visibly upset and as she spoke, she began crying.

I directed her to breathe into her heart, and Lauri reported an image of a hard leather strap around her chest that was attached to a wagon of heavy bricks that she was forced to pull.

The heavy bricks were her large family, in which she had experienced abuse and neglect. It became clear that Lauri's heart was holding pain from past traumatic experiences that had begun in early childhood and lasted until adulthood.

Due to being hit when she would cry or express emotion, Lauri had a voice that was barely audible at times, and she would spend long silent periods not being able to talk at all. Vocal psychotherapy was very important for Lauri, as the holding chords would just repeat and hold as long as Lauri needed, until she could let out some sounds. These were initially *oo*'s and *ah*'s and eventually a few simple words.

Lauri sang in vocal psychotherapy for many years, sorting through and expressing the intense pain, fear, and sadness that had never been listened to. On occasion, I would say something that hurt Lauri, and then I would help her to express her hurt and anger. Lauri would sing for 20 to 30 minutes, and the consistency of these chords ever moving back and forth to comfort and soothe her would slowly heal her deep wounds.

In one remarkable session after expressing intense pain, Lauri took a pillow and began cradling it like a child. Lauri was deeply altered, and she and I began singing, "I'm here. I've got you. I'm not going anywhere." She mostly sang "I'm here" over and over again. Lauri was singing to a very young, fragile, tender part of herself. These were the beginnings of Lauri learning to hold herself.

TRANSPERSONAL EXPERIENCES

"Transpersonal literally means beyond or through the personal. It refers to experiences, processes, and events in which our normal limiting sense of self is transcended" (Daniels, 2005). Transpersonal experiences include a mystical union with nature.

Kyra had been in cognitive behavior therapy for nine years and still struggled with depression and anxiety due to emotional abandonment by a narcissistically injured mother and sexual abuse at the hands of her uncle. Kyra needed her trauma validated and a safe place to express beyond words what it was like growing up with emotional deprivation.

Resourcing Kyra was essential, but it was difficult to find a nurturing figure in her past. Kyra was very connected to her loving aunt, who tried to be present, but her mother would become furious when she noticed their bond, so Kyra had to disconnect from her aunt's love.

Kyra sang with holding chords for 20 to 30 minutes during every session, as the therapist worked to help her learn not to push herself. In searching for some sense of object constancy, the therapist asked, "Was there anything that was there for you ... a pet ... a grandparent?" Kyra pictured her room and replied, "A tree."

Initially, it was painful for Kyra to realize that a tree was the most consistent living thing in her life, and deep mourning ensued. In one session, she sang to the tree, "How can you help me? You can't move." She then stepped into the role of the tree and sang to her young self, "Maybe I can wrap my arms around you and hold you safe."

One day, Kyra became the tree. She sang about feeling her "roots" running deep into the ground and sap running through her veins. Her back or trunk felt very strong. She also felt the wind through her branches and a squirrel tickling as it ran up her. At one point, she reached into her childhood room and picked up little Kyra with her branches, giving her a safe, beautiful room inside her trunk. The therapist witnessed, held the ground, doubled, and validated with singing.

This experience gave Kyra the knowledge that even though her human childhood had been fraught with pain, she could transcend this hardship by connecting to concepts "beyond the boundaries of normal ego-consciousness" (Laughlin, 2013).

Chapter 21

TOOLBOX

The Toolbox methods are organized alphabetically.

CALL-AND-RESPONSE

This is a beautiful method that can be used for many different goals. In jazz, improvisers find it relieving when trading fours (two soloists trade by playing every other four measures) rather than soloing through the form. The soloist feels less pressure to create extended ideas.

In the same way, there may be clients who really want to sing but feel confronted by the idea of letting the voice out for a whole song. Call-and-response creates contained, brief spaces for expression as well as very direct musical cues for how to sing each phrase.

It encourages the singer to shift from self-conscious focus to attentive focus on the leader. It is engaging as a kind of a game and motivates the singer to "keep up" with the leader. With the therapist as leader, this method can be used simply to keep the clients singing longer, or the therapist can use the leadership role to introduce expression. This expression can vary anywhere from being silly to being somber to powerful singing. Introducing different dynamic levels without changing the words can be quite effective for evoking emotions. Be careful with the words and dynamics chosen. Stay with safety first, and if the clients feel receptive, move gently into introducing more emotional topics or topics that express client goals.

It is also recommended that this method be designed so that the least musically skilled client can participate. If a client stops singing, it's possible that they can't execute the response phrases and are experiencing frustration.

CHANT

I have a friend who has been a Buddhist for 30 years. He chants *Nam Myoho Renge Kyo*. It is beautiful and has brought him much peace. However, even though I believe that expression through the speaking voice is important, this chant method is about singing. *Webster's Dictionary* has a number of definitions. For this method, I am using: 1. a song; melody, and 2. To celebrate in song (Webster, 2003).

To further illustrate, my own description of therapeutic chant involves the repetitive singing of words and melody of any length from three words (the "All is well" chant from chapter 10) to four simple sentences.

For example, Beatles choruses can be turned into chants. Stop reading right now and sing the chorus to "All You Need Is Love" (Lennon & McCartney, 1967). This is a solid four-short-sentences chant. You can also use "Let It Be" and the *na na na na* outchorus to "Hey Jude" (Lennon & McCartney, 1968); Christina Aguilera's "Beautiful" chorus (Perry, 2002); Chrissie Hynde's "Hymn to Her" (Keene, 1986); and so forth. Or, you can write your own chant. There are also prewritten chants in books such as *Rise Up Singing* (Blood & Patterson, 2004) and *Circle of Song* (Marks, 1993).

If you find a song whose melody fits your therapeutic needs and words do not, simply create new words.

An example of this is given in Stress Reduction.

If you choose to use more than one chant in a row, be careful to vary tempos slightly so that the clients don't fall asleep. It's important to promote relaxed, focused energy, as this is a place from which individuals can perceive reaching their goals, strive more comfortably, and problem-solve.

I might use a medium Latin (bossa nova) tempo song like the chorus of James Taylor's "Shower the People" (1976), then the chorus of the "Battle Hymn of the Republic" (Steffe & Howe, 1861) with alternate words from Stress Reduction, and then "Still, Still, Still" (Süß, 1865) from Stress Reduction.

The same chant can be sung at many different tempos. It is quite effective in reducing stress to use the song "This Little Light of Mine" (Loes, 1920) and change the tempo from a gospel-rhythmed 150 bpm to a flowing 80 bpm with suspended chords to an even slower a cappella. This is especially calming when repeating "Let It Shine" as a shorter chant.

When I worked with people with intellectual disabilities, I did not have to introduce chant technique because there was no resistance to singing the same phrase over and over.

However, when I began working with more verbally processing and socially aware populations, I found increased inhibition and judgment around singing repetitively.

Here's the scenario:

I introduce the chant. People join in after a few repetitions, so be prepared to sing the chant alone for a time. After a few repetitions, people begin to look at me with judgment, as if to say, "How many times are we going to sing this?" The first couple of times that I used chant technique, I felt quite insecure and thought, "Oh, this isn't working, but I don't know what else to do right now." Then I said (with a reassuring smile for both me and my clients), "Keep going." And, much to my surprise, after about four or five go-rounds, entrainment happened. Entrainment while singing chants feels rather like an elevator suddenly moving up from ground level to a higher floor. Once clients have become entrained, judgment is suspended and defenses are lowered. So, not only do clients feel the physical benefits of singing, but they can also take the message of the chant into their minds and bodies.

You will instinctively know when to end. Simply slow down, decrescendo, or repeat the last words. Then allow time for quiet breathing. If you reintroduce the chant each week, entrainment will happen sooner.

If someone cannot sing, therapeutic benefits are still possible through the therapist or others singing the chant for the client.

DIALOGUE

Dialogue techniques are listed in chapter 14. To ease into dialogue, the same techniques that are listed in call-and-response in chapter 10 can be used. Even though call-and-response keeps a structure so that the vocal expression is more contained and the goal—although some expression is involved—is largely about connecting to the body, it is a great way to introduce the back-and-forth pattern of dialogue.

Just as cooing with a very young child motivates her to explore, dialogue is about having a conversation in which the client is reflected, mirrored, and sometimes led. Dialogue is facilitated more easily as an individual method, but with a little creative stretching it can work as a group method as well.

As with all the methods, dialogue covers different goal areas, such as self-expression and communication, social interaction, cognitive development, and physical development (musculature for speech and lung capacity in developmental disabilities, Parkinson's disease, and rehabilitation from brain injuries).

Dynamics and Tempo

While rhythm and melody are the nuts and bolts that hold a song together, dynamics and tempo add color and variety. No one wants to live in a village where the houses are safe and sturdy but each one looks exactly the same. Imagine running a group with each song in the same dynamic and tempo. We wouldn't do that. Although it is second nature to us as musicians to vary these elements, let's talk about varying the elements while intentionally connected to therapeutic goals.

Guiding a client who has been discouraged from being "soft" to sing piano and, conversely, aiding someone in singing mezzo-forte when they have been rejected for being too much can be a very effective use of dynamics. For individuals whose survival has depended upon their silence, being supported in raising the singing voice above a whisper can make a huge difference in self-concept.

Slowing a song down can create space to breathe into emotions that come spontaneously, and playing faster can provide impetus to sing with assertiveness or energy.

Even those individuals who feel quite comfortable in expressing through singing can benefit from purposely introducing another dimension to explore.

Fill-Ins and One-Word Phrases

Gail and Herbert Levin's "Beat the Drum Once" (2012) is a great example of how filling in the ends of phrases can create safe, brief spaces for playing that motivate clients to pay attention, exhibit impulse control, and initiate interaction with the world around them.

Lorraine, an individual with severe intellectual disability, became a rock star when singing into the karaoke mic. She sang "Ghostbusters!" (Parker, 1984) at the end of every "Who ya gonna call?" Lorraine did not have the mental and physical capability to sing through an entire song. She was in a group with mostly men, and when they were powering through songs with rhythmic gusto, she was lost in another world. But when she sang, "Ghostbusters!," she was crushing it. There are many client populations for whom maintaining attention to the outside world as well as engaging with this world is quite difficult. Eliciting a vocal response from some clients of this nature can feel effortful, requiring much energy.

The more the client is lost in the world of "self," the more focus the therapist has to have in order to draw the client out. Often when we work with these clients, our goals are rhythm-based. We work on decreasing perseverative percussing, increasing synchronization with the therapist, or increasing a percussive response overall.

Vocal expression is important, too. Marvin's vocal cords had been used so little that by the time he was 18, they had atrophied and he could only grunt. Can you imagine barely using your voice for 18 years?

Although it takes a lot of energy to motivate more limited populations to sing, I have seen clients' demeanor change from slumped over to looking up, from peaked to having facial color, from completely withdrawn to aware that they exist—after singing one note.

The therapeutic benefit of fill-ins is worth the effort.

This method is helpful for client populations of all abilities because of the safety within the brevity.

LISTENING

We are a unique lot, we music therapists. We come into the field because we love music and want to "share" it. A large part of our music experience involves being "listened to" by friends, parents, audiences, teachers, and so forth. Even in most of our work, we are actively and with great analysis and intuition co-creating sounds. Yet, some of the most compelling moments I have had in my practice have involved being completely still and listening. Listening is one of our most potent tools.

Here are some thoughts on listening:

1. Many times when I thought I was listening, I became aware sooner or later that I was thinking, planning, or having an opinion. At these times, I noticed a stubborn feeling in my body and the fact that I was covertly pushing the client to do what I think is right.
2. When I am truly listening, I feel like a completely blank slate. I feel a trust in the process (the music) and an open acceptance and the willingness to let the session move forward in its own time and rhythm. At these times, miracles happen.
3. In every phase of life and with each different challenge, I need to have a therapist listen to me in order to stay present in listening for others.
4. For some clients, it can be uncomfortable to be held with listening, even though they need it. At times of discomfort, you can switch the focus by playing an instrument, listening to a recorded voice, singing silly music, and so on.
5. You can listen to a client's breathing, body sounds, groans, nonverbal sounds, spoken words, and singing/playing.
6. It's important to feel delight when listening to a client engaged in pure vocal expression (I put earplugs in for very loud clients). If this is not happening for you, do some self-inquiry.

LYRIC WRITING

Lyric writing, or lyric replacement/revision/substitution (Johnson, 2016; Ellis, 2016), is simply what it says: taking a song prewritten by the music therapist or a published composer and helping the client(s) to write original lyrics to it.

Kurta (2016) employed a step-by-step method in which she gently introduced a hesitant client to lyric writing by first introducing a song for lyric analysis. As the client shared her thoughts on the song, Kurta took notes and interpreted emerging themes. She then improvised the themes on voice and guitar and watched to see what resonated with the client. Finally, she wrote a song outside of the session using the client's words and then later presented this song. This technique maintained the flow of the creative dynamic and was effective. This was evidenced by the client crying and expressing feeling confidence and strength.

Baker and Tamplin (2007) describe a nine-step process for creating lyrics, including generating ideas and brainstorming around these ideas by encouraging the client to explore their personal connection to the topic.

Tamplin (2006) also developed a lyric writing technique called "song collage." This involves taking lyrics from various pre-existing songs and arranging them like puzzle pieces to form new lyrics.

Schmidt (1983) encouraged each client in a group setting to provide one lyrical phrase from a precomposed song. These would then be arranged to form new lyrical content.

Baker also wrote a chapter in *Therapeutic Songwriting* (2015, chapter 9) that includes a lyric creation method called FITB (Fill in the Blank; Schmidt, 1983) or Cloze Procedure (Freed, 1987).

To use this technique, blank out key lyrics from a pre-existing song and then, while encouraging clients to express thoughts and feelings around a specific topic, take key words that emerge from these expressions and fill in the blanks to create a new version of the lyrics.

Although lyric writing has many benefits, for the purpose of this book, the end goal of lyric writing is singing.

RECEPTIVE METHODS

Listening to a recording of a song chosen by a client is wildly popular as a music therapy go-to method. While it is a powerful method, it is concerning for two reasons: (1) It is seductive in its comfort and passivity to rely on this method more and more. Because some clients are indeed resistant and frightened to make their own sounds, it truly takes much commitment to uphold goals of making live music. Yet, it is important that receptive methods be used for therapeutic efficacy rather than because we are giving in to the client's resistance. (2) Any psychologist, social worker, recreation therapist, or nurse can run a group using recorded music. We know that they are not trained like we are, but others don't.

So, in suggesting this method, it is highly recommended that listening lead to some kind of music-making, no matter how brief.

SING-ALONGS

Sing-alongs are one of those very simple yet highly effective methods. Like a good Nordoff and Robbins (2020) session, the therapy is completely contained within the dynamic of the music. It is pure music therapy. There are wonderful techniques, such as lyric analysis, songwriting, improvisation, chant, singing and imagery, and so forth. Sometimes clients just want to sing through one song after another.

As mentioned in chapter 10, with continuous singing, clients become entrained, blood pressure lowers, oxygen intake increases, and—although this is not proven—it is possible that oxytocin (the hormone associated with love) is released. At these times, it is the therapist's job to let the music be the primary therapist and co-facilitate. If the group process is waning, step in and fan the flames. If the ball is rolling, keep your hands off.

Pay attention to the vertical (individuals in the group) and horizontal (whole group) process. If Sean is withdrawing, try to find out what he likes to sing or call his name occasionally. If Chelsea is singing too loudly or making too many requests, guide her to tone down or give her attention "Chelsea, come sit by me." Or, "Chelsea, can you hand out these lyric sheets?"

Help with song choices and requests and initiate songs when needed.

When music therapy students begin fieldwork, they borrow song lists from their practicum supervisors and from each other. While we are doing internships and working in the field, our music therapy repertoire builds and becomes more creative. We start to learn "workhorse" songs and eventually have a good stock base of material. From this stock base, you probably can think of 10 songs that are sturdy go-tos.

These are mine:

"Amazing Grace" (Newton, 1779)
"Lean on Me" (Withers, 1972)
"Stand by Me" (King, 1961)

"Beautiful" (Perry, 2002)
Peace Chant ("Peace on Earth") (Marks, 1993)
"Let It Be" (Lennon & McCartney, 1970)
"Three Little Birds" (Marley, 1977)
"This Little Light of Mine" (Loes, 1920)
"Hallelujah" (Cohen, 1984)
"River Come Down (Bamboo)" (Van Ronk, 1961)

What does your list look like? Of course, the list will change as your clients and your experience in the field changes. Be willing to let go of songs that don't work anymore and to add songs that are not your favorites but are effective. This is going to sound ancient, but in times when I really needed new material, I would go to a school library or local library. Putting my hands on the hard copy and actually seeing the music inspires much more creative design than searching for music online. You can also go to a peer's house and look through their personal music library to generate song ideas. Finally, there are music therapy songlists on the Internet.

It's okay for clients to derive benefit from singing the same song frequently, and it's also okay to introduce new songs.

SINGING AND IMAGERY

For years, I had attempted to assuage my own issues of anxiety and fear with many methods, including guided imagery recordings, but my mind was too scattered. Then I discovered GIM and was blown away by the power of music and imagery together. As I continued exploring music and imagery in both GIM and vocal psychotherapy, these techniques became quite useful in my day-to-day life. I found that I could recall resourcing images in times of distress and from these access the feelings of the music.

Imagery, for me, was the key to overcoming 10-plus years of severe performance anxiety while singing.

Instead of seeing people stare at me while I sang, I would become completely lost in the music and see images the lyrics evoked. I had finally found a safe place to be, which was right in the middle of the music.

Not everyone feels as powerfully connected to imagery, but it can still be a useful technique.

There are so many creative ways to connect singing with imagery, such as:

1. Grounding and running energy (from chapter 10).
2. Singing "Here Comes the Sun" (Harrison, 1969) or sun songs with images of the sun's golden glow and warmth.
3. Singing songs or chants about light while imaging light glowing from the body or surrounding the body.
4. Singing river songs or chants while imagining letting something float down the river.
5. Singing "What a Wonderful World" (Thiele & Weiss, 1967) or "Moonlight in Vermont" (Blackburn & Suessdorf, 1944) and picturing the imagery of the lyrics.
6. Singing vocal exercises while imagining a color that has been a resource.
7. Creating a song of your own.

SINGING AND MANDALA

Mandala drawing can be used in conjunction with imagery directives or alone. Before, during, or after singing with imagery, have your clients draw a mandala. Mandala drawing can also be used with very little instruction. For example, after singing for 10 to 15 minutes, the therapist can say, "What color(s) look like the feeling of your singing? Can you draw with these colors?" This intervention can be used with many different populations. Although the logistics can be complicated in terms of having a room with a table and getting wheelchairs to the table, this can be navigated with the right resourcefulness.

Mandala drawing can have a calm, focusing effect on clients, so use this resource accordingly. Adversely, on occasion, clients can become regressed to an earlier age through "coloring," so be aware of this possibility and have an alternative plan ready. For example, sit beside the individual and redirect them to draw something specific and grounding like a tree, the beach, a heart, a flower, and so on.

For further instruction on how to set up a mandala, go to the self-inquiry section of Therapist Training.

Singing for Entrainment

"In human-human interactions, entrainment is a naturally occurring phenomenon that happens when interlocuters mutually adapt their behaviors through the course of an interaction" (Lee et al., 2014).

Many approaches to entrainment use instruments and are rhythm-based. Yet, upon examination of the three components of music therapy entrainment, there is a place for voice, as well. The three theories are: (1) the iso principle—matching the client's emotional state through music; (2) resonance vibration—the therapist empathizing with the client and the client sensing that empathy; and (3) the entrainment principle—through matching and empathy, the therapist and client are now in the same vibrational experience and the therapist can exert a "pull" to another experience (Dileo & Bradt, 1999).

The voice can easily match and empathize as well as shift. Dimaio (2010) gives a beautiful illustration of using voice to match a hospice client's moans of pain and slowly, over the course of an hour, moving back and forth from pained voice to soothing voice until finally the client fell asleep.

Voice can also be used to sing in the rhythm of a client's breathing, helping them to slow down their breathing and relax.

Singing in Harmony

In my first vocal psychotherapy session, the therapist sang in unison with me. My jazz singer snotty self thought that this was boring, and I kept moving to harmony. No matter where my therapist moved, I moved away. I later learned that I wasn't ready to be doubled. The connection of a unison was too intimate for me. Yet, in working with clients—except in vocal psychotherapy—I can honestly say that I almost always use unison singing. The reason for this is that most often I would have to stop the therapeutic process to teach harmony, and many of my clients could not execute harmony anyway.

Below are some considerations for a positive benefit from therapist or client(s) singing harmonies:

1. Singing harmonies is highly enjoyable for the client(s).

2. Use of harmonies promotes a greater sense of self for the client(s).
3. Use of harmony increases emotional expression for the client(s).
4. Singing in harmony increases group connection and social interaction.
5. Singing in harmony increases connection for the therapist and individual client.

More thoughts:

1. If a client wants to experience harmony and can't, it's okay for the therapist to harmonize while the client(s) holds the ground. The client will still experience the harmonic resonance.
2. If singing harmonies causes some clients to stop singing because they can't hear the melody or themselves, instruct the clients to return to unison frequently.
3. If clients have a strong desire to sing harmony but struggle, try introducing simple chants and teach a harmony on the last note or sing the chant repeatedly for rote learning of harmony.
    Simple rounds can also be used—for example, "Amen" (Hairston, 1964), "Lovely Evening" (Crosby, 1961), "Banuwa Yo" (Seeger, 1955).
4. Find songs with easy descant parts or write a descant. There is a pretty descant for "All Through the Night" in *The Fireside Book of Children's Songs* (1966). Here is a descant part for the chorus of "Stand by Me" (King, 1961). (See Figure 14.)

Figure 14. Descant for the chorus of "Stand by Me."

5. When you are singing harmonies for the client, stay with consonance to begin and gradually add suspended seconds and fourths. Try to use the part pf your vocal range that resonates best with the clients(s).

Singing Lighthearted Fun, Joyful, and Silly Songs

Research is beginning to prove the health benefits of laughter. These benefits include:

1. Social bonding (Manninen et al., 2017)
2. Decreased anxiety and depression while grieving (Dunbar et al., 2011; Keltner & Bonanno, 1996)
3. Relief from emotional and physical pain in palliative and medical care (Adamle & Ludwick, 2005)
4. Physical health: lowered blood pressure (Eshg et al., 2017), boosted immune efficiency (Bennett & Lengacher, 2009; Shin et al., 2011), heart health (Miller & Fry, 2009), increased oxygen consumption (Filippelli et al., 2001), reduced negative emotions (Hatzipapas et al., 2017)

Of course, it is safe to assume that most clients will not be laughing for entire sessions and that some clients will not laugh at all. Although the goal of singing lighthearted, fun songs is not necessarily about outright laughter, there is no definitive research on measuring fun. For the purpose of encouraging therapists to embrace musical fun and humor as a viable tool, consider the possibility that simply playing may carry some of the same benefits as laughter.

Dr. Stuart Brown, founder of the National Institute for Play and author of the book *Play* (2009), connects lack of play with depression, decreased immune efficiency, and stress-related diseases. He claims that there is a strong connection between the practice of play and the emotional and cognitive development of the brain. "[R]esearchers have written volumes, explaining how play shapes brains, makes animals smarter and more adaptable, fosters empathy, and makes possible complex social groups. And, for humans, play lies at the core of creativity and innovation" (Aguilar, 2018, p. 250).

There are moments when a therapist's intuition says, "We really need to shift energy now." Of course, with children this is much easier. Introducing humor or joy, especially with adolescents and adults, can feel awkward. The therapist has to be willing to stick her neck out and work with resistance to playing.

After a session of singing and imagery in which clients were working on feeling their own well-being, I introduced Three Dog Night's "Joy to the World" (Axton, 1971). The clients stared at me in disbelief that I would introduce such a random song about Jeremiah the bullfrog, but I kept on singing. I think someone even said, "I can't believe you got that song out." But, in a bit, they were caught up in the contagion and smiling with delight while singing many rounds of the chorus and wishing joy to the fishes in the deep, blue sea. The energy had officially shifted. The group had let go of left-brain judgment and allowed themselves to stop working so hard on well-being and just have fun.

Admittedly, this was a fairly easy group with which to introduce humor. Yet, this episode exemplifies its effectiveness.

Lighthearted, silly, playful songs say to the client, "You've worked so hard. It's time to play." Some clients can shift and some can't, but you won't know until you try.

Here is a place to start:

"Down by the Bay" (Raffi, 1976)
"Funiculì Funiculà" (Denza & Turco, 1880)
"Supercalifragilisticexpialidocious" (Sherman & Sherman, 1964)
"Bibbidi-bobbodi-boo" (Hoffman et al., 1948)
"Do-Re-Mi" (Rogers & Hammerstein, 1959)
"Mercedes Benz" (Joplin et al., 1970)
"Joy to the World," by Three Dog Night (Axton, 1971)
"Werewolves of London" (Mannell et al., 1977)
"Bad to the Bone" (Thorogood, 1982)
"Proper Cup of Coffee" (Weston & Lee, 1926)
"Singing Tongue Twisters A–Z" (Kane, 2005)

SINGING SONGS IN UNISON

While this may seem like an obvious method, there are certain elements to be considered for successful facilitation. How exactly does one go about leading singing for an entire session and avoid tedium ... that sensation that you *have* to do one more song because the session time isn't over? How does a therapist move from song to song without losing the dynamic energy of the music and the effective focus on the goal?

We all know how to tell when a song is working well. When running a group, how do you tell the difference between a song that is "good enough" for group members to keep the singing going and a song that is okay for most but triggers one member? When running an individual session, how do you tell when encouraging a client to sing through reluctance is companioning them through fear or inducing them to sing to please you?

Using songs for part of a session, all of a session, and all or part of a process takes intuition and observational skills. As for a good physical workout, there is a warm-up, a more active time or two, a portion for slowing down and maintaining, and a warm-down. The song-singing process has to have a rise and fall, and this rise and fall is different for each group or individual. If the songs are all calming, the clients may get bored. If the songs are all in one tempo, the music may lose its meaning. To this day, when I plan a music therapy singing group, beyond knowing the goal, I sit and think about song choices and each member of the group. I think about how to vary the tempo, meter, style, and intensity while still maintaining the flow and purpose of the session.

Then, when I run the session, I allow myself to throw out the session plan and just go from my songlist if need be.

Here is where we separate trained music therapists from sing-along leaders and nursing home entertainers. With our training and knowledge, we constantly make observations and decisions in the moment.

How do we avoid tedium? By planning and using the musical elements. How do we read the difference between healthy reluctance and harm? By using the information in the chapter 9.

Simple methods like singing songs in unison can be so effective if the therapist plans ahead, facilitates creatively, and then gets out of the way to let the music do its magic.

SONGWRITING

Songwriting as a therapeutic intervention has been most commonly used in psychiatry, autistic spectrum disorder, developmental disability, oncology, dementia, and neurorehabilitation (Aasgaard &

Blichfeldt Ærø, 2015). In a survey of songwriting in music therapy (Baker et al., 2008, p. 120), goal areas were identified as:

1. Experiencing mastery, developing self-confidence, and enhancing self-esteem
2. Choice- and decision-making
3. Developing a sense of self
4. Externalizing thoughts, fantasies, and emotions
5. Telling the client's story
6. Gaining insights or clarifying thoughts and feelings

Therapists who are interested in using music on a more visceral level only may not choose songwriting as a method. However, in viewing the goals above, for those clients who gain benefit from grounding experiences in words, songwriting provides a highly effective way to connect mind and body as well as an avenue for cognitive behavior therapy and developing rational thinking techniques. Songwriting is also a way to do life review and create a memento.

Here are a few of the simplest ways to write songs:

1. Although lyrics substitution is not really writing an original song, writing only lyrics is an effective way to create a song container that can feel original to the client and bring the same amount of pride and validation.
2. Take the chords and form of a precomposed song and completely rewrite the melody and lyrics.
3. After choosing a key, tempo, meter, and style, find a very simple chord progression and write the melody and lyrics from this repetitive progression. For example, "Stand by Me" (King, 1961) is a moving song that is built solely on the chords I–VI–IV–V–I.

You can find more techniques for songwriting with clients in *Songwriting: Methods, Techniques, and Clinical Applications for Music Therapy Clinicians and Students* (Baker & Wigram, 2005); *Songwriting as a Therapeutic Procedure* (Schmidt, 1983); and *Guided Original Lyrics and Music* (O'Brien, 2014).

TONING

"Toning is a form of vocalizing that utilizes the natural voice to express sounds ranging from cries, grunts, and groans to open vowels and humming on the full exhalation of the breath" (Snow et al., 2018). "Toning is the use of personal vocal sound to change a state of being" (Deak, 1990). It is "the use of vowel sounds to restore vibratory patterns of the body within a perfect electromagnetic field, thereby enabling the body and all of its parts to function in harmony" (Bruscia, 1989, p. 25).

Responses to toning vocal sounds include mental alertness, relaxation, catharsis, and altered states of consciousness. In 1960, Von Bekesy (1960) determined that "self-produced vocal sound does produce measurable vibrations over a major portion of the body" (Deak, 1990).

One of the benefits of toning is that there is no thought or specific execution involved. It is pure vocal expression for the goal of shifting the energy of the body to one of well-being. Vowels and consonants can be explored, as well as vocal range and dynamics. Also, body sounds such as grunts and groans can be used.

It may be necessary to release tension and negative feelings through toning before the body can shift to comfort. Keyes (1973) recommends starting with groaning. It is also helpful to begin with a breathing exercise and then introduce releasing sounds on each exhale.

Because of the nonverbal aspect, the spontaneous nature, and the similarity to the self-calming behavior of babies, toning can have a deeply altering and regressive nature. Due to this, it may be important with some clients to supply some structure and limit the amount of time engaged in toning. Structured toning methods are given in chapter 10. There are many resources on toning the chakras, and Stephen Chung (1991) provides six therapeutic sounds that correspond to the heart, spleen, lungs, solar plexus, liver, and kidneys.

Toning can be used for stress reduction, pain management, increasing sense of safety, and encouraging connection with others. Keyes also talks about the effectiveness of toning for others.

Vocal Exercises

When vocal exercises are used in lessons, the goal is to advance as a performer. In this way, vocal exercises are like a gym workout for vocal cords, designed to increase range, flexibility, strength, and endurance. The main objective is to be able to perform a piece of music at an optimum level. So, this is very much like training as an athlete.

Vocal exercises for therapy have a biopsychosocial purpose. The therapist and client are not concerned with tone quality, correct pitches, precision, and so on. In fact, in the Singing for Stress Reduction group, a few of the singers could not hold correct pitch, and this did not affect the goal outcome for the group members.

Vocal exercises accomplish the benefits of singing, such as increased oxygen and pleasant vibrations, without the pressure of connecting to a song.

For some clients, taking away the need for executing words, varied rhythms, and specific melodies greatly reduces the fear and resistance to singing. This act pares the singing down to such a simple level without being patronizing ("Let's do a vocal warm-up"), so that a client can pretend they are not really singing yet.

In the meantime, they are still gaining all of the benefits of singing, including learning that it is safe to let one's voice express and be heard.

Vocal Improvisation

"The evidence suggests that vocal improvisation enables profound expression and contact with the self, as it is seen as a tangible and creative medium through which the singers playfully let the sound guide them past their judgmental mind into vulnerable places within" (Sauve, 2004).

"[When we sing,] we breathe deeply to sustain the tones we create and our heart rate slows down and our nervous system is calmed. Our voices resonate inward to help us connect to our bodies and express our emotions, and they resonate outward to help us connect to others" (Austin, 2009, p. 20).

Although this connection to self is more flexible with improvisation than with singing re-creatively, outside of my work in music psychotherapy private practice (not in a psychiatric facility) and with nonverbal individuals, I have used mostly structured improvisation techniques, such as those of fill-ins, dialogue, toning, and the blues. These can be found in the empowerment (chapter 10), self-expression (chapter 14), and social interaction (chapter 17) sections.

The reason for this is that for many clients, improvisation can be threatening. The immediacy of the experiences expressed in vocal improvisation can cause clients to feel way too vulnerable way too fast and encourage shutting down from music.

At the same time, there are many benefits from encouraging clients to let their voices out creatively in the moment. So, experiment and see what works for you.

For more resources on the use of vocal improvisation, read:

1. *Toning: The Creative Power of the Voice* (Keyes, 1973)
2. *Therapeutic Voicework* (Newham, 1998)
3. *Embodied VoiceWork: Beyond Singing* (Sokolov, 2020)
4. *Authentic Voice, Authentic Singing: A Multi-Cultural Approach to Vocal Music Therapy* (Uhlig, 2006)

Chapter 22

Conclusion

The use of voice in music therapy is quite a paradox. For clients and therapists, there can be an aversion to singing because the intimacy and connection to the body can be immediate, and yet the connection to the body is exactly what makes voice therapeutic.

In my late 40s, I suddenly developed a fear of bridges. I've been told that this is not uncommon for women in midlife. I started avoiding bridges, which is pretty hard to do in my city. One day, in an unforeseen moment, I found myself heading over the largest bridge in Philadelphia (Girard Point Bridge) with three boys and a teacher in my little hatchback. I had a full-blown panic attack. I thought I was going to have to pull over and stop, but somehow I made it over. It was then that I realized when you avoid something, the fear gets stronger and stronger.

I stopped avoiding bridges and, believe it or not, I began singing lip trills before, during, and after my bridge journey. By the fourth time over a bridge, the fear had become minimal and I had a system for dealing with it.

Maybe you stay away from singing altogether and run drum circles; possibly you steer clear of vocal improvisation; instead of singing pop tunes, you may put on recordings; there could be a client with whom you abstain from singing because they are raw and cause intense emotions; you might shelve singing angry or sentimental songs; or you could be one of the lucky ones who feels totally comfortable with any and all vocal expression.

However, if you are in the category of some type of avoidance, here is Lesson #1: You are not alone. "Avoidance of genuinely threatening stimuli or situations is a key characteristic of adaptive fear" (Krypotos et al., 2015). In the Introduction, the many ways that one can become disconnected from expression were discussed. Being laughed at by peers on the playground for crying, being told to "Quiet down!" in a moment of free expression, or being told to stop singing altogether are genuinely threatening to one's sense of self and social well-being.

At some point during my semester of Functional Voice, I have my students raise their hands and repeat after me, "I [state name] do solemnly swear that when I find myself feeling nervous about introducing a singing activity, I will forgive myself." Avoidance happens. You are not alone. Forgive yourself.

Lesson #2: After forgiving yourself, understand that giving in to fear only powers it to grow ever larger. "Excessive avoidance in the absence of threat can severely impair an individual's quality of life and may stop them from encountering anxiety-correcting information" (Barlow, 2002, in Krypotos et al., 2015). Such "anxiety-correcting information" could be "I can lead my group in call-and-response singing" or "Harry wants to improvise a blues—I can do this."

Hopefully, this book has given you at least one or two—if not more—metaphoric lip trills to help you over the vocal methods resistance bridge because on the other side is a whole new land of therapeutic experiences and opportunities to grow as a therapist and a human being.

Even if you don't identify as a "vocal avoider," the techniques shared here provide avenues for becoming unstuck when you are out of ideas or bored and for expanding skills.

From basic vocal exercises to exploring vocal self-identity and self-awareness to many different types of techniques for use with clients, the information is designed to help you to overcome fears of singing, understand how to use singing, be comfortable in singing, and derive joy from singing with clients.

Even more important than our vocal comfort level and continued growth is the client's therapeutic vocal needs.

Voice is most likely the original musical instrument. "There is no human culture, no matter how remote or isolated, that does not sing." Singing is "ancient and universal" (Koopman, 1999).

Singing helped Gloria to be less alone in her dementia (social interaction, self-expression and communication, emotional pain). During sessions, Gloria would suddenly lean far forward in her wheelchair, bump her forehead against the music therapist's forehead, and hold it there. It was as though Gloria was holding on with fervor to a connection with another human being. Gloria initiated this interaction with the music therapist only during singing. At these times, the music therapist felt her deep sorrow, and for these moments, Gloria was able to share this sorrow with another.

Singing helped Bill to continue to be a part of the society he so loved in spite of his aphasia (social interaction, self-expression and communication [self-esteem], cognitive development). Armed with his two favorite phrases from MIT therapy, "I am Bill" and "I have two kids," Bill could continue to be an extrovert and delight in the company and attention of others, as well as share his joy and love for his children.

Singing helped Carl come to believe he could gain control of his panic attacks (physical pain, emotional pain, empowerment, and resourcing). Carl had two attacks so severe his workplace called an ambulance, thinking that he was having a heart attack. This pattern could have continued to escalate and severely affect Carl's quality of life. Singing over the simple two-chord (V7–I) pattern held Carl in the present and connected him to his body so that he could breathe through the panic and diminish its effect.

Whether grounded in physical goals such as Dylan working on tongue flexibility; facilitating a healthier social life and education by motivating Andy to go to the bathroom; focusing on cognitive behavior therapy, as with Lee, who practiced assertive expression by singing "Don't Rain on My Parade" (Styne & Merrill, 1963); or supporting Liz's journey through acceptance of deep grief, the use of vocal methods within the music therapy relationship changed these individuals' lives for the better.

It can be surprising to discover those clients whose therapeutic process hinges on vocalizing.

Lee's voice was extremely soft and limited, while Dylan's was rough and, at times, off pitch. Yet, these factors did not inhibit pleasure and sense of achievement. For some clients, it's obvious why they need to sing. Lee needed to let her voice be heard after growing up with an overbearing mother, and Dylan needed to express his anger through his rock music. With others, it will not be as clear.

However, one thing is clear: If vocal opportunities are not explored within the session, the therapist will never know who might respond and who might benefit. If you choose to stretch yourself by using voice more or introducing "riskier" vocal techniques, you will be stepping into your own vocal journey and inviting clients to explore theirs.

Never in a million years would I have been able to foresee the depth of the self-knowledge, healing, and self-compassion to which my singing journey has brought me. I know firsthand the power of this sublime instrument (the vocal cords literally look like two gossamer, mother-of-pearl bands).

I encourage you to:

1. Buy the sheet music so that original melodies live on (this is greatly concerning to me).
2. Set a goal:
    a. "I will introduce one vocal method per session or per week."
    b. "I will develop 20 minutes of vocal interventions to use with one specific group or client."
    c. "I will improvise vocally for five minutes with one client."
3. Seek support and/or supervision if discomfort comes up consistently while singing.
4. Embark on your own vocal journey.

My beloved mentor, Dr. Diane Austin, once said to me, "Kelly, your biggest fear will become your greatest joy." Dear reader, take some vocal chances and get ready to experience great joy!

APPENDIX

LISA SOKOLOV DUET GAMES

(These are my shortened simplifications of Lisa Sokolov's Game descriptions. For more detail and understanding of the games, refer to her book *Embodied VoiceWork: Beyond Singing* (Barcelona Publishers, 2020).

> These games are about listening. These games are about relationship. What is it like to listen, stay inwardly connected, and be related to the other? You can communicate during the game process. If you need more sound or more support from your partner, you can say, "I need more, please." If you feel overwhelmed by the partner, you can say, "I need less, please." Simple …
>
> These games will bring you to your growing edge. It is important for partners to recognize where their partner's growing edge is and to not go past it, making it too hard, which is discouraging. Do not make it too easy, either. Find the sweet spot. Everyone is at a different place in their work. There is no shame in being wherever you are …
>
> What is it to sing with another person? What is it to really listen to what is happening? To allow two tones to flow into each other and become one sound? When I "really" listen, I hear how tones fit together. Each tone and its overtones fit together, birthing new overtones. The sound shines and becomes more than

the sum of its parts. The carving of the vessel, whether it is one's body or the relational body created by two people singing together, has integrity, cohesion, and wholeness. It becomes a home of shining, rich tone. (Sokolov, 2020)

Game 1: Intervals
Partner 1 holds a low tone while partner 2 begins in unison and moves up slowly in half-steps until the octave is reached. Listen deeply into the intervals.

Game 2A: Flying
The duo agrees on a ground tone together. Partner 1 holds the ground while partner 2 flies in a short solo over the ground tone. It is important that partner 2 be aware of and related to the ground tone while flying. When partner 2 lands back on the ground tone, partner 1 takes off, continuing in this alternating pattern.

Game 2B
Again, partner 1 holds ground while partner 2 flies, but when partner 2 lands, partner 1's job is to fly exactly the same path. This happens four times, and then the roles are switched. The game challenges you to hold the ground and listen at the same time. If possible, understand the four phrases as being connected and developing, as in a paragraph.

Game 3: Time
This is similar to Game 2 but focused on time. The partners establish a pulse together using a syllable beginning with a consonant. For example, quarter notes on *dun, dun, dun, dun*. Partner 1 holds time and partner 2 dances off and on the beat. When partner 2 comes back to the pulse, it is partner 1's turn to dance. Keep alternating.

Game 4: The Bus
This game emulates a bus that takes many turns on its route while a skateboarder hangs on to the back of it for a ride.
    Partner 1 is the bus, singing freely without concern for partner 2 and simply singing what she needs to sing in the moment. Partner 2—

the skateboarder—sings exactly what partner 1 sings, a millisecond later. It will sound like they are singing in unison. Switch roles.

Game 5: The Dream
Partner 1 sings her dream of the moment—that is, what she really needs to sing in the moment. Partner 2 sings what partner 1 would sing if partner 1 had two voices. Partner 2 is singing what is implied by partner 1 rhythmically and tonally, but not actually being sung aloud. Do not add anything that is not already implied. Try not to limit or lead your partner.

Your goal is to allow them to be free and to change whenever they want. Notice moments when you inadvertently manipulated your partner. When finished, ask your partner if he felt the duet remained his dream. Change roles.

Game 6: Breathing Game
There is one constant rule for this game. You must always show your breathing with your hands. As you inhale, your arms float up with palms up. As you exhale, your arms float down, palms down.

In section 1, when partner 1 inhales, partner 2 exhales. Find a rhythm of breath that works for both partners.

In section 2, continue with oppositional breathing but let sound happen when you exhale.

In section 3, continue to sound when you exhale, but you no longer have to stay in oppositional breathing. You can breathe any way that you like, long or short breaths, and sing in phrases of any length. Inhale in long, or short, or any length of breath that you wish and exhale while making sound in the same way. You can sing however you like, as long as your arms float up when inhaling and down when making sound.

Game 7: No Rules/All Games
This game is a free duet, no rules. Notice that many of the earlier games will emerge. Recognize them. This is the first game involving shared leadership.

Game 8A: Following the Call of the Music

This is an advanced game. Partner 1 sings a long tone and holds it. Then, partner 2 sings another long tone and holds it. They both listen to the interval. Partner 1 listens to where the interval is leading and moves there. They both listen. Partner 2 listens to where the interval is leading and moves there. Allow the pace to move at the speed of a slow heartbeat. Harmonic movement will emerge. Continue until a cadence arises and you arrive "home."

Game 8B

Replicate the game above. Allow harmonic movement to be established, and at some point, one partner conducts both players into a brief suspended silence and then conducts both back in at the same time. Continue in this way and notice what emerges until you arrive home.

Again: These descriptions are brief and intended to inspire the reader to research more about the method. Recorded versions of these exercises can be found at EmbodiedVoiceWork.com.

Song Resources

Adkins, A., & Epworth, P. (2010). Rolling in the deep.

Aebersold, J. (1981). *Nothin' but blues, vol. 2.*

Agrell, J., & Ward-Steinman, P. (2014). *Vocal improvisation games for singers and choral groups.* GIA Publications.

All through the night. (1966). In *The fireside book of children's songs* (pp. 27–28). Simon and Schuster.

Angels watching over me [Recorded by Sara Grove]. On *Station wagon.* Fair Trade Services. (2007)

Arlen, H., & Harburg, E. (1939). Somewhere over the rainbow.

Arlen, H., Arburg, Y., & Rose, B. (1933). It's only a paper moon. Victor Records.

Axton, H. (1971). Joy to the world. Dunhill.

The banana boat song (Day-o) [Recorded by Harry Belafonte] On *Calypso.* RCA Victor. (1956)

Banuwa yo [Recorded by Pete Seeger]. On *Folk songs of four continents.* (1955)

Bareilles, S. (2007). Love song. Epic Records.

Bareilles, S., Antonoff, J., & Anderson, M. (2013). Chasing the sun. Epic Records.

Barney and Friends. (1992). Clean up. On *Barney's favorites, Vol. 1.* [CD]. Hollywood, CA: Lyons Partnership. (1993)

Bhasker, J., Ruess, N., Dost, A., & Antonoff, J. (2012). Carry on. Fueled by Ramen, Atlantic, Elektra.

Bingo. [Printed by Fox, D.]. (2008). *World's greatest children's songs.* Alfred Music Publishing.

Blood, P., & Patterson, A. (2004). *Rise up singing.* Sing Out! Corporation.

Bowers, B. (2000). Friend for life. Flying Fish Records.

Brumley, A. (1932). I'll fly away.

Calloway, C., Mills, I., & Gaskill, C. (1931). Minnie the moocher. Brunswick BR 6074.
Chauliac, L., Trenet, C., & Beach, A. (1957). I wish you love. Capitol Records.
Cohen, L. (1984). Hallelujah. Columbia Records.
Cole, N., & Mills, I. (1943). Straighten up and fly right.
Corea, C., & Potter, N. (1973). Open your eyes, you can fly.
Crawford, J., Hawkins, B., Hawkins, R., & Johnson, J. (1965). Iko. Red Bird.
Dacre, H. (1892). Daisy bell. Edison Phonograph Company.
Davis, J., & Mitchell, C. [Disputed]. (1939). You are my sunshine.
Denza, L., & Turco, P. (1880). Funiculì funiculà.
DeSylva, B., & Meyer, J. (1925). If you knew Susie like I knew Susie.
Down by the Riverside [Recorded by W. Nelson & W. Marsalis]. On *Two men with the blues.* Lincoln Center: New York. (2008)
Dylan, B. (1965). Like a rolling stone. Columbia Records.
Dylan, B. (1968). I shall be released. Capitol Records.
Dylan, B. (1997). To make you feel my love. Columbia Records.
Edwards, G. (1909). By the light of the silvery moon.
Ellington, D., & Mills, I. (1932). It don't mean a thing (If it ain't got that swing).
Everybody loves Saturday night [Recorded by The New Christy Minstrels]. On *In person.* (1963)
Five Little Ducks [Recorded by Raffi]. On *Rise and shine.* (1982)
Fogerty, J. (1970). Have you ever seen the rain? Fantasy Records.
Folds, B. (2012). Do it anyway [CD]. ImaVeePee Records.
Ford, V., & Marley, B. (1974). No woman, no cry. [Sheet music]. Island.
Gilmore, P. (1863). The ants go marching.
Giordani, G. (1785). Caro mio ben.
Goodman, S. (1989). Cordon chicken blues. Special Music (Buddha).
Greensleeves [Recorded by P. Hollens & T. Faust]. On *Legendary folk songs.* (2018)
Greg and Steve. (1978). Months of the year.
Greg and Steve. (1980). Days of the week.
Guthrie, W. (1954). Put your finger in the air. Folkways Music.
Hairston, J. (1964). Amen. ABC, Paramount.
Hamilton, A. (1955). I can sing a rainbow.

Hansard, G. (2012). Song of good hope. Anti.
Hansard, G., & Irglová, M. (2006). Falling slowly. Overcoat Recordings.
Harrison, G. (1969). Here comes the sun. EMI Studios.
Head and shoulders, knees and toes [Recorded by Lucy Sparkles]. On *Lucy Sparkles and friends*. (2018)
Henderson, R., Lewis, S., & Young, J. (1925). Five foot two, eyes of blue.
Here we go 'round the mulberry bush [Recorded by the Countdown Kids] On *100 songs for happy kids*. (2009)
Herman, J. (1964). Hello, Dolly! Columbia Records.
Hoffman, A., David, M., & Livingston, J. (1948). Bibbidi-bobbidi-boo.
Howard, B. (1954). Fly me to the moon. Decca.
Hynde, C., Kelly, T., & Steinberg, B. (1994). I'll stand by you. Sire, Warner Brothers, WEA.
Isley, O., Isley, R., & Isley, R. (1959). Shout! RCA Victor.
I've been working on the railroad [Recorded by Raffi]. On *More singable songs*. (1977)
Jenkins, E. (1974). Barreling on down the highway. Smithsonian Folkways.
Jenkins, E. (1998). Long John. Adventures in Rhythm: Smithsonian Folkways.
Jobim, A., & Gimbel, N. (1964). The girl from ipanema. A&R Recording Studios.
Jobim, A., & Lees, G. (1965). Quiet nights of quiet stars (Corcovado).
Joplin, J., McClure, M., & Neuwirth, B. (1970). Mercedes Benz.
Kane, B. (2005). Singing tongue twisters A–Z. Jazz Path Publishing.
Kane, B. (2007). Sing after me. Jazz Path Publishing.
Keene, M. (1986). Hymn to her. Warner Music Group.
Keys, A., Brothers, K., & Harry, G. (2007). No one. J Records.
King, B. (1961). Stand by me.
Kumbaya [Recorded by Joan Baez]. On *Joan Baez in concert*. (1962)
Lennon, J., & McCartney, P. (1966). Good day sunshine. Parlophone, Capitol Records.
Lennon J., & McCartney, P. (1966). Yellow submarine. Parlophone, Capitol Records.
Lennon, J., & McCartney, P. (1967). All you need is love. Capitol Records.

Lennon, J., & McCartney, P. (1968). Blackbird. Apple.
Lennon, J., & McCartney, P. (1968). Hey Jude. Trident Studios.
Lennon, J., & McCartney, P., (1970). Let it be. EMI Studios.
Lennon J., & McCartney, P. (1970). The long and winding road. EMI Studios.
Levin, G., & Levin, H. (2012). Beat the drum once. In *Learning through music*. Barcelona Publishers.
Loes, H. (1920). This little light of mine.
Lovely Evening [Recorded by Bing Crosby]. On *101 gang songs*. (1961).
Mack, L., & Wilkerson, M. (1985). Oreo cookie blues. Alligator Records.
Madonna. (1990). Hanky panky. Sire-Warner Brothers.
Mancini, H., & Mercer, J. (1960). Moon river. RCA Records.
Mannell, L., Wachtel, W., & Zevon, W. (1977). Werewolves of London. Asylum Records.
Marks, K. (1993). Circle of song. Full Circle Press.
Marks, K. (1993). Peace on earth. In *Circle of Song* (p. 244). Full Circle Press.
Marley, B. (1977). Three little birds. Tuff Gong.
Marley, B., & Tosh, P. (1973). Get up, stand up. Tuff Gong, Island.
May, B. (1977). We will rock you [CD]. EMI Elektra.
Mayer, J. (2006). Gravity.
McLachlan, S. (1998). Angel. Arista: Warner Brothers.
Miles, A. (1912). In the garden.
The more we are together [Recorded by Raffi]. On *Singable songs for the very young*. (1976)
My Lord, what a morning [Recorded by Harry Belafonte]. On *My Lord, what a morning*. RCA Victor. (1960)
Nash, J. (1972). I can see clearly now. Epic.
Near, H. (1979). Singing for our lives. Hereford Music.
Newley, A., & Bricusse, L. (1964). Feeling good.
Newton, J. (1779). Amazing grace.
Nobody knows the trouble I've seen [Recorded by Sam Cooke]. On *Night beat*. (1963)
Norworth, J., & Von Tilzer, A. (1908). Take me out to the ball game.
Old MacDonald had a farm [Recorded by Bing Crosby]. On *Join Bing and sing along*. (1959)

Old MacDonald had a farm [Recorded by Ella Fitzgerald]. On *Whisper not.* (1967)

Palmer, H. (1969). What are you wearing?

Palmer, H. (1973). Ideas, thoughts, and feelings. Activity Records.

Parker, R. (1984). Ghostbusters.

Peace Like a River [Recorded by the Mormon Tabernacle Choir]. On *Peace like a river.* Temple Square. (2004)

Perren, F., & Fekaris, D. (1978). I will survive. Polydor.

Perry, K., Eriksen, M., Hermansen, T., Wilhelm, S., & Dean, E. (2010). Firework. Capitol Records.

Perry, L. (2002). Beautiful. RCA Sony.

Polisar, B. (1978). Don't put your finger in your nose. Rainbow Morning Music.

Raffi. (1976). Brush your teeth. Troubadour Records.

Raffi. (1976). Down by the bay. Troubadour Records.

Rhiannon. (1999). *Flight: Rhiannon's interactive guide to vocal improvisation.*

Rogers, R., & Hammerstein, O. (1959). *Do-re-mi.*

Row, row, row your boat [Recorded by Bing Crosby]. On *101 songs.* (1961)

Schultz, W., & Fraites, J. (2012). Ho hey. Dualtone.

Schwartz, S. (2003). Defying gravity.

She'll be coming 'round the mountain [Recorded by David Hudspeth]. On *Classic songs for kids to sing along to.* (2017)

She'll be coming 'round the mountain [Recorded by Neil Young]. On *Americana.* (2012)

Sherman, B., & Sherman, R. (1964). Supercalifragilisticexpialidocious.

Smith, J., & Key, F. (1773, 1814). The star-spangled banner.

S lem, P., Wilde, D., Crane, D., Koffman, M., Skloff, M., & Willis, A. (1995). I'll be there for you. East West, Atlantic.

Songs for teaching: Using music to promote learning. www.songsforteaching.com

Spector, P., Barry, J., & Greenwich, E. (1963). Da doo ron ron. Phillies Records.

Stefani, G., Thiam, A., & Tuinfort, G. (2006). The sweet escape. Interscope.

Steffe, W., & Howe, J. (1861). Battle hymn of the republic.

Stevens, C. (1971). If you want to sing out, sing out. A&M.
Stoloff, B. (1999). *SCAT! Vocal improvisation techniques* (2nd ed.). Gerard and Sarzin.
Stoloff, B. (2012). *Vocal improvisation*. Boston, MA: Berklee Press.
Styne, J., & Merrill, B. (1963). Don't rain on my parade.
Swing low, sweet chariot [Recorded by Etta James]. On *Blowin' in the wind: The gospel soul of Etta James*. K-Tel. (2002)
Süß, M. (1865). Still, still, still. Folksong Collection.
Taylor, James. (1970). Steamroller blues. Warner Brothers Records.
Taylor, James. (1976). Shower the people. Warner Brothers Records.
Taylor, Jane. (1806). Twinkle, twinkle, little star. (lyrics).
Thiele, B., & Weiss, G. (1967) What a wonderful world. ABC.
Thorogood, G. (1982). Bad to the bone. EMI America.
Tunstall, K. T. (2004). Heal over.
Van Ronk, D. (1961). River come down. Smithsonian Folkways.
Wainright, L., III. (1972). There's a dead skunk in the middle of the road. Columbia Records.
We shall overcome [Recorded by Pete Seeger]. On *We shall overcome*. Carnegie Hall. (1963)
Welch, F., & Epworth, P. (2011). Shake it out. Island.
Weston, R., & Lee, B. (1926). What I want is a proper cup of coffee [Recorded by Trout Fishing in America]. On *Big trouble*. (1991)
When the saints go marching in [Recorded by Louis Armstrong]. On *When the saints go marching in*. Decca. (1938)
Withers, B. (1972). Lean on me. Sussex.
Williams, P. (2013). Happy. Back Lot Music.
Young, N. (1970). Helpless. Atlantic.

REFERENCES

Aasgaard, T., & Blichfeldt Ærø, S. (2015). *Songwriting techniques in music therapy practice.* Retrieved January 25, 2020, from https://www.oxfordhandbooks.com/view/10.1093/oxfordhb/9780199639755.001.0001/

Ackerman, C. (2019). *What is self-expression and how to foster it? (20 activities + examples).* Retrieved January 28, 2020, from https://positivepsychology.com/self-expression/

Adamle, K., & Ludwick, R. (2005). Humor in hospice care: Who, where, and how much? *American Journal of Hospice and Palliative Medicine, 22*(4), 287–290. doi:10.1177/104990910502200410

Agheana, V. (2016). *Music therapy for children with intellectual disabilities.* Retrieved January 26, 2020, from https://www.researchgate.net/publication/328686368_Music_Therapy_for_children_with_intellectual_disa

Aguilar, E. (2018). *Onward: Cultivating emotional resilience in educators.* San Francisco, CA: Jossey-Bass.

American Speech–Language–Hearing Association. (2019). https://www.asha.org/

Amichai-Hamburger, Y., & Schneider, B. H. (2014). Loneliness and internet use. In R. J. Coplan & J. C. Bowker (Eds.), *The handbook of solitude: Psychological perspectives on social isolation, social withdrawal, and being alone* (pp. 317–334). Hoboken, NJ: Wiley-Blackwell.

Anshel, A., & Kipper, D. (1988). The influence of group singing on trust and cooperation. *Journal of Music Therapy, 25*(3), 145–155. doi:10.1093/jmt/25.3.145

Arriaga, G., Zhou, E., & Jarvis, E. (2012). Of mice, birds, and men: The mouse ultrasonic song system has some features similar to humans and song-learning birds. *PLOS One, 7*(10), e46610. doi:10.1371/journal.pone.0046610

Ashley, M. (2015). *Singing in the lower secondary school.* Oxford, UK: Oxford University Press.

Austin, D. (2009). *The theory and practice of vocal psychotherapy.* London, UK: Jessica Kingsley Publishers.

Baker, E. (2002). *Caring for ourselves: A therapist's guide to personal and professional well-being.* Researchgate.net. doi:10.1037/10482-000

Baker, F. (2015). Songwriting methods that emphasize lyric creation. In *Therapeutic songwriting: Developments in theory, methods, and practice.* London, UK: Palgrave Macmillan.

Baker, F., Tamplin, J., & Kennelly, J. (2007). *Music therapy methods in neurorehabilitation.* Palo Alto, CA: Ebrary.

Baker, F., & Wigram, T. (2004). Finding climax and cadence in the uninflected voice. *Music Therapy Perspectives, 22*(1), 4–10. doi:10.1093/mtp/22.1.4

Baker, F., & Wigram, T. (2005). *Songwriting: Methods, techniques, and clinical applications for music therapy clinicians, educators, and students.* London, UK: Jessica Kingsley Publishers.

Baker, F., Wigram, T., & Gold, C. (2005). The effects of a song-singing programme on the affective speaking intonation of people with traumatic brain injury. *Brain Injury, 19*(7), 519–528. doi:10.1080/02699050400005150

Baker, F., Wigram, T., Stott, D., & McFerran, K. (2008). Therapeutic songwriting in music therapy. Part I: Who are the therapists, who are the clients, and why is songwriting used? *Nordic Journal of Music Therapy, 17*(2), 105–123. doi:10.1080/08098130809478203

Barlow, D. (2002). *Anxiety and its disorders.* New York, NY: Guilford Press.

Beck, A. (1979). *Cognitive therapies and emotional disorders* (1st ed.). New York, NY: Penguin Group.

Bennett, M., & Lengacher, C. (2009). *Humor and laughter may influence health. IV. Humor and immune function.* Retrieved January 29, 2020, from https://www.ncbi.nlm.nih.gov/pmc/articles/PMC2686627/_ doi:10.1093/ecam/nem149

Bergman, T. (2016). Music therapy for people with autism spectrum disorder. In J. Edwards (Ed.), *The Oxford handbook of music therapy* (p. 186). Oxford, UK: Oxford University Press.

Bernhard, T. (2015). *How to live with chronic pain and illness: A mindful guide.* Somerville, MA: Wisdom Publications.

Bieleninik, U., Ghetti, C., & Gold, C. (2016). Music therapy for preterm infants and their parents: A meta-analysis. *Pediatrics, 138*(3), e20160971–e20160971. doi:10.1542/peds.2016-0971

Bodner, M., Turner, R., Schwacke, J., Bowers, C., & Norment, C. (2012). Reduction of seizure occurrence from exposure to auditory stimulation in individuals with neurological handicaps: A randomized controlled trial. *PLOS One, 7*(10), e45303. doi:10.1371/journal.pone.0045303

Bonilha, A., Onofre, F., Prado, M., & Martinez, J. (2009). Effects of singing classes on pulmonary function and quality of life of COPD patients. *International Journal of Chronic Obstructive Pulmonary Disease, 4*, 1–8. doi:10.2147/copd.s4077

Braaten, D. (Ed.). (2009). *The neurosciences and music III: Disorders and plasticity, 1169*(1), 1–569. Retrieved January 12, 2020, from https://nyaspubs.onlinelibrary.wiley.com/toc/17496632/2009/1169/1

Bradt, J., Norris, M., Shim, M., Gracely, E., & Gerrity, P. (2016). Vocal music therapy for chronic pain management in inner-city African-Americans: A mixed methods feasibility study. *Journal of Music Therapy, 53*(2), 178–206. doi:10.1093/jmt/thw004

Bremner, J. D. (2006). Traumatic stress effects on the brain. *Dialogues in Clinical Neuroscience, 8*(4) 445–461.

Bright, R. (1999). Music therapy in grief resolution. *Bull Menninger Clin, 63*(4), 481–498. Retrieved January 19, 2020, from https://www.ncbi.nlm.nih.gov/pubmed/10589140

Brown, S. (2000). Evolutionary models of music: From sexual selection to group selection. Retrieved January 12, 2020, from https://link.springer.com/chapter/10.1007/978-1-4615-1221-9_9

Brown, S. (2009). *Play. How it shapes the brain, opens the imagination, and invigorates the soul.* New York, NY: Penguin Press.

Bruscia, K. (1989). *Defining music therapy.* Spring City, PA: Spring House Books.

Bruscia, K. (1998). *The dynamics of music psychotherapy* (chapter 24). Gilsum, NH: Barcelona Publishers.

Budd, J. (2020). https://www.linkedin.com/in/jayebudd/

Burnett, S., & Blakemore, S. (2009). The development of adolescent social cognition. *Annals of the New York Academy of Sciences, 1167*(1), 51–56. doi:10.1111/j.1749-6632.2009.04509.x

Burns, D. (1999). *The feeling good handbook*. New York, NY: Plume.

Cameron, H. (2017). Long-term music therapy for people with intellectual disabilities and the NDIS. *Australian Journal of Music Therapy*. Retrieved January 12, 2020, from https://www.austmta.org.au/journal/article/long-term-music-therapy-people-intellectual-

Castillo-Pérez, S., Gómez-Pérez, V., Velasco, M., Pérez-Campos, E., & Mayoral, M. (2010). Effects of music therapy on depression compared with psychotherapy. *The Arts in Psychotherapy, 37*(5), 387–390. doi:10.1016/j.aip.2010.07.001

Chadwick, D., & Platt, T. (2018). Investigating humor in social interaction in people with intellectual disabilities: A systematic review of the literature. *Frontiers in Psychology, 9.* doi:10.3389/fpsyg.2018.01745

Chapman, A. (1983). Humor and laughter in social interaction and some implications for humor research. Retrieved January 29, 2020, from https://link.springer.com/chapter/10.1007/978-1-4612-5572-7_7

Cheever, T., Taylor, A., Finkelstein, R., Edwards, E., Thomas, L., & Bradt, J. (2018). NIH/Kennedy Center workshop on music and the brain: Finding harmony. *Neuron, 97*(6), 1214–1218. doi:10.1016/j.neuron.2018.02.004

Cheng, J., Tracy, J., Ho, S., & Henrich, J. (2016). Listen, follow me: Dynamic vocal signals of dominance predict emergent social rank in humans. *Journal of Experimental Psychology: General, 145*(5), 536–547. doi:10.1037/xge0000166

Cheng, S. (1991). *The Tao of voice: A new East-West approach to transforming the singing and speaking voice*. New York, NY: Destiny Books.

Cornwell, E., & Waite, L. (2009). Social disconnectedness, perceived isolation, and health among older adults. *Journal of Health and Social Behavior, 50*(1), 31–48. doi:10.1177/002214650905000103

Cuncic, A. (2019). How to develop and use self-regulation in your life. Retrieved January 25, 2020, from https://www.verywellmind.com/how-you-can-practice-self-regulation-4163536

Dalton, T., & Krout, R. (2005). Development of the grief process scale through music therapy songwriting with bereaved adolescents. *The Arts in Psychotherapy, 32*(2), 131–143. doi:10.1016/j.aip.2005.02.002

Daniels, M. (2005). *Shadow, self, spirit.* Charlottesville, VA: Imprint Academic.

Davidovic, G., Iric-Cupic, V., Milanov, S., Dimitijevic, A., & Petrovic-Janicijevic, M. (2013). *When heart goes "BOOM" too fast. Heart rate greater than 80 as mortality predictor in acute myocardial infarction.* Retrieved January 12, 2020, from https://www.ncbi.nlm.nih.gov/pmc/articles/PMC3751677/

Davis, M., Eshelman, R., & McKay, M. (1995). *The relaxation and stress reduction workbook* (2nd ed.). Oakland, CA: New Harbinger Publications.

Davis, M., Eshelman, R., & McKay, M. (2008). *The relaxation and stress reduction workbook* (7th ed.). Oakland, CA: New Harbinger Publications.

Deak, M. (1990). *Toning: Definition and usage in music therapy.* Master's thesis, Hahnemann University, Philadelphia, PA.

Dileo, C. (2011). Final notes: Therapeutic uses of the voice with imminently dying patients. In S. Uhlig & F. Baker (Eds.), *Voicework in music therapy: Research and practice.* London, UK: Jessica Kingsley Publishers.

Dileo, C., & Bradt, J. (1999). Entrainment, resonance, and pain-related suffering. In C. Dileo (Ed.), *Music therapy and medicine: Clinical and theoretical applications* (pp. 181–188). Silver Spring, MD: American Music Therapy Association.

Dimaio, L. (2010). Music therapy entrainment: A humanistic music therapist's perspective of using music therapy entrainment with hospice clients experiencing pain. *Music Therapy Perspectives, 28*(2), 106–115. doi:10.1093/mtp/28.2.106

Dogan, T. (2018). The effects of the psychodrama in instilling empathy and self-awareness: A pilot study. *Psych Journal, 7*(4), 227–238. doi:10.1002/pchj.228

Dunbar, R., Baron, R., Frangou, A., Pearce, E., van Leeuwen, E., & Stow, J. (2011). Social laughter is correlated with an elevated pain threshold. *Proceedings of the Royal Society B: Biological Sciences, 279*(1731), 1161–1167. doi:10.1098/rspb.2011.1373

Dunbar, R., Kaskatis, K., MacDonald, I., & Barra, V. (2012). Performance of music elevates pain threshold and positive affect: Implications for the evolutionary function of music. *Evolutionary Psychology, 10*(4). doi:10.1177/147470491201000403

Edwards, J. (Ed.). 2016. *The Oxford handbook of music therapy*. Oxford, UK: Oxford University Press.

Elefant, C., Baker, F., Lotan, M., Lagesen, S., & Skeie, G. (2012). The effect of group music therapy on mood, speech, and singing in individuals with Parkinson's disease—A feasibility study. *Journal of Music Therapy, 49*(3), 278–302. doi:10.1093/jmt/49.3.278

Ellis, A. (2016). Lyric revision & substitution—Music therapy with adolescents. Retrieved January 26, 2020, from http://blogs.cuit.columbia.edu/are2126/2016/12/13/lyric-revision/

Engel, G. (1981). The clinical application of the biopsychosocial model. *The Journal of Medicine and Philosophy: A Forum for Bioethics and Philosophy of Medicine, 6*(2), 101–124. doi:10.1176/ajp.137.5.535

Eshg, Z., Ezzati, J., Nasiri, N., & Ghafouri, R. (2017). *Effect of humor therapy on blood pressure of patients undergoing dialysis*. Retrieved January 12, 2020, from https://www.researchgate.net/publication/322715145_Effect_of_Humor_Therapy_on_Blood

Ezegbe, B., Ede, M., Eseadi, C., Nwaubani, O., Akaneme, I., & Aye, E. (2018). Effect of music therapy combined with cognitive restructuring therapy on emotional distress in a sample of Nigerian married couples. *Medicine, 97*(34), e11637. doi:10.1097/md.0000000000011637

Fallis, J. (2019). *How to stimulate your vagus nerve for better mental health*. Optimal Living Dynamics. Retrieved January 27, 2020, from https://www.optimallivingdynamics.com/blog/how-to-stimulate-your-vagus-nerve-for-better-mental-health-brain-vns-ways-treatment-activate-natural-foods-depression-anxiety-stress-heart-rate-variability-yoga-massage-vagal-tone-dysfunction

Fan, P., Xiao, W., Huo, S., & Jiang, X. (2009). Singing behavior and singing functions of black-crested gibbons *(Nomascus concolor jingdongensis)* at Mt. Wuliang, central Yunnan, China. *American Journal of Primatology, 71*(7), 539–547. doi:10.1002/ajp.20686

Fancourt, D., Williamon, A., Carvalho, L., Steptoe, A., Dow, R., & Lewis, I. (2016). Singing modulates mood, stress, cortisol, cytokine, and neuropeptide activity in cancer patients and carers. *Ecancermedicalscience, 10.* doi:10.3332/ecancer.2016.631

Fang, R., Ye, S., Huangfu, J., & Calimag, D. (2017). Music therapy is a potential intervention for cognition of Alzheimer's Disease: a mini-review. *Translational Neurodegeneration, 6*(1). doi:10.1186/s40035-017-0073-9

Ferrari, A. J., Charlson, F. J., Norman, R. E., Patten, S. B., Freedman, G., Murray, C. J., ... & Whiteford, H. A. (2013). Burden of depressive disorders by country, sex, age, and year: findings from the global burden of disease study 2010. *PLOS Medicine, 10*(11), e1001547. doi:10.1371/journal.pmed.1001547

Filippelli, M., Pellegrino, R., Iandelli, I., Misuri, G., Rodarte, J., & Duranti, R. (2001). Respiratory dynamics during laughter. *Journal of Applied Physiology, 90*(4), 1441–1446. doi:10.1152/jappl.2001.90.4.1441

Freed, B. (1987). Songwriting with the chemically dependent. *Music Therapy Perspectives, 4*(1), 13–18. doi:10.1093/mtp/4.1.13

Gardner-Gordon, J. (1993). *The healing voice: Traditional and contemporary toning, chanting, and singing.* Freedom, CA: Crossing Press.

Gaskill, C., & Erickson, M. (2008). The effect of a voiced lip trill on estimated glottal closed quotient. *Journal of Voice, 22*(6), 634–643. doi:10.1016/j.jvoice.2007.03.012

Gawain, S., & Shimoff, M. (2016). *Creative visualization.* Novato, CA: New World Library.

Glazer, J. (2016). *Self-expression.* Retrieved January 28, 2020, from https://www.psychologytoday.com/us/blog/conversational-intelligence/201602/self-expression

Grant, M. (2012). *Ten tips for communicating with a person suffering from chronic pain. Overcoming pain.* Retrieved January 26, 2020, from https://overcomingpain.com/ten-tips-for-communicating-with-a-person-suffering-from-chronic-pain/

Grant, M. (2019). OvercomingPain.com.

Grape, C., Sandgren, M., Hansson, L., Ericson, M., & Theorell, T. (2002). Does singing promote well-being? An empirical study of professional and amateur singers during a singing lesson. *Integrative Physiological & Behavioral Science, 38*(1), 65–74. doi:10.1007/bf02734261

Grossman, L. (2011). Why harmony pleases the brain. Retrieved January 8, 2020, from https://www.newscientist.com/article/dn20930-why-harmony-pleases-the-brain/

Harman, S. (2010). *Mind the fire: Managing and preventing burnout.* Retrieved January 27, 2020, from https://www.healio.com/hematology-oncology/practice-management/news/print/hemonc-today/%7B14f195cc-2c5d-44b2-970f-8630a4f21274%7D/mind-the-fire-managing-and-preventing-burnout

Hartley, C., & Phelps, E. (2009). Changing fear: The neurocircuitry of emotion regulation. *Neuropsychopharmacology, 35*(1), 136–146. doi:10.1038/npp.2009.121

Harvard Health Publishing. (2011). *Understanding the stress response.* Retrieved January 27, 2020, from https://www.health.harvard.edu/staying-healthy/understanding-the-stress-response

Hatzipapas, I., Visser, M., & Janse van Rensburg, E. (2017). Laughter therapy as an intervention to promote psychological well-being of volunteer community care workers working with HIV-affected families. *SAHARA-J: Journal of Social Aspects of HIV/AIDS, 14*(1), 202–212. doi:10.1080/17290376.2017.1402696

Hicks, M. (2019, May). *Personal interview.*

Hilliard, R. (2001). The effects of music therapy-based bereavement groups on mood and behavior of grieving children: A pilot study. *Journal of Music Therapy, 38*(4), 291–306. doi:10.1093/jmt/38.4.291

Hoffmann, S., Trost, L., Voigt, C., Leitner, S., Lemazina, A., & Sagunsky, H. (2019). Duets recorded in the wild reveal that interindividually coordinated motor control enables cooperative behavior. *Nature Communications, 10*(1). doi:10.1038/s41467-019-10593-3

HowStuffWorks/Science/Physical Science/Acoustics. (2020). *What is a decibel, and how is it measured?* Retrieved January 26, 2020, from https://science.howstuffworks.com/question124.htm

Hsieh, F., Miao, N., Tseng, I., Chiu, H., Kao, C., & Liu, D. (2019). Effect of home based music intervention versus ambient music on breast cancer survivors in the community: A feasibility study in Taiwan. *European Journal of Cancer Care, 28*(4). doi:10.1111/ecc.13064

Hudgins, K. (2007). *The effect of music therapy on the grief process and group cohesion of grief support groups.* Retrieved January 28, 2020, from https://core.ac.uk/display/47015895

Iliya, Y. (2015). Music therapy as grief therapy for adults with mental illness and complicated grief: A pilot study. *Death Studies, 39*(3), 173–184. doi:10.1080/07481187.2014.946623

Ismail, A. (2019, May). *Personal interview.*

Johnson, E. (2016). *How did I, as a student music therapist, use songwriting techniques to facilitate self-expression with adolescents in a mental health school setting?* Retrieved January 26, 2020, from https://pdfs.semanticscholar.org/13c3/a9acdd3fcf35a6f8fd38801c26bd67dc4cc9.pdf

Jung, C., Henderson, J., Franz, M., Jaffe, A., & Jacobi, J. (1964). *Man and his symbols.* New York, NY: Dell Publishers.

Kahloul, M., Mhamdi, S., Nakhli, M., Sfeyhi, A., Azzaza, M., Chaouch, A., & Naija, W. (2016). Effects of music therapy under general anesthesia in patients undergoing abdominal surgery. *Libyan Journal of Medicine, 12*(1), 1260886. doi:10.1080/19932820.2017.1260886

Kane, B. (2005). *Singing tongue twisters A–Z.* Jazz Path Publishing.

Kane, B. (2007). *Sing after me.* Jazz Path Publishing.

Karmel, M. (2005). *Thank you, Dr. Lamaze.* London, UK: Pinter & Martin.

Katok, D. (2016). *The versatile singer: A guide to vibrato and straight tone.* Retrieved January 12, 2020, from https://academicworks.cuny.edu/gc_etds/1394/

Keeler, J., Roth, E., Neuser, B., Spitsbergen, J., Waters, D., & Vianney, J. (2015). The neurochemistry and social flow of singing: Bonding and oxytocin. *Frontiers in Human Neuroscience, 9.* doi:10.3389/fnhum.2015.00518

Kellogg, J. (1992). *Mandala: Path of beauty.* Williamsburg, MA: Graphic Publishing of Williamsburg.

Keltner, D., & Bonanno, G. (1997). A study of laughter and dissociation: Distinct correlates of laughter and smiling during bereavement. *Journal of Personality and Social Psychology, 73*(4), 687–702. doi:10.1037/0022-3514.73.4.687

Kern, P., Wakeford, L., & Aldridge, D. (2007). Improving the performance of a young child with autism during self-care tasks using embedded song interventions: A case study. *Music Therapy Perspectives, 25*(1), 43–51. doi:10.1093/mtp/25.1.43

Keyes, L. (1973). *Toning: The creative power of the voice.* Marina del Rey, CA: De Vorss & Co.

Khan, H. (2005). *The music of life.* New Lebanon, NY: Omega Press.

Kim, H., & Ko, D. (2006). Culture and self-expression. Retrieved January 28, 2020, from https://www.researchgate.net/publication/267794252_Culture_Self-Expression_1_Culture_and_Self-Expression

Kington, A., Gates, P., & Sammons, P. (2013). Development of social relationships, interactions and behaviours in early education settings. *Journal of Early Childhood Research, 11*(3), 292–311. doi:10.1177/1476718x13492936

Koda, H., Lemasson, A., Oyakawa, C., Rizaldi, Pamungkas, J., & Masataka, N. (2013). Possible role of mother–daughter vocal interactions on the development of species-specific song in gibbons. *PLOS One, 8*(8), e71432. doi:10.1371/journal.pone.0071432

Koopman, J. (1999). A brief history of singing. Retrieved January 12, 2020, from https://www2.lawrence.edu/fast/ KOOPMAJO/brief.html

Kraus, K., & Canlon, B. (2012). Neuronal connectivity and interactions between the auditory and limbic systems. Effects of noise and tinnitus. *Hearing Research, 288*(1–2), 34–46. doi:10.1016/j.heares.2012.02.009

Kreutz, G. (2014). Does singing facilitate social bonding? *Music and Medicine: An Interdisciplinary* Journal, *6*(2), 51–60.

Kreutz, G., Bongard, S., Rohrmann, S., Hodapp, V., & Grebe, D. (2004). Effects of choir singing or listening on secretory immunoglobulin A, cortisol, and emotional state. *Journal of*

Behavioral Medicine, 27(6), 623–635. doi:10.1007/s10865-004-0006-9

Krishnakumar, D., Hamblin, M., & Lakshmanan, S. (2015). Meditation and yoga can modulate brain mechanisms that affect behavior and anxiety: A modern scientific perspective. *Ancient Science, 2*(1), 13. doi:10.14259/as.v2i1.171

Krout, R. (2001). The effects of single-session music therapy interventions on the observed and self-reported levels of pain control, physical comfort, and relaxation of hospice patients. *American Journal of Hospice and Palliative Medicine, 18*(6), 383–390. doi:10.1177/104990910101800607

Krypotos, A., Effting, M., Kindt, M., & Beckers, T. (2015). Avoidance learning: a review of theoretical models and recent developments. *Frontiers in Behavioral Neuroscience, 9*(189). doi:10.3389/fnbeh.2015.00189

Kurta, T. (2018). *Therapeutic song writing in healthcare: How song writing promotes creative self-expression.* Cancer Knowledge Network. Retrieved January 26, 2020, from https://cancerkn.com/therapeutic-song-writing-healthcare-song-writing-promotes-creative-self-expression/

Kwan, M., & Seah, A. (2013). Music therapy as a non-pharmacological adjunct to pain management: Experiences at an acute hospital in Singapore. *Progress in Palliative Care, 21*(3), 151–157. doi:10.1179/1743291x12y.0000000042

Ladden, M. (2019). *Creative communities are addressing social isolation.* Retrieved January 13, 2020, from https://www.rwjf.org/en/blog/2019/01/what-communities-are-doing-to-address-social-isolation.html

Laughlin, C. (2013). Transpersonal anthropology, then and now. *Transpersonal Review, 1*(1), 7–10.

Leanderson, R., Sundberg, J., & von Euler, C. (1987). Role of diaphragmatic activity during singing: A study of transdiaphragmatic pressures. *Journal of Applied Physiology, 62*(1), 259–270. doi:10.1152/jappl.1987.62.1.259

Lee, C., Katsamanis, A., Black, M., Baucom, B., Christensen, A., Georgiou, P., & Narayanan, S. (2014). Computing vocal entrainment: A signal-derived PCA-based quantification scheme with application to affect analysis in married couple interactions. *Computer Speech & Language, 28*(2), 518–539. doi:10.1016/j.csl.2012.06.006

Lesiak, M. (2017). *Mindfulness-based music therapy group protocol for individuals with serious mental illnesses and chronic illnesses: A feasibility study.* Retrieved January 26, 2020, from https://kuscholarworks.ku.edu/handle/1808/25394

Lim, H. (2010). Effect of "developmental speech and language training through music" on speech production in children with autism spectrum disorders. *Journal of Music Therapy, 47*(1), 2–26. doi:10.1093/jmt/47.1.2

Lindenfelser, K., Grocke, D., & McFerran, K. (2008). Bereaved parents' experiences of music therapy with their terminally ill child. *Journal of Music Therapy, 45*(3), 330–348. doi:10.1093/jmt/45.3.330

Linehan, M. (2015). *DBT skills training manual.* New York, NY: Guilford Press.

Levine, P. (1997). *Waking the tiger.* Berkeley, CA: North Atlantic Books.

Loewy, J., Stewart, K., Dassler, A., Telsey, A., & Homel, P. (2013). The effects of music therapy on vital signs, feeding, and sleep in premature infants. *Pediatrics, 131*(5). doi:10.1542/peds.2012-1367

Louie, D., Brook, K., & Frates, E. (2016). The laughter prescription. *American Journal of Lifestyle Medicine, 10*(4), 262–267. doi:10.1177/1559827614550279

Lund, D., Utz, R., Caserta, M., & de Vries, B. (2009). Humor, laughter, and happiness in the daily lives of recently bereaved spouses. *OMEGA—Journal of Death and Dying, 58*(2), 87–105. doi:10.2190/om.58.2.a

Lyu, J., Zhang, J., Mu, H., Li, W., Champ, M., & Xiong, Q. (2018). The effects of music therapy on cognition, psychiatric symptoms, and activities of daily living in patients with Alzheimer's disease. *Journal of Alzheimer's Disease, 64*(4), 1347–1358. doi:10.3233/jad-180183

MacDonald, R. (2013). Music, health, and well-being: A review. *International Journal of Qualitative Studies on Health and Well-Being, 8*(1), 20635. doi:10.3402/qhw.v8i0.20635

MacLeod, A., Lewis, A., & Robertson, C. (2013). "CHARLIE: PLEASE RESPOND!" Using a participatory methodology with individuals on the autism spectrum. *International Journal of Research & Method in Education, 37*(4), 407–420. doi:10.1080/1743727x.2013.776528

Malloch, S. (1999). Mothers and infants and communicative musicality. *Musicae Scientiae, 3*(1, suppl), 29–57. doi:10.1177/10298649000030s104

Manninen, S., Tuominen, L., Dunbar, R., Karjalainen, T., Hirvonen, J., & Arponen, E. (2017). Social laughter triggers endogenous opioid release in humans. *The Journal of Neuroscience, 37*(25), 6125–6131. doi:10.1523/jneurosci.0688-16.2017

McCollum, E. (2015). *Mindfulness for therapists.* New York, NY: Routledge.

Mercado, E., Schneider, J., Pack, A., & Herman, L. (2010). Sound production by singing humpback whales. *The Journal of the Acoustical Society of America, 127*(4), 2678–2691. doi:10.1121/1.3309453

Miller, M., & Fry, W. (2009). The effect of mirthful laughter on the human cardiovascular system. *Medical Hypotheses, 73*(5), 636–639. doi:10.1016/j.mehy.2009.02.044

Mills, H., Reiss, N., & Dombeck, M. (2018). *Types of stressors (eustress vs. distress).* Retrieved January 7, 2020, from https://www.mentalhelp.net/stress/types-of-stressors-eustress-vs-distress/

Mindful.org. Getting started with mindfulness. (2020). Retrieved January 27, 2020, from https://www.mindful.org/meditation/mindfulness-getting-started/

Morton, C. (2020). *Singing in unison, singing in harmony: Civic mentorship and choral communities.* Retrieved January 8, 2020, from http://journals.library.mun.ca/ojs/index.php/singing/article/view/640

Mueller, P., & Oppenheimer, D. (2014). The pen is mightier than the keyboard. *Psychological Science, 25*(6), 1159–1168. doi:10.1177/0956797614524581

Müller, V., & Lindenberger, U. (2011). Cardiac and respiratory patterns synchronize between persons during choir singing. *PLOS One, 6*(9), e24893. doi:10.1371/journal.pone.0024893

Newham, P. (1998). *Therapeutic voicework.* London, UK: Jessica Kingsley.

Niu, N., Perez, M., & Katz, J. (2011). Singing intervention for preoperative hypertension prior to total joint replacement: A case report. *Arthritis Care & Research, 63*(4), 630–632. doi:10.1002/acr.20406

Nordoff, P., & Robbins, C. (1971). *Therapy in music for handicapped children.* London, UK: Victor Gollancz Ltd.

Nordoff, P., & Robbins, C. (2020). *Nordoff-Robbins center for music therapy.* https://research.steinhardt.nyu.edu/music/nordoff

Norton, A., Zipse, L., Marchina, S., & Schlaug, G. (2009). Melodic intonation therapy: Shared insights on how it is done and why it might help. *Annals of the New York Academy of Sciences, 1169*(1), 431–436. doi:10.1111/j.1749-6632.2009.04859.x

O'Brien, E. (2014). View of the language of guided song writing with a bone marrow transplant patient. *Voices: A World Forum for Music Therapy.* Retrieved January 29, 2020, from https://voices.no/index.php/voices/article/view/1645/1405

O'Callaghan, C., & Michael, N. (2015). *Music therapy in grief and mourning.* Retrieved January 19, 2020, from https://oxfordindex.oup.com/view/10.1093/oxfordhb/9780199639755.013.42

Oesch, N. (2019). Music and language in social interaction: Synchrony, antiphony, and functional origins. *Frontiers in Psychology, 10.* doi:10.3389/fpsyg.2019.01514

Okamoto, M. (2005). *Effects of music therapy interventions on grief and spirituality of family members of patients in a hospice setting.* Retrieved January 19, 2020, from http://diginole.lib.fsu.edu/islandora/object/fsu%3A180515/

O'Kelly, J. (2016). Music therapy and neuroscience: Opportunities and challenges. *Voices: A World Forum for Music Therapy, 16*(2). doi:10.15845/voices.v16i2.872

Oxford Online Dictionary. (2020). *English dictionary, thesaurus, & grammar help.* Retrieved January 28, 2020, from https://www.lexico.com/

Pagani, M., Di Lorenzo, G., Verardo, A., Nicolais, G., Monaco, L., & Lauretti, G. (2012). Neurobiological correlates of EMDR monitoring: An EEG study. *PLOS One, 7*(9), e45753. doi:10.1371/journal.pone.0045753

Palmer, J., Lane, D., & Mayo, D. (2015). Surgical music therapy: The significance and implementation of music therapy in the operating arena: Table 1. *Music Therapy Perspectives, 35*(1), 30–35. doi:10.1093/mtp/miv036

Pearce, E., Launay, J., & Dunbar, R. (2015). The ice-breaker effect: Singing mediates fast social bonding. *Royal Society Open Science, 2*(10), 150221. doi:10.1098/rsos.150221

Pearce, E., Launay, J., van Duijn, M., Rotkirch, A., David-Barrett, T., & Dunbar, R. (2016). Singing together or apart: The effect of competitive and cooperative singing on social bonding within and between subgroups of a university fraternity. *Psychology of Music, 44*(6), 1255–1273. doi:10.1177/0305735616636208

Pemberton, C., McCormack, P., & Russell, A. (1998). Have women's voices lowered across time? A cross-sectional study of Australian women's voices. *Journal of Voice, 12*(2), 208–213. doi:10.1016/s0892-1997(98)80040-4

Planck-Gesellschaft, M. (2019). *Brains of birds synchronize when they sing duets.* Retrieved January 28, 2020, from https://www.sciencedaily.com/releases/2019/06/190612141406.htm

Prat, Y., Taub, M., & Yovel, Y. (2016). Everyday bat vocalizations contain information about emitter, addressee, context, and behavior. *Scientific Reports, 6*(1). doi:10.1038/srep39419

Rainey, S. (2013). *All together now: Singing is good for your body and soul.* Retrieved January 8, 2020, from https://www.telegraph.co.uk/news/health/10168914/All-together-now-singing-is-good-for-your-body-and-soul.html

Redfield, A. (2017). *An analysis of the experiences and integration of transpersonal phenomena induced by electronic dance music events.* Retrieved January 26, 2020, from https://digitalcommons.ciis.edu/cgi/viewcontent.cgi?article=1513&context=ijts-transpersonalstudies

Reece, A. (2015). *The interaction between music and language in learning and recall in children with autism spectrum condition.* Retrieved January 26, 2020, from https://ethos.bl.uk/OrderDetails.do?uin=uk.bl.ethos.680461

R k, P. (2017). Multimodal coordination enhances the responses to an avian duet. *Behavioral Ecology, 29*(2), 411–417. doi:10.1093/beheco/arx174

Richards, K., Campenni, C., & Muse-Burke, J. (2010). Self-care and well-being in mental health professionals: The mediating effects of self-awareness and mindfulness. *Journal of Mental Health Counseling, 32*(3), 247–264. doi:10.17744/mehc.32.3.0n31v88304423806

Riley, J., & Breland, K. (2020). *Songwriting and lyric convergence.* Retrieved January 26, 2020, from https://musictherapyactivities.fandom.com/wiki/Category:Songwriting_and_Lyric_Convergence

Rosenfeld, J. (2018). *11 scientific benefits of having a laugh.* Retrieved January 9, 2020, from https://www.mentalfloss.com/article/539632/scientific-benefits-having-laugh

Rosner, R., Kruse, J., & Hagl, M. (2010). A meta-analysis of interventions for bereaved children and adolescents. *Death Studies, 34*(2), 99–136. doi:10.1080/07481180903492422

Russo, F. (2020). https://www.researchgate.net/profile/Frank_Russo

Satoh, M., Yuba, T., Tabei, K., Okubo, Y., Kida, H., Sakuma, H., & Tomimoto, H. (2015). Music therapy using singing training improves psychomotor speed in patients with Alzheimer's disease: A neuropsychological and fMRI study. *Dementia and Geriatric Cognitive Disorders Extra, 5*(3), 296–308. doi:10.1159/000436960

Sauvé, M. (2004). *The therapeutic effects of vocal improvisation.* Retrieved January 22, 2020, from http://citeseerx.ist.psu.edu/viewdoc/summary?doi=10.1.1.550.9034

Schaefer, H. (2017). Music-evoked emotions—Current studies. *Frontiers in Neuroscience, 11.* doi:10.3389/fnins.2017.00600

Schlaug, G., Norton, A., Marchina, S., Zipse, L., & Wan, C. (2010). From singing to speaking: Facilitating recovery from nonfluent aphasia. *Future Neurology, 5*(5), 657–665. doi:10.2217/fnl.10.44

Schlesinger, L. (2016). *5 reasons fantasizing is good for you.* Retrieved January 27, 2020, from https://www.huffpost.com/entry/five-reasons-fantasizing-is-good-for-you_b_8060884

Schmidt, J. (1983). Songwriting as a therapeutic procedure. *Music Therapy Perspectives, 1*(2), 4–7. doi:10.1093/mtp/1.2.4

Schwartz, E., Boyle, S., & Engen, R. (2018). *Functional voice skills for music therapists.* Dallas, TX: Barcelona Publishers.

Selye, H. (1956). *The stress of life. (Implications and applications.)*. New York, NY: McGraw-Hill Book Co.

Shapiro, F. (1995). *Eye movement desensitization and reprocessing: Basic principles, protocols, and procedures* (1st ed.). New York, NY: Guilford Press.

Shin, H., Ryu, K., & Song, Y. (2011). Effects of laughter therapy on postpartum fatigue and stress responses of postpartum women. *Journal of Korean Academy of Nursing, 41*(3), 294. doi:10.4040/jkan.2011.41.3.294

Shoemark, H. (2008). Infant-directed singing as a vehicle for regulation rehearsal in the medically fragile full-term infant. *Voices: A World Forum for Music Therapy, 8*(2). doi:10.15845/voices.v8i2.437

Snow, S., Bernardi, N., Sabet-Kassouf, N., Moran, D., & Lehmann, A. (2018). Exploring the experience and effects of vocal toning. *Journal of Music Therapy, 55*(2), 221–250. doi:10.1093/jmt/thy003

Sokolov, L. (2020*). Embodied voicework: Beyond singing.* Dallas, TX: Barcelona Publishers.

Stacy, R., Brittain, K., & Kerr, S. (2002). Singing for health: an exploration of the issues. *Health Education, 102*(4), 156–162. doi:10.1108/09654280210434228

Stegemoller, E., Zaman, A., & Shirtcliff, E. (2018). *Effects of group singing on stress and motor symptoms in persons with Parkinson's disease.* Presentation, Neuroscience Conference, Nov 7, 2018. Retrieved January 12, 2020, from https://www.abstractsonline.com/pp8/#!/4649/presentation/39439

Summers, K. (2019, May). *Personal interview.*

Summers, S. (2011). The vocal hello space model in hospice music therapy. In S. Uhlig & F. Baker, *Voicework in music therapy: Research and practice.* London, UK: Jessica Kingsley Publishers.

Suttie, J. (2016). *How music bonds us together.* Retrieved January 8, 2020, from https://greatergood.berkeley.edu/article/item/how_music_bonds_us_together

Tamplin, J. (2006). Song collage technique: A new approach to songwriting. *Nordic Journal of Music Therapy, 15*(2), 177–190. doi:10.1080/08098130609478164

Tamplin, J. (2008). A pilot study into the effect of vocal exercises and singing on dysarthric speech. *Neurorehabilitation, 23*(3), 207–216.

Tamplin, J., Baker, F., Jones, B., Way, A., & Lee, S. (2013). "Stroke a chord": The effect of singing in a community choir on mood and social engagement for people living with aphasia following a stroke. *Neurorehabilitation, 32*(4), 929–941. doi:10.3233/nre-130916

Tamplin, J., & Grocke, D. (2008). A music therapy treatment protocol for acquired dysarthria rehabilitation. *Music Therapy Perspectives, 26*(1), 23–29. doi:10.1093/mtp/26.1.23

Thaut, M. (2005). *Neurologic music therapy techniques and definitions.* Retrieved January 26, 2020, from https://nmtacademy.files.wordpress.com/2015/07/nmt-definitions.pdf

Thaut, M., McIntosh, G., & Hoemberg, V. (2015). Neurobiological foundations of neurologic music therapy: Rhythmic entrainment and the motor system. *Frontiers in Psychology, 5.* doi:10.3389/fpsyg.2014.01185

Trimble, M., & Hesdorffer, D. (2017). Music and the brain: The neuroscience of music and musical appreciation. *Bjpsych International, 14*(2), 28–31. doi:10.1192/s2056474000001720

Trimmer, C., Tyo, R., & Naeem, F. (2016). Cognitive behavioural therapy-based music (CBT–Music) group for symptoms of anxiety and depression. *Canadian Journal of Community Mental Health, 35*(2), 83–87. doi:10.7870/cjcmh-2016-029

Tucci, G., & Houghton Brodrick, A. (1961). *Theory and practice of the mandala.* London, UK: Rider and Company.

Tull, M. (2019). *The importance of emotional awareness in PTSD.* Retrieved January 25, 2020, from https://www.verywellmind.com/increasing-emotional-awareness-2797603

Turner, C. (2014, Sept. 10). *"This is your brain. This is your brain on music."* NPR audio article transcript. National Public Radio. http://www.npr.org/templates/transcript/transcript.php?storyId=343681493

Uhlig, S. (2006). *Authentic voices, authentic singing.* Dallas, TX: Barcelona Publishers.

Uhlig, S., & Baker, F. (2011). *Voicework in music therapy: Research and practice.* London, UK: Jessica Kingsley Publishers.

Urdang, E. (2010). Awareness of self—A critical tool. *Social Work Education, 29*(5), 523–538. doi:10.1080/02615470903164950

Van der Kolk, B. (2000). Posttraumatic stress disorder and the nature of trauma. *Dialogues in Clinical Neuroscience, Mar.* 2(1), 7–22.

Van der Kolk, B. (2014). *The body keeps the score: Mind, brain, and body in the transformation of trauma.* New York, NY: Penguin Books Limited.

Van Der Meulen, I., Van De Sandt-Koenderman, M., Heijenbrok, M., Visch-Brink, E., & Ribbers, G. (2016). Melodic intonation therapy in chronic aphasia: Evidence from a pilot randomized controlled trial. *Frontiers in Human Neuroscience, 10.* doi:10.3389/fnhum.2016.00533

Vickhoff, B., Malmgren, H., Åström, R., Nyberg, G., Ekström, S., & Engwall, M. (2013). Music structure determines heart rate variability of singers. *Frontiers in Psychology, 4,* 334. doi:10.3389/fpsyg.2013.00334

Wade, J. (2019, July). *Personal interview.*

Wan, C., Rüber, T., Hohmann, A., & Schlaug, G. (2010). The therapeutic effects of singing in neurological disorders. *Music Perception, 27*(4), 287–295. doi:10.1525/mp.2010.27.4.287

Wheeler, B. (2015). *Music therapy handbook.* New York, NY: Guilford Press.

Webster's Dictionary. (2003). Merriam-Webster, Inc.

Westle, L. (2019, May). *Personal interview.*

Wikipedia.org. 2019. *Bilateral stimulation.* Retrieved January 28, 2020, from https://en.wikipedia.org/wiki/Bilateral_stimulation

Winter, K. (2009). *A phenomenological experience of singing vocal harmony with another person.* iDEA: Drexel Libraries E-Repository and Archives. Retrieved January 8, 2020, from https://idea.library.drexel.edu/islandora/object/idea:3044

Wolk, L., Abdelli-Beruh, N., & Slavin, D. (2012). Habitual use of vocal fry in young adult female speakers. *Journal of Voice, 26*(3), e111–e116. doi:10.1016/j.jvoice.2011.04.007

Wöllner, C. (2018). Call and response: Musical and bodily interactions in jazz improvisation duos. *Musicae Scientiae, 24*(1), 44–59. doi:10.1177/1029864918772004

Yen, H., & Lin, L. (2018). A systematic review of reminiscence therapy for older adults in Taiwan. *Journal of Nursing Research, 26*(2), 138–150. doi:10.1097/jnr.0000000000000233

Yinger, O., & Lapointe, L. (2012). The effects of participation in a group music therapy voice protocol (G-MTVP) on the speech of individuals with Parkinson's disease. *Music Therapy Perspectives, 30*(1), 25–31. doi:10.1093/mtp/30.1.25

Index

A

accents, 19, 53, 60
adolescents, 135, 203, 228, 230, 233, 240
age, 5, 15, 17, 20, 52, 55, 152, 161, 187, 200, 231
anger, 5, 21, 56, 79, 100, 103, 118–19, 140, 188–89, 213
anxiety, 8, 16–17, 77, 117, 148, 150, 152, 159, 162, 189, 199, 226, 235, 242, 249
    social, 171–72
arrhythmic, 130, 182–83
Authentic Voices, 32, 50, 209, 243
autism, 3, 6, 15, 89, 91, 128, 171–72, 175, 234, 249
avoidance, 38, 40, 211–12

B

bereavement, 146, 148, 160, 234
blues, 46–49, 103–4, 209, 212, 219–20
body, 3–5, 33–34, 59–60, 74–75, 78, 84, 90, 92–94, 96, 100–101, 111–13, 158–59, 193, 206–8, 211
boys, 6–7, 26, 89, 162, 211
brain, 85, 93–94, 111–12, 118, 125, 153, 166, 175–78, 203, 227–28, 232, 242–43
brain injury, 8, 142, 175, 178, 181–82, 194, 226, 249
breath, 3, 7, 9, 16–20, 34–36, 65, 75, 78, 84, 100, 113–14, 145, 155, 207, 217
breathe, 72, 74–75, 78, 84, 92, 94, 120, 142, 146–47, 186, 189, 194, 208, 213, 217
breathing, 3, 17, 19, 33, 78, 94, 101, 104–5, 115, 124, 143, 146, 148, 156–57, 188
    shallow, 33, 84, 101
breath support, 33–35, 51, 92, 112

C

call-and-response, 89, 98, 102, 129, 167–68, 191, 193
CBT (Cognitive behavior therapy), 117, 189, 206, 213, 242
chant, 11, 27, 37, 102–3, 113–14, 124, 129, 132, 157, 192–93, 198, 200, 202
children, 40, 52, 55, 117, 135, 138, 161, 169, 171, 175, 203, 213, 225, 236, 239
chords, 16, 22, 24, 44, 47–48, 61, 87, 94–95, 98, 102, 130–32, 134, 149, 155, 187–90, 206
chorus, 27, 79, 83, 102, 115, 121, 148, 192, 202, 204
circle, 57, 59, 72–73, 83, 90, 142, 167
client dynamics, 71, 73, 75, 77, 79
clients, nonverbal, 84–85, 129
colors, 59, 73, 80, 84, 142, 177, 194, 200

comfort, 4, 38, 62, 85, 92, 96, 150, 155, 189, 197, 207
communication, 15, 81, 89, 127–29, 131, 133, 135, 137, 139, 141, 143, 153, 194, 212–13
connect, 4–5, 27, 30, 32, 35, 66–68, 72, 75, 90, 92, 99, 102–3, 129–30, 166, 208
connection, 8–9, 26–27, 29, 56, 85, 109–10, 138, 140, 142, 146, 148, 154, 201–2, 211, 213
consonance, 44, 47, 92, 149, 202
containers, 26, 31, 148, 150, 159
conversation, 20, 49, 61, 107, 125, 131, 162, 167, 171, 173, 176, 194
Core belief, 118–19
countertransference, 71–72, 186

D

depression, 4, 8, 17, 119, 148, 150, 152, 162, 189, 203, 228, 242, 249
dialogue, 27, 49, 129–35, 150, 193–94, 209
disabilities, intellectual, 77, 129, 142, 175, 193, 195, 225, 228
discomfort, 36, 44, 66–67, 77, 81, 84–85, 97, 154, 186, 196, 214
distress, 17, 27, 117, 120–21, 132, 156, 199, 237
downbeat, 16, 18–19, 52, 149
dreams, 131, 133, 161, 217, 246
drums, 4, 15, 19, 22–23, 30, 32, 54, 65, 89, 98, 102, 160, 222
dynamics, 23, 44, 47, 58, 60–61, 92–93, 137–39, 164, 168, 173, 191, 194, 207

E

Embodied VoiceWork, 50, 187, 209, 241
emotional pain, 84, 145, 147–51, 159, 212–13
Emotional Regulation, 117, 119, 121, 123, 125
emotions, 4, 21, 23–24, 38, 54, 56–57, 59–61, 69–70, 82–83, 117, 119, 124–25, 127, 145, 148
empathy, 82, 161, 172, 201, 203
empowerment, 90–92, 97–98, 100–103, 107, 112, 209, 213
energy, 18–19, 21, 23, 30, 59, 91, 96, 101, 149, 192, 194–95, 204, 207
entrainment, 93, 107, 109, 149, 154–59, 193, 201, 229
ethics, 65, 67, 69
exercises, 32, 35–39, 41, 44, 50, 57, 60, 73, 92–94, 96, 104, 115, 130–31, 160, 181–83

F

family, 91, 119–20, 148, 150
favorite songs, 4, 120, 136, 142, 148, 151, 159–60, 166, 173, 176
feet, 3, 17, 75, 105, 163
field, 30, 32, 52, 65–66, 69–70, 81, 187, 195, 198
fill-ins, 135–36, 166–67, 194–95, 209
focus, 10, 30, 33, 35, 58–59, 75, 89, 91, 95–97, 101–3, 155–56, 158–59, 166, 171–72, 195–96
fun, 5, 34, 62, 65, 74, 110, 115, 164, 171, 204

G

game, 77, 168, 191, 215–18

gravity, 131–32, 222
grief, 7, 21, 68, 146, 186, 188, 213, 238
ground, 22, 27, 49, 77, 90, 92, 96, 101, 120, 126, 139, 190, 202, 216
grounding, 86, 90–91, 95, 97–98, 101–2, 124, 126, 130, 149, 187, 200, 206
group, 4–5, 50, 74, 80–83, 93–95, 107, 109, 113, 129–30, 137–38, 141–42, 163, 172–73, 197–98, 204–5
group cohesion, 90, 107, 109
group members, 5, 19, 82, 85, 101, 137, 141, 166–67, 172, 205, 208
guitar, 3, 15, 31, 44, 47, 57, 130, 137, 160, 181, 196

H

hands, 3, 10, 26, 35, 59, 76, 125, 137, 154, 169–70, 188–89, 198–99, 212, 217, 245–46
harmony, 21–22, 58, 67, 77, 92–93, 96–97, 109, 113, 147, 173, 201–2, 207, 232, 237, 243
head, 26, 35–36, 43, 71–72, 75–76, 96, 145, 177, 221
heart, 17, 20, 107, 111, 114–15, 126, 189, 200, 207, 229
hum, 3, 36, 74, 92–93
humor, 90, 103, 150, 168, 203–4, 226, 228, 236

I

imagery, 95–97, 105, 114–15, 147, 157–60, 198–200, 204
images, 66, 74, 96–97, 115, 188–89, 199–200
imitate, 25, 48–49, 60, 127, 129–30

improvisation, 31, 43–45, 47, 49–50, 60, 78, 92, 124, 150, 198, 208–9, 223
improvise, 26, 43–47, 49–50, 62, 72, 78, 97, 103, 131, 153, 212, 214
improvising, 26, 43, 48–49, 61, 188
inhale, 4, 16, 18, 33–36, 78, 92–93, 100, 104, 112–13, 146, 217
instruments, 18, 21–22, 34, 38, 45, 50, 57, 66–67, 72, 92, 130, 154, 156, 196, 201
intervals, 21–22, 182, 216, 218

J

jaw, 25, 33, 37, 53
jazz, 26–27, 34, 43, 47, 52, 87, 163, 191
joy, 31, 55, 61, 68, 86, 135, 147, 150, 163, 203–4, 212–14, 219, 250

K

keys, 22, 29, 32, 38–40, 43–44, 47–48, 101, 119, 130, 199, 206, 211, 221, 223

L

laughter, 103, 109–10, 116, 203, 228, 231, 234, 236
listening, 7, 59–60, 71, 78, 99, 127–29, 140–42, 148, 151, 154, 163, 195–98, 215
loneliness, 9, 107–8, 161–62, 166, 225
loss, 67–68, 108, 187–88
lungs, 32–33, 78, 111, 124, 155, 182, 194, 207
lyric analysis, 38, 101, 148, 196, 198

lyrics, 26–27, 85–86, 114, 118, 121, 135, 138, 141, 151, 158, 160, 168–69, 196–97, 199–200, 206

M

mandala, 59–61, 72–73, 78–79, 101, 115, 142, 188, 200, 234, 242
melody, 20–22, 26, 28, 31, 40, 43, 47, 52, 87, 159–60, 178, 192, 194, 206, 208
meter, 18–19, 98, 122, 131, 164, 205–6
mindfulness, 79, 123–24, 159, 237, 240
mirror, 37, 66, 69–70
mother, 9, 20–21, 91, 150, 162–63, 171, 190, 234, 237
mouth, 3, 25, 29, 33, 35–37, 39, 53–54, 110
music psychotherapy, 68, 71–72, 185, 187–88, 208, 228
music therapy entrainment (MTE), 155, 201, 229

N

NICU, 23, 146, 148–50, 155

P

pain, 20–21, 24, 56, 83, 121, 147, 149, 153–56, 158–60, 186, 188–90, 201, 231, 246
parents, 29, 32, 55, 119–20, 148, 150, 177, 185, 187, 195, 227, 246
Parkinson's Disease, 8, 182, 184, 194, 230, 241, 244
partner, 5, 119, 121, 178, 215–18
patients, 30, 77, 145, 148, 150, 154–55, 157, 175, 233, 236, 238, 240

phrases, 34, 53, 61, 91, 95–96, 98, 120, 132, 136, 162, 176–78, 188, 191, 193–94, 216–17
physical pain, 153, 155, 157, 159, 203, 213
piano, 4, 15, 22, 32, 39, 44, 47, 126, 130, 149, 156, 160, 162, 178, 181
pitches, 28, 120, 149, 156, 178, 213
populations, 6–7, 23, 56, 66, 81, 86, 90, 135, 142, 166–67, 173, 193, 200
power, 67, 69, 99, 155, 171, 176, 187, 199, 212, 214
process, 8, 43, 59, 90–91, 100–101, 127–28, 132, 153, 167–68, 173, 186, 189, 196, 198, 205
pulse, 16–17, 20, 53, 167, 216

R

Raffi, 39, 135, 170, 177, 204, 220–23
range, 6, 25–26, 33, 38–40, 44, 47, 52–53, 56, 92, 148, 187, 208
recorded, 218–24
relaxation, 5, 24, 111, 113, 115, 154, 156, 207, 235
release, 4, 8, 18, 22, 24, 76, 92, 94, 97, 103, 113, 145, 147, 152–54
reminiscing, 148, 176
research, 8, 44, 52, 108, 112, 124, 141, 145, 155, 166, 175–76, 183–84, 203, 241, 243
resonance, 20, 22, 33, 35–36, 53, 92, 143, 155–56, 229
retrieved, 225–44
rhythm, 3, 15–16, 46–47, 52–53, 58, 101–3, 155–58, 170–71, 178, 183–84, 194, 196, 201, 217, 221
rhythmic singing, 53

S

safety, 9, 15–17, 73, 82, 90–91, 97–98, 103, 112, 173, 191, 195, 207
scale, 21, 43–45, 47, 49, 93, 96, 112–13, 139
scat-sing, 62, 68, 131
self-awareness, 57, 65, 67, 69, 71, 76, 78, 80, 212, 229, 240
self-care, 32, 54, 62, 156, 160, 240
self-esteem, 29, 31–32, 51, 54, 161, 213
self-expression, 55–57, 59–62, 127, 129, 131, 133, 135, 137–41, 143, 165–66, 168, 212–13, 225, 231, 233–34
sharing songs, 140–41
silence, 10, 83–84, 109, 115, 129, 194
sing-alongs 163, 198
singing bowl, 17, 61, 92, 147
singing harmonies, 201–2
singing voice, 6, 58, 140, 145, 194
social interaction, 15–16, 22, 26, 67, 77, 161–63, 165–67, 169, 171–73, 194, 202, 209, 212–13, 228, 238
social skills, 161, 169, 171–72
song choices, 54, 166, 198, 205
songs, familiar, 47, 86, 93, 102, 169, 173, 175, 178, 182
songwriting, 121, 150–51, 158–60, 198, 205–6, 226, 231, 241–42
spaces, 76, 108, 110, 129, 135, 153, 160, 163, 171–72, 191, 194–95
stomach, 3, 33–34, 40, 67, 71, 155
strength, 29, 32, 38, 56, 117, 140, 145, 155, 197, 208
stress, 33, 92, 94, 111–13, 118, 145, 183, 231, 241
stress reduction, 5, 22, 33, 86, 90, 111–13, 173, 192, 207–8
styles, 45, 49, 52, 131, 151, 205–6, 245, 249
supervision, 56, 66, 69–70, 73, 76, 186, 214, 245
supervisor, 18, 67, 70–71, 73, 81–82, 86, 89, 187

T

tempos, 18, 30, 114, 139, 164, 168, 192
tensing muscle groups, 33, 75, 112
tension, 4, 7, 22, 34, 37, 75, 78, 80, 84, 97, 113, 116, 132
textures, 25–26, 29, 59, 61–62, 130, 188
therapy, melodic intonation, 175, 178–79, 243
thoughts, 20, 72–76, 87, 118–22, 128, 145, 159, 171–72, 177, 196–97, 202, 206, 223
throat, 34–36, 39, 41, 53, 111, 124
timbre, 24–25
tone, 24, 35–36, 40, 95–96, 129–30, 155, 198, 208, 215–16
tongue, 22, 25, 110, 181–82
toning, 92–98, 124, 146–47, 155, 207, 209, 229, 234
  word, 94, 96–97
Toolbox, 116, 173, 191, 193, 195, 197, 199, 201, 203, 205, 207, 209
trauma, 17, 77, 90–91, 130, 140, 150, 152, 189, 243, 249
trust, 7–9, 15, 17, 66, 107, 146, 161, 196, 225

U

unison, 22, 24, 92, 96, 107–9, 111, 128–29, 131–32, 138, 147, 162, 201–2, 204, 216–17, 237

V

variations, 23, 163–65, 182
verbal processing, 17, 27, 91, 108
verses, 9, 19, 23, 103, 121, 163, 168, 170, 172, 177
vibrations, 3–4, 9, 24, 27, 36, 40, 66, 85, 96, 129–30, 149
vocal cords, 3–4, 9, 28, 39, 93, 156, 208, 214
vocal exercises, 32, 57, 93, 112–13, 115, 124, 129, 145, 181–82, 188, 208, 242
vocal identity and self-expression, 55, 57, 59–61
vocal improvisation, 29, 43, 49–50, 62, 149, 151, 208–9, 211, 224, 240
vocal methods, 7, 10, 82, 97, 114, 124, 213–14
vocal psychotherapy, 32, 60, 145, 151–52, 185–86, 189, 199, 201, 226
vocal range, 29, 31, 33, 35, 37–39, 41, 149, 202, 207
voice, speaking, 38, 184, 192, 228
voice changes, 6
Voicework, 229, 241, 243
vowels, 36–39, 53, 74, 92, 110, 131, 149, 156, 160, 181–82, 207

W

warm-ups, 24, 36–37, 39, 93, 205, 245
women, 5-7, 9, 38, 79, 107–8, 117, 148, 163, 171. 211, 220
words, 21, 27–28, 33–34, 37–38, 47–49, 59, 61–62, 85–86, 94–95, 98–99, 101–3, 128–29, 138–41, 146–51, 190–93
worries, 3, 115, 120, 125, 142